Plans and the
Structure
of Behavior

Plans and the Structure of Behavior

George A. Miller, Princeton University
Eugene Galanter, Columbia University
Karl H. Pribram, Stanford University

with a foreword by

Donald E. Broadbent, University of Oxford

COLLEGE FOR HUMAN SERVICES
LIBRARY
345 HUDSON STREET
NEW YORK, N.Y. 10014

Adams-Bannister-Cox
New York

Adams, Bannister, Cox, New York 10027

© 1960 by Holt, Reinhart and Winston, Inc.
© 1979, 1986 by George A. Miller, Eugene Galanter, and Karl H. Pribram
All rights reserved
Printed in the United States of America

Library of Congress Cataloging in Publication Data
Miller, George A., Galanter, Eugene, and Pribram, Karl H.
    Plans and the Structure of Behavior
Library of Congress Catalogue Card Number 86-25934
ISBN 0-937431-00-1

ACKNOWLEDGMENTS

It is an ill-kept secret that many more people than the authors participate in the creation of every book. In our case, an entire institution was involved in a supporting role; it is one of our most pleasant chores to acknowledge our debt to the Center for Advanced Study in the Behavioral Sciences in Stanford, California. The Director of the Center, Dr. Ralph Tyler, won our deep and lasting affection by making available to us the time and facilities we needed for our collaboration, and by giving us the freedom to exploit them. But the Center is a great deal more than an institution, a pleasant place to work; it is a collection of scholars and scientists drawn from all the different branches of the behavioral sciences. Many of those men and women spent time with us when we were confused and gave freely of their wisdom and experience. Those who read some of the preliminary drafts and tried to save us from our mistakes included Cora Dubois, Helen Peak, Frank Barron, Frank Beach, Jerome Frank, Roman Jakobson, James Jenkins, Thomas Kuhn, Charles Osgood, Seymour Perlin, and Willard V. Quine. Of course, this expression of our gratitude to them does not mean that they endorse the views expressed in the following pages.

An early draft of the manuscript was sent to some of our friends. Many of them found or made the time to reply to us, some at great length, and so we gratefully acknowledge the corrections and improvements suggested by Robert R. Bush, Noam Chomsky, Frederick C. Frick, Burt Green, Francis W. Irwin, R. Duncan Luce, Allen Newell, Herbert A. Simon, and Donald W. Taylor. The fact that they criticized an early version, of course, does not deprive them of their right to criticize the present one as well.

We count ourselves particularly fortunate to have had the very best kind of assistance in getting our words into print. Katherine J. Miller and Phyllis Ellis typed our visions and revisions quickly and accurately, correcting our spelling and grammar as best they could.

In addition, we wish to express our thanks to the individuals, publishers, and journals who gave us permission to reprint passages from their articles or books.

January 1960

G.A.M.
E.G.
K.H.P.

CONTENTS

	Prologue	1
1.	Images and Plans	5
2.	The Unit of Analysis	21
3.	The Simulation of Psychological Processes	41
4.	Values, Intentions, and the Execution of Plans	59
5.	Instincts	73
6.	Motor Skills and Habits	81
7.	The Integration of Plans	95
8.	Relinquishing the Plan	103
9.	Nondynamic Aspects of Personality	117
10.	Plans for Remembering	125
11.	Plans for Speaking	139

12. *Plans for Searching and Solving*   159

13. *The Formation of Plans*   177

14. *Some Neuropsychological Speculations*   195

    Epilogue   211

    Index of Authors   217

    Index of Subjects   221

FOREWORD

There are a number of reasons why a book on psychology may be worth republishing even twenty-five years after it first appeared. To start with the least important, the older reader can enjoy the sheer nostalgia of being reminded of the way things used to be. More seriously, if the book has had a major impact, those interested in history will want to see in the text the echoes of still earlier influences; or the germs of ideas that were taken up later by others. As always with history, there are lessons to be learned for the future as well, from seeing the methods by which an area can be changed.

Most important of all, there may be things in the book that have been neglected, but are still true. They may be even more timely than when they were first published. There are two good examples cited in this volume that illustrate how this can happen. Alan Turing published in 1937 a paper, mentioned in Chapter 3, that was a key step in the development both of the electronic computer and of the simulation of psychological processes. Yet when it first came out, Turing received only two requests for reprints.[1] The world was not ready in 1937 to understand what had been achieved. Again, a publication can be welcomed from one point of view and ignored from others.

[1] A. Hodges, *Alan Turing: The Enigma* (London: Burnett Books, 1983). The paper itself was A. M. Turing, On computable numbers, with an application to the Entscheidungsproblem, *Proceedings of the London Mathematical Society*, 1937, 42, 230–265.

² The 1932 book by F. C. Bartlett, cited in Chapter 1, was originally a great success amongst those psychologists who valued phenomenological accounts of human experience. The theoretical language was however too uncongenial for it to be widely accepted amongst experimental psychologists seeking a language that uses publicly defined terms. The advent of computational methods made it possible to discuss the issues that concerned Bartlett in such terms; concepts of schema or frame have now become major parts of artificial intelligence, and the book has gained a new vogue of citation as a result.

The present volume is worth rereading for all these reasons; or reading for the first time for those who meet it afresh. Of course a lot has happened in psychology during twenty-five years; much of it happened because this book existed. One ought therefore to look back at the crucial insights; what was it that made these views so influential? Most of all there are parts of this book that have not yet had their full impact. Currently, signs of interest in these topics can be seen in the academic community. Future research may well start from ideas that are still slumbering in the following pages.

The Background and Significance of 'Plans'

As a simple mythic account of history, some people would say that, before the 1950s, psychology was dominated by theories based on simple association. Experiments were frequently done on animals rather than people, and concerned observable stimuli and responses between which the associations were supposed to occur. Even if the experiments were on people, the theoretical structure was often of the same type. In the 1980s however the dominant approach in psychology concerns internal events, which may be related to each other in ways much more complex than mere association; and since the experiments involve language, imagery, or problem-solving, they are usually performed on human beings. By an ironic reversal, animal researchers also now use theories that postulate internal operations and representations. Theories of such a kind are usually called 'cognitive.'

The swing from the associationist to the cognitive approach was naturally not instantaneous, but the origins of the current view can be located in the second half of the 1950s. Certain meetings, papers, and books from that time are seen as stating particularly clearly the manifesto of the newer approach; and 'Plans' is one of the books. That is why it is historically important, and one of the reasons for looking at it again.

This simple picture is of course *too* simple. It slides easily into thinking of psychologists of the 1950s as falling into two warring camps, the goodies and the baddies. In some ways it may be more helpful to think of a single community gradually tackling a series of problems. Elsewhere I have suggested that there have been three such problems.[2] First, can science be applied to human beings (or indeed animals) since they show purposive behavior? Second, must the processes inside them be described in specific physiological terms, or can one find another scientific language independent of physiology? Third, are the processes always the same, so that one can seek and find 'the' mechanism of reading or theorem-proving; or can one give a scientific account of processes that interact with each other and vary between and within individuals?

The first of these problems has been with us ever since Aristotle distinguished two kinds of causality; if not longer. It was solved in the 1930s by the realization that the cause of a purposive action is not a future event, requiring a different kind of causality. Rather, the cause is a past or present event, namely a state of the person or animal before the action appears. This solution was hit upon by various people in both the 'good' (cognitive) and 'bad' (behaviorist) camps; some of the clearest statements come from Clark Hull, the dean of the behaviorists.[3] (Notice also the quotation from him in Chapter 3, on the advantages of models from engineering.) There is however no doubt that this age-old problem is now solved; nobody in these days cites purposive behavior as making scientific psychology impossible. On the other hand, at the present time we are in the throes of the third problem, and cannot claim to have solved it; more of this later.

'Plans' was written after the first problem had been solved, al-

[2] D. E. Broadbent, *In Defence of Empirical Psychology* (London: Methuen, 1973).
[3] C. L. Hull, Knowledge and purpose as habit mechanisms, *Psychological Review*, 1930, 37, 511–525, C. L. Hull, Mind, mechanism, and adaptive behavior, *Psychological Review*, 1937, 44, 1–32.

though relics of past dilemmas are still detectable in its pages.² The second problem however was in 1960 still very much on the agenda. Even when one has agreed that purpose can be built into a physical system, many people would then think that the system should be explained in terms of its components. The performance of a car is explained by the number of its carburetors, or the shape of the combustion chambers. On that view, the explanation of behavior would be in terms of physiology. If one cannot observe the physiology directly, then like Hebb one should use physiological entities for theorizing about a Conceptual Nervous System.⁴

The answer to this view, we would all see now, is that abstract descriptions can be produced, that fit several physical systems; and these abstractions can be discussed without needing to go into the physical reality. The equations that fit the performance of the carburetor, the combustion chamber, and other components of the car can be implemented in a computer just as well as in metal. One can explore whether it would be advantageous to change the performance of a component in a certain way, before one is quite sure how to shape the metal to achieve that performance. In the same way we can discuss the computations that the visual system must perform to decide the distance of an object, without knowing how the neurons perform those computations.

Nobody now disputes this; and it is quite hard to recall the different attitudes of the 1950s. Neuroscientists then would study the firing of single cells, or the concentrations of transmitter substances at synapses, as they do now. Nowadays however it is respectable and usual for them to measure the behavior of animals or people at the same time, using sophisticated cognitive tests, and to try and link the events at the neural level to the computational mechanisms implied by the tests. In the 1950s this was mostly in the future; neurologists would try to assess the state of a brain-damaged patient by pulling out of their pocket the first common object they could find and asking the patient to name it. For psychological theory, they would fall back on the language of everyday life. A respected 1955 textbook

⁴ D. O. Hebb, *The Organization of Behavior* (Chichester: Wiley, 1949). For a philosophical view from the period, see B. A. Farrell, On the limits of experimental psychology, *British Journal of Psychology,* 1955, 46, 165–177.

of physiology, in the chapter on the cerebral cortex, jumps uneasily between words such as consciousness, ambition, responsibility, imagination, or propriety, and the familiar anatomical vocabulary of cingulate gyrus, pulvinar, and orbitofrontal cortex.[5]

It is hard now to realise that it was two years after 'Plans' appeared, before Hubel and Wiesel showed a relationship between the firing of single cortical cells and the presence of complex or moving visual events.[6] The entire effort to understand the nervous system was being hindered by the absence of a common functional language in which to discuss brain and behavior. The merit of the behaviorists was that they were using stimulus-response terms that could be mapped physiologically, and indeed the 1955 physiology text quotes data on the way brain lesions disturb animal learning, using behavioristic techniques and terms. These terms however became impossibly complicated when applied to complex performances; whereas the cybernetic or information-processing language could produce more manageable descriptions.

A profitable way of seeing 'Plans,' therefore, is as an act of persuasion, an attempt to show that a scientifically acceptable language could discuss real human functions such as those disturbed in brain injury; but without unwarranted assumptions about the actual physiological mechanisms. From this aspect, notice in the following pages the clear, simple, and appealing accounts of earlier cybernetic work. The analysis of computability by Turing, of neural nets by McCulloch and Pitts, of precise formulations of grammar by Chomsky, and of concept learning by Bruner, Goodnow, and Austion, had already appeared. They were however technical, specific, and did not make it obvious to the general psychologist that a whole different attitude to the subject was implicit in these scattered publications. The summaries of this work in 'Plans' have probably never been bettered either for accuracy or for level of literary quality. The readers then, and the readers now, could see without effort what was being claimed, why it was important, and the promise it gave for the future. 'Plans' was a turning point therefore as a summary and integration of prog-

[5] J. F. Fulton, ed., *A textbook of physiology*, 17th edition (Philadelphia: W. B. Saunders, 1955).
[6] D. H. Hubel and T. N. Wiesel, Receptive fields, binocular interaction and functional architecture in the cat's visual cortex, *Journal of Physiology*, 1962, 160, 106–154.

ress in solving the second of my three historic problems. It communicated to many people what the answer was, and carries a high proportion of the credit for the now near-universal acceptance of that answer.

If it were only a summary of pre-existing ideas, however, the book might merely have had its persuasive effect and then been forgotten. It added other ideas as well, less visible in earlier work. One in particular, the concept of the TOTE unit, is probably the most frequently cited by later writers. It is fair to say that it was remembered, but has not as yet given rise to further behavioral research. It has been important as clearing up a difficulty and letting people get on with other things; more of this in a moment. In addition to the TOTE unit, there were a number of other ideas that are not usually quoted as coming from this book; but whose influence is clearly visible in later research.[3] Finally, there is a last group of ideas that are still dormant and may, in my view, bear on the third and still unsolved problem of psychology. Hence the suggestion that 'Plans' has still a further part to play.

The Concept of the TOTE

The construction of a cybernetic or information processing language required some basic unit, with which more complex processes could be built. One might think, and in the 1930s some people did think, that one could use as a unit the fact that the system produces a particular output; in situation X the animal or person contracts muscle group A, in situation Y muscle group B. Learning at that time was thought about as a change in the conditions under which A would occur rather than B. The mechanical analogy was with open-chain systems in which the input caused a particular output, as pressure on a bell-push causes the bell to ring, or as hitting a typewriter key causes a certain letter to be printed; with a switching system to take care of learning. (See for instance the footnote at the start of Chapter 3).

By the time of 'Plans,' however, it had long been clear that this would not do. The conditioned response, the salivation of a dog when a bell is rung after prolonged experience of bell plus food, looks like a simple output being transferred from one situation to another. It is not; in Pavlov's original paradigm, the composition of the saliva is different. When muscular movement rather than secretion is involved, one can see that the pattern of movement after learning is different from that in the unlearned reaction. If we use instrumental learning, giving a rat a pellet of food each time it presses a bar, we shall increase the frequency of bar-presses. It does not follow however that the rat is repeating the muscle-twitches that have been followed by food; because it may press the bar with one paw or with another, with its nose, or sit on it. What is learned is the achievement of some end-result, not the contraction of certain muscles. The behaviorists adopted various methods for dealing with this, of which the most successful was probably that of Skinner; he suggested that the unit of behavior should be the class of actions that were followed by a single later event. (For this reason, much of the critique of Skinner by Chomsky, quoted in Chapter 2, is misconceived.)

Although Skinner's formulation went part of the way towards a sound unit of analysis, it had two snags. First, the words used were so similar to those of Pavlov or Watson that readers could blur the important difference in concept. They could readily imagine that Skinner was still, like his predecessors of thirty years previously, thinking in terms of a fixed output; rather than a family of outputs linked by some achievement. (Indeed, there is a faint impression that 'Plans' itself makes this simplification). The TOTE unit, like Skinner's 'operant,' is defined by what it achieves; it tends towards goals rather than producing an invariant output. But it breaks away from the word 'reflex' that Skinner still used in the 1930s, and by doing so, as well as by drawing boxes and arrows for the flow of control, it brings home clearly to readers the fact that the concept is one of a closed-loop rather than an open-chain. Skinner's operant was assimilated by most readers to the very different notion of a door-bell ringing when a bell-push was pressed; the TOTE unit was never mistaken in that way.

The second advantage of the TOTE unit was the way it encouraged the notion of units existing simultaneously at different hierarchic levels. The temptation was to regard an operant as equivalent to a single bar-press; there were known to be strange phenomena that pointed to different interpretations, but these were exceptional. For example, in 'fixed-ratio reinforcement,' an animal gains a food pellet for ten bar-presses rather than one; and the rate of bar-pressing may become higher than it is when every press is successful. It was possible to regard the ten presses, not each one, as a single action; in that case the rate of emitting actions per unit time would be reasonable, and one would escape from the apparent paradox that the animal works harder for fewer rewards. In general however it was too difficult to see how in that case another animal could be taught with a different ratio; surely one could not have two, or more, sizes of unit simultaneously? With the concept of the TOTE unit, however, one could see that a larger unit of 'make ten presses' could well coexist with a smaller unit of 'make one press,' the achievement of the latter being part of the process of succeeding in the former. Similarly, a general unit of 'fixing the fence' might exist, and smaller units of 'buying the wood,' 'taking the wood to the fence,' 'nailing the wood to the gap'; and the latter might include, amongst other TOTE units, the 'hammering' unit discussed in Chapter 2. In contrast to operants, TOTE units can readily be thought of as potentially present even while lower-order units are deciding what will happen in the immediate future.

The TOTE unit therefore set at rest the worries of psychology as a whole, that a mechanical analysis of human function would founder on the obvious differences between the way we behave and the operation of a door-bell, a typewriter, or any other open-chain mechanism. Within a few years there disappeared from the journals and textbooks the concerned discussions of differences between the Unconditioned and the Conditioned Responses; it ceased to be an insuperable stumbling block that a rat taught to run through a maze would swim through it if the maze was full of water. Closed-loops, it was realized, can make that problem melt away. We are therefore entitled to seek computational principles that explain perception, decision, or memory without the nagging doubt that the whole enterprise is misconceived. It was this relief that caused the grateful citation of the TOTE unit in a succession of later contributions.

Interestingly, the TOTE was cited but not, in that era, further developed; the journals did not fill up with diagrams of hierarchic trees describing the way TOTEs combine to produce gardening, courtship, or counseling. There are reasons for this, which we shall discuss later. They do not undermine however the importance of setting psychology free from the conceptual problem of the open-chain link from input to output.

What Happened Afterwards

One of the shocks of re-reading 'Plans' is to encounter the casual and fairly frequent use of the phrase 'cognitive psychology.' Most of us associate it with a book of the same name by Ulric Neisser,[7] not published until 1967. That book, like 'Plans,' assumed that one can talk about events within the person and perform experiments to shed light upon them. In contrast to 'Plans,' however, it was able to quote a substantial body of experimental work, mostly performed since 1955, and all based on the same assumption. This body of hard data was seen by the psychological community as the cash payment that honored the cheque written by 'Plans,' and since then the number of people regarding themselves as cognitive psychologists has grown until it is now probably the majority of the discipline.

Looking back, the areas studied in the 1960s stayed pretty close to the sense-organs. The actual experimental techniques remained, as they had been for pre-cognitive human experimentalists, the delivery of isolated stimuli and the comparison of reaction to one kind of stimulus rather than another. Thus, a person might be presented with artificially generated sounds and asked what speech sound they perceive. Alternatively, a visual stimulus might be presented, consisting of several rows of letters, and a later signal would then indicate which row the person was to report. This kind of technique is of course the one to which open-chain thinking leads, but it was the one for which methods existed. The change introduced by the shift to a cognitive approach was a change to theories of a more active, top-down, kind; it was not a large change in experimental technique. Consequently while 'Plans' is full of people actively moving from sub-goal to sub-goal until their purposes are achieved, the cognitive laboratory of the 1960s was equally full of people sitting passively until the experimenter fired a stimulus at them.

[7] U. Neisser, *Cognitive Psychology* (New York: Appleton-Century-Crofts, 1967).

Neisser's book was largely devoted to studies of perception, and to some extent of relatively short-term memory. Perhaps the line of work closest to the spirit of 'Plans' was that on language; where the important developments in formal linguistics, summarized in Chapter 11, produced new kinds of stimuli to compare. Can one understand two sentences equally quickly when they have highly similar words but different syntactic depth? Such studies gave striking results; and as the decade wore on, the study of language became almost the dominant field of human experimental psychology. On the theoretical side it left totally behind the analogy with open-chain systems, even those with switches; and though the method was still usually to present some situation to an awaiting person, the 'stimulus' was now a long stream of written or acoustic events. The key experimental variable was the structure of the stream rather than its isolated members.

During the decade after the publication of Neisser's book, the quantity of research increased explosively. For one thing, small computers found their way into psychological laboratories. This made it much easier both to present complex stimuli such as sentences, and also to collect large numbers of reaction times. Previously, experimenters had the problem of reading clocks and writing down the times while the experimental subject waited impatiently. Now, the computer could take care of such details without interrupting the flow of signals. Particular ingenuity was shown by experimenters such as Sternberg and Posner, in devising tasks where the stimulus input was complex, needing a number of internal operations, but where the person could indicate a decision by pressing one of two keys. (Say, one key for 'these two letters are the same although one is upper-case and one lower-case' and the other key for 'these two letters are different'). The complex mechanisms that underlie pattern analysis, sentence comprehension, and temporary memory, were greatly illuminated in this way.

Two developments in particular stemmed from notions that are set out in 'Plans'. In Chapter 4, there is introduced the idea of a 'working memory,' some system that holds necessary information while a plan is being executed. The information need not however be retained after the plan is completed; indeed, it should not. If I act today on an intention that I had yesterday, disaster may ensue. What is wanted is a device to hold the intention only while it is in play. Computationally, such a mechanism is essential for all kinds of operations. The traditional approach to memory amongst psychologists had however concentrated on one particular task; presenting people with material, leaving them for an interval, and then asking them to recall it. This approach leads one, for parsimony, to think of memory as a single system; and in the 1960s the main achievement was to separate relatively short-term, temporary, memory, from longer-term retention, so as to show that memory was not a single monolithic entity. With the onset of the 1970s, however, it began to become clear that there are a number of different modes of temporary memory. People can say things to themselves, image them, recall them for relatively unanalyzed sensory storage; and above all they use these varying forms of representation to 'park' information that has been computed earlier, and that will be needed shortly. If for instance you are trying to add two numbers, each made up of several digits, you add pairs of digits and hold the results temporarily while you are adding the next pair. You may also have to hold the need to 'carry one'; and only at the end of the whole task can you clear the temporary memories. The study of 'working memory' is now a large and flourishing experimental area.[8] Most of the research is admittedly done by the traditional method of asking people to learn and recall items, under various conditions of difficulty; but the emphasis on the topic in 'Plans' is clearly justified by the experimental results.

The second area in which 'Plans' showed particular prescience was that of retrieval schemes, mnemonics, and organization of longer-term memory; discussed in Chapter 10. A wealth of experiments in the later 1960s and through the 1970s studied such processes. They confirmed up to the hilt the notion of long term retention and recall as being the result of active building of structures by the memorizer. When something is to be learned, the success of later retrieval is largely determined by the level or extent of processing that the material has received at input.[9] The relations between various items in

[8] A. D. Baddeley, Working memory, *Philosophical Transactions of the Royal Society of London*, 1983, B 302, 311–324. A. D. Baddeley, *Working Memory* (Oxford: Oxford University Press, in press).
[9] F. I. M. Craik and R. S. Lockhart, Levels of processing: A framework for memory research, *Journal of Verbal Learning and Verbal Behavior*, 1972, 11, 671–684.

Foreword ■ xxi

the material itself can also have a large influence; words that are linked into hierarchic groupings, and so amenable to the kind of scheme discussed in Chapter 10, are particularly memorable.[10] In fact, of course, much of our semantic knowledge falls into categories in such a way; it is obviously true that arbitrary names do so, with the result that cities fall within nations, and nations within continents. In addition however our pet Tweety is a canary, a canary is a bird, and a bird is an animal. Some properties of Tweety are unique, some shared with all canaries, and some indeed with all animals. The resulting network of properties and relationships can be shown to determine the speed with which we decide that a sentence about canaries or animals is true or false; and also the changes in speed that may occur in a task as a result of earlier activation of some other part of the network.

Nowadays therefore we appeal regularly to structures that cannot be directly observed, to explain the results of experiments on the speed or accuracy with which a person can react to, or remember, an observable stimulus. The whole body of knowledge that has been built up is too large for a foreword; there are plenty of lengthy books that summarize it.[11] The main point to assert is that the seeds of all this development lie here in the pages of 'Plans.'

Some Clouds and Uncertainties

It would be fantasy to argue that the developments of twenty-five years were accurately foreseen by a single book, however distinguished. A number of things have happened that fit badly into the scheme proposed by this volume. Perhaps the best way of introducing them is to look at the more recent work of Newell and Simon, whose earlier contributions provided much of the rationale for 'Plans.'

In the studies before 1960, computational models of problem-solving proceeded firmly in a hierarchic manner (see Chapter 13). In playing chess, the program would first decide whether it was its

---

[10] G. H. Bower, M. C. Clark, A. M. Lesgold, and D. Winzenz, Hierarchical retrieval schemes in recall of categorized word lists, *Journal of Verbal Learning and Verbal Behavior*, 1969, 8, 323–343.

[11] For instance, M. W. Eysenck, *A Handbook of Cognitive Psychology* (Hillsdale, NJ: Lawrence Erlbaum, 1983).

turn to play, then select a move, then evaluate that move, and so on. The program could be represented by a tree of nested sub-routines each called up in turn after the manner of the TOTE hierarchy. By the 1970s however Newell and Simon were proposing programs built as 'production systems.'[12] In such a system, the movement of the program through the problem can turn in a variety of directions whenever a choice point is encountered. At each such point a series of 'productions' is examined; a 'production' is a rule which states a possible situation that might be present, and says what is to be done if that situation does apply. If more than one condition is true, there is some rule for deciding the resulting conflict. Such a rule might, for example, be to take the first production on the list whose condition is satisfied. One can readily state single TOTE units as production systems; for example, here is one for hammering:

(1) IF goal = hammering AND Nail-head flush

THEN goal = next goal (That is, give up hammering and go on to the next job)

(2) IF goal = hammering AND Nail-head not flush AND hammer up

THEN strike nail

(3) IF goal = hammering AND Nail-head not flush AND hammer down

THEN lift hammer

If there are a number of TOTE units, however, they may not fit together in a simple hierarchy. For instance, one might imagine an extra rule in the above system:

(1a) IF goal = hammering AND wood has split

THEN goal = buy wood (That is, abandon hammering without a satisfactory outcome and go back to an earlier TOTE unit that you thought you had finished).

In a production system therefore it is not necessary for each sub-sub-goal to be achieved before one moves to the next sub-goal; nor for each sub-goal to be satisfied before one stops trying to achieve a main goal. The effect is to give the whole system much more flexibility. Just as the TOTE unit is less rigid than an open-chain machine,

---

[12] A. Newell and H. A. Simon, *Human Problem Solving* (Englewood Cliffs, NJ: Prentice-Hall, 1972).

so the production system is less rigid than a fixed hierarchy of goals.[13]

The extra flexibility is needed; attempts to program many kinds of problem show that the inflexible sequence will not work. Take for example the parsing of sentences. The insights achieved by the time of 'Plans' might suggest that one could first decode the syntactic structure, and then consider the semantics or meaning of the message. A well-known example from the late 1960s, however, was the contrast between the two sentences

(1) He had some dirt from his farm near the Hudson river.
(2) He had some dirt from his farm near his foot.

The correct parsing differs from these two sentences, because the final phrase modifies different earlier words in each case.[14]

One needs to know facts about the structure of the world in order to get the syntax right. A program attempting to place syntactic markers on each phrase would need to break off and go into a semantic process before returning to complete the syntactic part of the total task.

Modern programs for handling language, and solving other problems, therefore incorporate a good deal of knowledge about the topic that is going to be discussed, and their organization is sometimes described as 'heterarchic, not hierarchic.' In one sense this gives the whole system the same principle of flexibility that 'Plans' asserted at the level of the TOTE unit. The production, however is getting very similar to the old stimulus-response link in a more sophisticated guise. It is a condition-action rule. That is, in a situation, certain actions take place; just as the old theories used to assert that a stimulus was followed by a response. Nowadays the situation may include states of working memory, and the action may be entirely unobservable from outside the person; but the working of a single condition-action rule is an open-chain mechanism. One can see this in everyday life; as Chapter 11 argues, when we are faced with a fresh problem, we adopt a heuristic without any feedback, without being certain that our action is actually taking us in the direction we want. A consultant faced with the accounts of a new business will proclaim "You

---

[13] Ibid.

[14] The example comes from M. R. Quillian; for a general account of the complex interaction between syntax and semantics, see H. H. Clark and E. V. Clark, *Psychology and Language* (New York: Harcourt Brace, 1977).

must increase market share!" and then go through a number of TOTE units designed to meet that goal; but the choice of the goal is only reversed after a long period of failure.

In so far as the choice of a goal is an open-chain effect of the appearance of a problem, the person cannot report any intention which will justify it; something is done because it feels right, not because there is a plan that can be reported. The choice itself has been most studied in relatively simple situations, measuring reaction time and errors. From the results, it seems fairly definite that such choices are the outcome of a statistical process within the person. Some evidence in the situation points one way, some another, and gradually the person cumulates evidence until one alternative or the other wins out. Less evidence may be demanded for probable alternatives. Hence, people see what is probable even if it is not there, do what is usually appropriate even though this time it isn't, and generally show an impact of stochastic as well as determinate factors in a way that Chapter 3 rather resists.[15] The effect of this is that plans may be adopted for apparently unjustifiable and 'irrational' reasons, and that strange errors and slips of action occur in the execution of the plan.

To return to the problems of language, Chapter 11 introduced transformational grammar as if it provided a model for the actual mechanisms responsible for human utterance and perception. One must record that the verdict of the decades has gone against that idea. Some of the formal arguments of the Chapter are now regarded with more scepticism than they were in 1960; but that on its own is perhaps a matter of linguists, since it would be perfectly possible for the best and most elegant description of a language to be different from the mechanism that produced it. (In the same way, geometry describes a circle as $x^2 = a^2 - y^2$, but in the neurons and muscles of a man who draws a circle there is no corresponding equation.) The main point for us is that there are too many psychological experiments whose results are inconsistent with the hierarchies of Chapter 11. Rather, people seem to understand speech by applying a series of heuristic strategies, dropping one and picking up another depend-

---

[15] For an account of some of the evidence, see J. M. Wilding, *Perception: From sense to object* (especially Chapter 7) (London: Hutchinson, 1982).

ing on the difficulties they encounter.[16] The interaction of syntax and semantics, mentioned earlier, is just one aspect of this bewildering heterarchic medley of processes.

One can summarize the discrepancies and uncertainties that have arisen by raising again my third problem. The search for 'the' way in which people parse sentences is vain; so is the search for 'the' way in which they do anything else. The second problem, to which 'Plans' was addressed, can now be taken as solved; we are entitled to discuss the computations that must be involved in human performance, even when we do not know the physiology that underlies them. Twenty-five years of research of this kind have shown however that different people do the same task by using different computations, and that the same individual may do the same task on different occasions by different means depending on temporary purposes or states. There is a real difficulty in deciding how scientific accounts of human nature shall now proceed; but it is not a problem of 'Plans' alone, rather of the whole psychological community.

The Hope of the Future

The story of 'Plans' is unusual therefore. It is usually quoted for the concept of the TOTE unit; yet few other workers have in fact pursued that line further. It is less often quoted as a place where cognitive psychology was discussed very early on; yet that was so. Its discussions of working memory, and of systematic retrieval strategies, seem to have slept in the literature and only come to flower after a long interval. Finally, its expectation of a clear and consistent mechanism unrolling in a determinate and universal fashion, according to the assumptions of classical mechanics and classical psychology, has turned out invalid.

The most curious gap, between the fame of the book and the actions of its followers, lies in the kind of experiment that has occupied cognitive psychologists. As we have seen, in the laboratory the

---

[16] J. A. Fodor, T. G. Bever, and M. F. Garrett, *The psychology of language* (New York: McGraw-Hill, 1974). See also H. H. Clark and E. V. Clark, op. cit., and H. C. Longuet-Higgins, J. Lyons, and D. E. Broadbent, eds., *The Psychological Mechanisms of Language* (London: Royal Society, British Academy, 1981).

technique of study has continued to be through firing stimuli at a person who sits and awaits them. Theory has become more dynamic; not so empirical work. The reason is, of course, technological. If we leave people free to construct their own plans, to achieve those plans by a variety of routes, and even more to drop unachieved goals and move laterally to others as modern psycholinguistics suggests, then we have an enormous problem of recording and analyzing data. There was no way of doing this in 1960; nor indeed until recently. Research wisely took the insight of the TOTE unit as an assurance that cognitive psychology would in the end be possible; and got on with the perceptual and memory processes that could be studied by traditional paradigms.

Even in the 1950s there was one area where experiments of a different kind could be performed; the one of motor skill, attacked in Chapter 6. If one asks a person to move a pointer to a certain target, they will not do so in a totally open-chain fashion but will show the flexible and variable, and yet lawful, sequence of movements that one would expect from the involvement of TOTE units. In the United States, Paul Fitts had by 1960 performed numbers of elegant experiments on the mechanisms involved; and in Britain Craik had gone on from *The Nature of Explanation* to launch a programme of such research continued by Gibbs, Leonard, and Poulton. As they showed, the achievement of a skilled movement involved a smooth interplay of closed-loop mechanisms with ballistic open-chain ones, and with long range anticipatory actions intelligible only in the light of the overall plan.[17] All this work however lay in the area of engineering psychology rather than in traditional academic circles, and it depended heavily on funding from agencies that wanted practical answers. After 1960 the need for such work waned, and the pace of experimentation decreased; the investigators who seized on the possibilities of cognitive psychology did not normally see the possibilities of manual skill. After 'Plans,' psychology became cognitive not only in the sense of allowing explanations from processes inside the person, but also in confining itself to verbal and intellectual processes rather than the manual and skilled ones of Chapter 6.

Recently however there have been signs that the special nature

[17] See for instance D. H. Holding, ed., *Human Skills* (Chichester: Wiley, 1980).

of motor skill, and its illumination of the connection between intention and action, have become of renewed interest in the academic community. Actions, as opposed to responses, are reviving in respectability.[18] This has coincided with a new concern for the errors and slips of action that occur in everyday life, when we take wrong turns, mislay property, or generate slips of the tongue.[19] Now that a long period of experiment has built up knowledge about the processes initiated by stimuli, scholars are ready to think about activities initiated by the person.

At the same time the technological problem is no longer so serious. As domestic computer games show us, it is easy to store in a small and cheap computer a surprisingly rich world through which people can move in any order they please. They can be (and often are in commercial games) left to explore with no clear instruction about what goal to set themselves. Even if they have an ultimate goal, they can reach it in a controllable variety of ways. There is no longer an insuperable problem of letting the person rather than the experimenter take the initiative, and yet being able to specify the consequences that will follow for any of a large set of chosen actions.

There is even a new practical demand, arising from the problems of devising large computer systems so that users can interact naturally with them. A modern 'expert system' will involve a substantial amount of stored information about the topic on which it is to give advice, and to control the inferences it draws from that knowledge; but it may also involve as much again to make itself intelligible to a human being. The builders of hardware and software need badly to understand the ways that a person is liable to approach their systems, and the goals, sub-goals, and principles which the person will use to interact with the machine.

The technology and the interest is now present to acquire empirical data about plans. We could now back up the study of action with data in the same way that the last twenty-five years have backed

---

[18] For example, W. Prinz and A. F. Sanders, *Cognition and Motor Processes* (Berlin: Springer-Verlag, 1984).

[19] J. Reason and K. Mycielska, *Absent-Minded?* (Englewood Cliffs, NJ: Prentice-Hall, 1982).

up cognitive theories of perception and memory with data. If so, the ideas in this book will take on a new significance and produce a new flowering.

Nostalgia: And Something More

From these cosmic considerations, let us come back to the personal and nostalgic. For those who lived through the period of 'Plans,' these pages carry a memory of sunshine and hope. The style, the gracefully worn scholarship, and the wide curiosity about all sorts of human phenomena, all contrast sharply with the turgid prose and narrow interests of so much psychological work in the 1980s. We are reading here of a secure world in which the human mind was beginning to reach out to understand its own nature; only shortly after Sputnik, before the Cuban missile crisis, in a day when Palo Alto seemed a long way from the troubles of Europe, let alone Africa or the Middle East. Of course it was also a time of capital punishment, of legal penalties for homosexuals, of racism that makes the current form look almost virtuous by comparison. But there were some good things amongst the bad; just as there are now. The achievement of 'Plans,' and of the men who wrote it, stands out as a model of the way that important problems should be tackled. Let us learn from them.

DONALD E. BROADBENT

PROLOGUE

As I sit at my desk, I know where I am. I see before me a window; beyond that some trees; beyond that the red roofs of the campus of Stanford University; beyond them the trees and roof tops which mark the town of Palo Alto: beyond them the bare golden hills of the Hamilton Range. I know, however, more than I see. Behind me, although I am not looking in that direction, I know there is a window, and beyond that the little campus of the Center for Advanced Study in the Behavioral Sciences; beyond that the Coast Range; beyond that the Pacific Ocean.

With these words the economist Kenneth E. Boulding begins a short treatise entitled *The Image*, in which he explores some of the dimensions of our picture of man and the universe.[1] He goes on to sketch some of the larger aspects of his own Image whereby he feels himself located in space and time and society and nature and his own personal history. He is not thinking here of simple visual images; blind men have Images, too. The Image is his knowledge of the world. His behavior depends upon the Image. Meaningful messages change

[1] Kenneth E. Boulding, *The Image* (Ann Arbor: University of Michigan Press, 1956).

the Image. He pursues men's Images through biology, sociology, economics, political science, and history, and he weaves together a tapestry of private and public Images, of personal and shared knowledge, which can best be described as a snapshot of a twentieth-century mind at work.

Boulding wrote *The Image* during the summer of 1955 at the close of an academic year spent in California at the Center for Advanced Study in the Behavioral Sciences. It was just three years later, during the academic year 1958–59, that the present authors assembled, not entirely accidentally, at that same Center. We had our individual problems. We had some shared problems that dated back to a summer together at Harvard in 1956. And we had a general commitment to continue our own education. It was in the course of that latter project that we came across *The Image* on the shelf of the Center's library. To psychologists who like alternatives to nickel-in-the-slot, stimulus-response conceptions of man, an Image has considerable appeal. (It is so reasonable to insert between the stimulus and the response a little wisdom. And there is no particular need to apologize for putting it there, because it was already there before psychology arrived.) *The Image* became a part of the Image we were building for ourselves, in our conversations and our arguments and our writings.

But as the year advanced and our Image grew, we slowly became convinced that Boulding—and cognitive psychologists generally—had not told a complete story. We thought we knew a part that was missing. Although we could accept, in spirit if not in detail, the argument that cognitive theorists made, it left an organism more in the role of a spectator than of a participant in the drama of living. Unless you can use your Image to do something, you are like a man who collects maps but never makes a trip. It seemed to us that a Plan is needed in order to exploit the Image.

The notion of a Plan that guides behavior is, again not entirely accidentally, quite similar to the notion of a program that guides an electronic computer. In order to discover how to get the Image into motion, therefore, we reviewed once more the cybernetic literature on the analogies between brains and computers, between minds and programs. In this survey we were especially fortunate in having at our disposal a large mass of material, much of it still unpublished, that Miller had obtained from Allen Newell, J. C. Shaw, and Herbert A. Simon in the course of a Research Training Institute on the Simulation of Cognitive Processes held at RAND Corporation, Santa Monica, California, July 1958, and sponsored by the Social Science Research Council. Unfortunately, however, when these materials were transported from the think-center in Santa Monica to the think-center in Stanford, the electronic computer, its attendants, and the research workers themselves had to be left behind. Without those supporting facilities, all we could do was try to understand the spirit of the work as simply and concretely as we could—but doubtless there was considerable distortion in the channel. Newell, Shaw, and Simon inspired us by their successes, but they should not be held responsible for our mistakes or embellishments. Nor should Wiener, Ashby, von Neumann, Minsky, Shannon, MacKay, McCulloch, Chomsky, or any of the other authors whose work we studied. Our only hope is that there really can be such a thing as creative misunderstanding.

Our fundamental concern, however, was to discover whether the cybernetic ideas have any relevance for psychology. The men who have pioneered in this area have been remarkably innocent about psychology—the creatures whose behavior they want to simulate often seem more like a mathematician's dream than like living animals. But in spite of all the evidence, we refused to believe that ignorance of psychology is a cybernetic prerequisite or even an advantage. There must be some way to phrase the new ideas so that they can contribute to and profit from the science of behavior that psychologists have created. It was the search for that favorable intersection that directed the course of our year-long debate.

With an Image, a Plan, and a debate simmering in our minds, it soon became necessary for us to write the argument down in order to remember what it was. And as things became clearer, suddenly it seemed necessary to make a book of the argument. It was to be a little book, even smaller than it turned out to be. It was to take only a few days to write, but those days stretched into months. It was to be our intellectual diary for the year, with none of the defensiveness or documentation that have since crept into it. But in spite of all those familiar academic vectors acting upon it, it has turned out to be a spontaneous, argumentative, personal kind of book that should irritate our sober-sided colleagues. That would be all right—sober-sided colleagues deserve to be irritated—except that more is at stake than the authors' reputations. Some of the ideas we have used are too good to lose. It would be unfortunate if our style were to conceal the true merit of the arguments we try to present. If we had had more time together, we might have been able to argue our way through to a better-balanced composition. But a year is only a year long. So, gentle reader, if your anger starts to rise, take a deep breath, accept our apologies—and push ahead.

CHAPTER 1

IMAGES AND PLANS

Consider how an ordinary day is put together. You awaken, and as you lie in bed, or perhaps as you move slowly about in a protective shell of morning habits, you think about what the day will be like—it will be hot, it will be cold; there is too much to do, there is nothing to fill the time; you promised to see him, she may be there again today. If you are compulsive, you may worry about fitting it all in, you may make a list of all the things you have to do. Or you may launch yourself into the day with no clear notion of what you are going to do or how long it will take. But, whether it is crowded or empty, novel or routine, uniform or varied, your day has a structure of its own—it fits into the texture of your life. And as you think what your day will hold, you construct a plan to meet it. What you expect to happen foreshadows what you expect to do.

The authors of this book believe that the plans you make are interesting and that they probably have some relation to how you actually spend your time during the day. We call them "plans" without malice—we recognize that you do not draw out long and elaborate blueprints for every moment of the day. You do not need to. Rough, sketchy, flexible anticipations are usually sufficient. As you brush your teeth you decide that you will answer that pile of letters you have been neglecting. That is enough. You do not need to list the names of the people or to draft an outline of the contents of the letters. You think simply that today there will be time for it after lunch. After lunch, if you remember, you turn to the letters. You take one and read it. You plan your answer. You may need to check on some information, you dictate or type or scribble a reply, you address an envelope, seal the folded letter, find a stamp, drop it in a mailbox. Each of these subactivities runs off as the situation arises—you did not need to enumerate them while you were planning the day. All you need is the name of the activity that you plan for that segment of the day, and from that name you then proceed to elaborate the detailed actions involved in carrying out the plan.

You *imagine* what your day is going to be and you make *plans* to cope with it. Images and plans. What does modern psychology have to say about images and plans?

Presumably, the task of modern psychology is to make sense out of what people and animals do, to find some system for understanding their behavior. If we, as psychologists, come to this task with proper scientific caution, we must begin with what we can see and we must postulate as little as possible beyond that. What we can see are movements and environmental events. The ancient subject matter of psychology—the mind and its various manifestations—is distressingly invisible, and a science with invisible content is likely to become an invisible science. We are therefore led to underline the fundamental importance of behavior and, in particular, to try to discover recurrent patterns of stimulation and response.

What an organism does depends on what happens around it. As to the way in which this dependency should be described, however, there are, as in most matters of modern psychology, two schools of thought. On the one hand are the optimists, who claim to find the dependency simple and straightforward. They model the stimulus-response relation after the classical, physiological pattern of the reflex arc and use Pavlov's discoveries to explain how new reflexes can be formed through experience. This approach is too simple for all but the most extreme optimists. Most psychologists quickly realize that behavior in general, and human behavior in particular, is not a chain of conditioned reflexes. So the model is complicated slightly by incorporating some of the stimuli that occur after the response in addition to the stimuli that occur before the response. Once these "reinforcing" stimuli are included in the description, it becomes possible to understand a much greater variety of behaviors and to acknowledge the apparently purposive nature of behavior. That is one school of thought.

Arrayed against the reflex theorists are the pessimists, who think that living organisms are complicated, devious, poorly designed for research purposes, and so on. They maintain that the effect an event will have upon behavior depends on how the event is represented in the organism's picture of itself and its universe. They are quite sure that any correlations between stimulation and response must be mediated by <u>an organized representation of the environment, a system of concepts and relations within which the organism is located</u>. A human being—and probably other animals as well—builds up an internal representation, a model of the universe, a schema, a simulacrum, a cognitive map, an Image. Sir Frederic C. Bartlett, who uses the term "schema" for this internal representation, describes it in this way:

> "Schema" refers to an active organisation of past reactions, or of past experiences, which must always be supposed to be operating in any well-adapted organic response. That is, whenever there is any order or regularity of behavior, a particular response is possible only because it is related to other similar responses which have been serially organised, yet which operate, not simply as individual members coming one after another, but as a unitary mass. Determination by schemata is the most fundamental of all the ways in which we can be influenced by reactions and experiences which occurred some time in the past. All incoming impulses of a certain kind, or mode, go together to build up an active, organised setting: visual, auditory, various types of cutaneous impulses and the like, at a relatively low level; all the experiences connected by a common interest: in sport, in literature, history, art, science, philosophy, and so on, on a higher level.[1]

[1] Frederic C. Bartlett, *Remembering, A Study in Experimental and Social Psychology* (Cambridge: Cambridge University Press, 1932), p. 201.

The crux of the argument, as every psychologist knows, is whether anything so mysterious and inaccessible as "the organism's picture of itself and its universe," or "an active organisation of past reactions," etc., is really necessary. Necessary, that is to say, as an explanation for the behavior that can be observed to occur.

The view that some mediating organization of experience is necessary has a surprisingly large number of critics among hard-headed, experimentally trained psychologists. The mediating organization is, of course, a theoretical concept and, out of respect for Occam's Razor, one should not burden the science with unnecessary theoretical luggage. An unconditional proof that a completely consistent account of behavior cannot be formulated more economically does not exist, and until we are certain that simpler ideas have failed we should not rush to embrace more complicated ones. Indeed, there are many psychologists who think the simple stimulus-response-reinforcement models provide an adequate description of everything a psychologist should concern himself with.

For reasons that are not entirely clear, the battle between these two schools of thought has generally been waged at the level of animal behavior. Edward Tolman, for example, has based his defense of cognitive organization almost entirely on his studies of the behavior of rats—surely one of the least promising areas in which to investigate intellectual accomplishments. Perhaps he felt that if he could win the argument with the simpler animal, he would win it by default for the more complicated ones. If the description of a rodent's cognitive structure is necessary in order to understand its behavior, then it is just that much more important for understanding the behavior of a dog, or an ape, or a man. Tolman's position was put most simply and directly in the following paragraph:

> [The brain] is far more like a map control room than it is like an old-fashioned telephone exchange. The stimuli, which are allowed in, are not connected by just simple one-to-one switches to the outgoing responses. Rather, the incoming impulses are usually worked over and elaborated in the central control room into a tentative, cognitivelike map of the environment. And it is this tentative map, indicating routes and paths and environmental relationships, which finally determines what responses, if any, the animal will finally release.[2]

[2] Edward C. Tolman, Cognitive maps in rats and men, *Psychological Review*, 1948, 55, 189–208.

We ourselves are quite sympathetic to this kind of theorizing, since it seems obvious to us that a great deal more goes on between the stimulus and the response than can be accounted for by a simple statement about associative strengths. The pros and cons cannot be reviewed here—the argument is long and other texts [3] exist in which an interested reader can pursue it—so we shall simply announce that our theoretical preferences are all on the side of the cognitive theorists. Life is complicated.

Nevertheless, there is a criticism of the cognitive position that seems quite important and that has never, so far as we know, received an adequate answer. The criticism is that the cognitive processes Tolman and others have postulated are not, in fact, sufficient to do the job they were supposed to do. Even if you admit these ghostly inner somethings, say the critics, you will not have explained anything about the animal's behavior. Guthrie has made the point about as sharply as anyone:

> Signs, in Tolman's theory, occasion in the rat *realization*, or *cognition*, or *judgment*, or *hypotheses*, or *abstraction*, but *they do not occasion action*. In his concern with what goes on in the rat's mind, Tolman has neglected to predict what the rat will do. So far as the theory is concerned the rat is left buried in thought; if he gets to the food-box at the end that is his concern, not the concern of the theory.[4]

Perhaps the cognitive theorists have not understood the force of this criticism. It is so transparently clear to them that if a hungry rat knows where to find food—if he has a cognitive map with the food-box located on it—he will go there and eat. What more is there to explain? The answer, of course, is that a great deal is left to be explained. The gap from knowledge to action looks smaller than the gap from stimulus to action—yet the gap is still there, still indefinitely large. Tolman, the omniscient theorist, leaps over that gap when he infers the rat's cognitive organization from its behavior. But that leaves still outstanding the question of the rat's ability to leap it. Apparently, cognitive theorists have assumed that their best course was

---

[3] See, for example, either E. R. Hilgard, *Theories of Learning* (New York: Appleton-Century-Crofts, ed. 2, 1956), or W. K. Estes *et al.*, *Modern Learning Theory* (New York: Appleton-Century-Crofts, 1954), or D. O. Hebb, *The Organization of Behavior* (New York: Wiley, 1949).
[4] E. R. Guthrie, *The Psychology of Learning* (New York: Harper, 1935), p. 172.

to show that the reflex theories are inadequate; they seem to have been quite unprepared when the same argument—that things are even more complicated than they dared to imagine—was used against them. Yet, if Guthrie is right, more cognitive theory is needed than the cognitive theorists normally supply. That is to say, far from respecting Occam's Razor, the cognitive theorist must ask for even *more* theoretical luggage to carry around. Something is needed to bridge the gap from knowledge to action.

It is unfair to single out Tolman and criticize him for leaving the cognitive representation paralytic. Other cognitive theorists could equally well be cited. Wolfgang Köhler, for example, has been subjected to the same kind of heckling. In reporting his extremely perceptive study of the chimpanzees on Tenerife Island during the first World War, Köhler wrote:

> We can . . . distinguish sharply between the kind of behavior which from the very beginning arises out of a consideration of the structure of a situation, and one that does not. Only in the former case do we speak of insight, and only that behavior of animals definitely appears to us intelligent which takes account from the beginning of the lay of the land, and proceeds to deal with it in a single, continuous, and definite course. Hence follows this criterion of insight: *the appearance of a complete solution with reference to the whole lay-out of the field.*[5]

Other psychologists have been less confident that they could tell the difference between behavior based on an understanding of the whole layout and behavior based on less cognitive processes, so there has been a long and rather fruitless controversy over the relative merits of trial-and-error and of insight as methods of learning. The point we wish to raise here, however, is that Köhler makes the standard cognitive assumption: once the animal has grasped the whole layout he will behave appropriately. Again, the fact that grasping the whole layout may be necessary, but is certainly not sufficient as an explanation of intelligent behavior, seems to have been ignored by Köhler. Many years later, for example, we heard Karl Lashley say this to him:

> I attended the dedication, three weeks ago, of a bridge at Dyea, Alaska. The road to the bridge for nine miles was blasted

[5] Wolfgang Köhler, *The Mentality of Apes* (translated from the second edition by Ella Winter; London: Routledge and Kegan Paul, 1927), pp. 169–170.

along a series of cliffs. It led to a magnificent steel bridge, permanent and apparently indestructible. After the dedication ceremonies I walked across the bridge and was confronted with an impenetrable forest of shrubs and underbrush, through which only a couple of trails of bears led to indeterminate places. In a way, I feel that Professor Köhler's position is somewhat that of the bridge. . . . The neurological problem is in large part, if not entirely, the translation of the afferent pattern of impulses into the efferent pattern. The field theory in its present form includes no hint of the way in which the field forces induce and control the pattern of efferent activity. It applies to perceptual experience but seems to end there.[6]

Many other voices could be added to this dialogue. Much detailed analysis of different psychological theories could be displayed to show why the cognitive theorists feel they have answered the criticism and why their critics still maintain that they have not. But we will not pursue it. Our point is that many psychologists, including the present authors, have been disturbed by a theoretical vacuum between cognition and action. The present book is largely the record of prolonged—and frequently violent—conversations about how that vacuum might be filled.

No doubt it is perfectly obvious to the reader that we have here a modern version of an ancient puzzle. At an earlier date we might have introduced the topic directly by announcing that we intended to discuss the will. But today the will seems to have disappeared from psychological theory, assimilated anonymously into the broader topic of motivation. The last serious attempt to make sense out of the will was the early work of Kurt Lewin and his students. Lewin's contributions are so important that we will treat them in detail in Chapter 4; we cannot dismiss them summarily by a paragraph in this introduction. In order to show what a psychology of will might be like, therefore, it is necessary to return to an earlier and more philosophical generation of psychologists. William James provides the sort of discussion that was once an indispensable part of every psychology text, so let us consider briefly how he handled the topic.

The second volume of *The Principles* contains a long chapter

---

[6] Lloyd A. Jeffress, ed., *Cerebral Mechanisms in Behavior* (New York: Wiley, 1951), p. 230.

(106 pages) entitled "Will." The first third of it is James's struggle against theories based on "sensations of innervation"—the notion that the innervation required to perform the appropriate action is itself a part of the cognitive representation. James maintains instead that it is the anticipation of the kinesthetic effects of the movement that is represented in consciousness. He then turns to the topic of "ideo-motor action," which provides the foundation for his explanation of all phenomena of will. If a person forms a clear image of a particular action, that action tends to occur. The occurrence may be inhibited, limited to covert tensions in the muscles, but in many cases having an idea of an action is sufficient for action. If there is anything between the cognitive representation and the overt action, it is not represented in consciousness. Introspectively, therefore, there seems to be no vacuum to be filled, and James, had he heard them, would have felt that criticisms of the sort made by Guthrie and Lashley were not justified.

But what of the more complicated cases of willing? What occurs when we force ourselves through some unpleasant task by "the slow dead heave of the will?" According to James, the feeling of effort arises from our attempt to keep our attention focused on the unpleasant idea. "The essential achievement of the will," he tells us, "is to *attend* to a difficult object and hold it fast before the mind." [7] If an idea can be maintained in attention, then the action that is envisioned in the idea occurs automatically—a direct example of ideo-motor action. All of which helps us not in the least. The bridge James gives us between the *ideo* and the *motor* is nothing but a hyphen. There seems to be no alternative but to strike out into the vacuum on our own.

The problem is to describe how actions are controlled by an organism's internal representation of its universe. If we consider what these actions are in the normal, freely ranging animal, we must be struck by the extent to which they are organized into patterns. Most psychologists maintain that these action patterns are punctuated by goals and subgoals, but that does not concern us for the moment. We wish to call attention to the fact that the organization does exist—configuration is just as important a property of behavior as it is of

[7] William James, *The Principles of Psychology*, Vol. II (New York: Holt, 1890), p. 561.

perception. The configurations of behavior, however, tend to be predominantly temporal—it is the *sequence* of motions that flows onward so smoothly as the creature runs, swims, flies, talks, or whatever. What we must provide, therefore, is some way to map the cognitive representation into the appropriate *pattern* of activity. But how are we to analyze this flowing pattern of action into manageable parts?

The difficulty in analyzing the actions of an animal does not arise from any lack of ways to do it but from an embarrassment of riches. We can describe an action as a sequence of muscle twitches, or as a sequence of movements of limbs and other parts, or as a sequence of goal-directed actions, or in even larger units. Following Tolman, most psychologists distinguish the little units from the big units by calling the little ones "molecular," the big ones, "molar." Anyone who asks which unit is the correct size to use in describing behavior is told that behavioral laws seem more obvious when molar units are used, but that just how molar he should be in any particular analysis is something he will have to learn from experience and observation in research.

The implication is relatively clear, however, that the molar units must be composed of molecular units, which we take to mean that a proper description of behavior must be made on *all levels simultaneously*. That is to say, we are trying to describe a process that is organized on several different levels, and the pattern of units at one level can be indicated only by giving the units at the next higher, or more molar, level of description. For example, the molar pattern of behavior X consists of two parts, A and B, in that order. Thus, $X = AB$. But A, in turn, consists of two parts, a and b; and B consists of three, c, d, and e. Thus, $X = AB = abcde$, and we can describe the same segment of behavior at any one of the three levels. The point, however, is that we do not want to pick one level and argue that it is somehow better than the others; the complete description must include all levels. Otherwise, the configurational properties of the behavior will be lost—if we state only $abcde$, for example, then $(ab)(cde)$ may become confused with $(abc)(de)$, which may be a very different thing.

This kind of organization of behavior is most obvious, no doubt, in human verbal behavior. The individual phonemes are organized into morphemes, morphemes are strung together to form phrases, phrases in the proper sequence form a sentence, and a string of sentences makes up the utterance. The complete description of the utterance involves all these levels. The kind of ambiguity that results when all levels are not known is suggested by the sentence, "They are flying planes." The sequence of phonemes may remain unchanged, but the two analyses *(They)(are flying)(planes)* and *(They)(are) (flying planes)* are very different utterances.[8]

Psychologists have seldom demonstrated any reluctance to infer the existence of such molar units as "words" or even "meanings" when they have dealt with verbal behavior, even though the actual responses available to perception are merely the strings of phones, the acoustic representations of the intended phonemes. Exactly the same recognition of more molar units in nonverbal behavior deserves the same kind of multi-level description. Unfortunately, however, the psychologist usually describes behavior—or some aspect of behavior—at a single level and leaves his colleagues to use their own common sense to infer what happened at other levels. The meticulous recording of every muscle twitch, even if anyone were brave enough to try it, would still not suffice, for it would not contain the structural features that characterize the molar units—and those structural features must be *inferred* on the basis of a *theory* about behavior. Our theories of behavior, in this sense of the term, have always remained implicit and intuitive. (It is rather surprising to realize that after half a century of behaviorism this aspect of the problem of describing behavior has almost never been recognized, much less solved.)

---

[8] The traditional method of parsing a sentence is the prototype of the kind of behavioral description we demand. Noam Chomsky, in Chapter 4 of his monograph, *Syntactic Structures* (The Hague: Mouton, 1957), provides a formal representation of this kind of description, which linguists refer to as "constituent analysis." We shall discuss Chomsky's method of representing verbal behavior in more detail in Chapter 11. The suggestion that linguistic analysis provides a model for the description of all kinds of behavior is, of course, no novelty; it has been made frequently by both linguists and psychologists. For example, in *The Study of Language* (Cambridge: Harvard University Press, 1953), John B. Carroll, a psychologist, observed that, "From linguistic theory we get the notion of a hierarchy of units—from elemental units like the distinctive feature of a phoneme to large units like a sentence-type. It may be suggested that stretches of any kind of behavior may be organized in somewhat the same fashion" (p. 106).

In those fortunate instances that do give us adequate descriptions of behavior—instances provided almost entirely by linguists and ethologists—it is quite obvious that the behavior is organized simultaneously at several levels of complexity. We shall speak of this fact as the "hierarchical organization of behavior."[9] The hierarchy can be represented in various ways. The diagram of a hierarchy usually takes the form of a tree, the arborizations indicating progressively more molecular representations. Or it can be cast as an outline:

    X.
       A.
          a.
          b.
       B.
          c.
          d.
          e.

This outline shows the structure of the hypothetical example introduced on page 13. Or it can be considered as a collection of lists: X is a list containing the two items, A and B; A is a list containing two items, a and b; B is a list containing three items, c, d, and e.[10] Or it can be considered as a set of rules governing permissible substitu-

---

[9] Many psychologists are familiar with the notion that behavior is hierarchically organized because they remember Clark Hull's use of the phrase "habit-family hierarchy." We must hasten to say, therefore, that Hull's use of the term "hierarchy" and our present use of that term have almost nothing in common. We are talking about a hierarchy of levels of representation. Hull was talking about an ordering of alternative (interchangeable, substitutable) responses according to their strengths. See, for example, C. L. Hull, The concept of the habit-family hierarchy and maze learning, *Psychological Review*, 1934, 41, 33–54; 134–152. Closer to the spirit of the present discussion is the system of behavioral episodes used by Roger G. Barker and Herbert F. Wright, in *Midwest and Its Children* (Evanston: Row, Peterson, 1954), to describe the molar behavior of children in their natural habitats. The work of Barker and Wright is a noteworthy exception to our assertion that psychologists have not tried to describe the structural features of behavior.

[10] The tree and outline forms of representation are quite ancient and familiar, but the use of list structures for representing such organizations is, we believe, relatively new. We first became acquainted with it through the work of Newell, Shaw, and Simon on the simulation of cognitive processes by computer programs. See, for example, Allen Newell and Herbert A. Simon, The logic theory machine: A complex information processing system, *IRE Transactions on Information Theory*, 1956, Vol. IT-2, No. 3, 61–79. Also, Allen Newell and J. C. Shaw, Programming the logic theory machine, *Proceedings of the Western Joint Computer Conference*, Los Angeles, February 1957, pp. 230–240.

tions: Where X occurs, we can substitute for it AB; where A occurs we can substitute ab; etc.[11] Each of these methods of presentation of a hierarchy has its special advantages in special situations.

Now, if the hierarchical nature of the organization of behavior can be taken as axiomatic, the time has come to set aside a few terms for the special purposes of the present discussions. Because definitions make heavy reading, we shall keep the list as short as possible.

Plan. Any complete description of behavior should be adequate to serve as a set of instructions, that is, it should have the characteristics of a plan that could guide the action described. When we speak of a Plan in these pages, however, the term will refer to a *hierarchy* of instructions, and the capitalization will indicate that this special interpretation is intended. *A Plan is any hierarchical process in the organism that can control the order in which a sequence of operations is to be performed.*

(2) A Plan is, for an organism, essentially the same as a program for a computer, especially if the program has the sort of hierarchical character described above. Newell, Shaw, and Simon have explicitly and systematically used the hierarchical structure of lists in their development of "information-processing languages" that are used to program high-speed digital computers to simulate human thought processes. Their success in this direction—which the present authors find most impressive and encouraging—argues strongly for the hypothesis that a hierarchical structure is the basic form of organization in human problem-solving. Thus, we are reasonably confident that "program" could be substituted everywhere for "Plan" in the following pages. However, the reduction of Plans to nothing but programs is still a scientific hypothesis and is still in need of further validation. For the present, therefore, it should be less confusing if we regard a computer program that simulates certain features of an organism's behavior as a theory about the organismic Plan that generated the behavior.[12]

[11] Chomsky, *op. cit.*, p. 26.
[12] It should be clearly recognized that, as Newell, Shaw, and Simon point out, comparing the sequence of operations executed by an organism and by a properly programmed computer is quite different from comparing computers with brains, or electrical relays with synapses, etc. See Allen Newell, J. C. Shaw, and Herbert A. Simon, Elements of a theory of human problem solving. *Psy-*

Moreover, we shall also use the term "Plan" to designate a rough sketch of some course of action, just the major topic headings in the outline, as well as the completely detailed specification of every detailed operation.[13]

Strategy and Tactics. The concept of the hierarchical organization of behavior was introduced earlier with the distinction between molar and molecular units of analysis. Now, however, we wish to augment our terminology. The molar units in the organization of behavior will be said to comprise the behavioral *strategy*, and the molecular units, the *tactics*.

Execution. We shall say that a creature is executing a particular Plan when in fact that Plan is controlling the sequence of operations he is carrying out. When an organism executes a Plan he proceeds through it step by step, completing one part and then moving to the next. The execution of a Plan need not result in overt action—especially in man, it seems to be true that there are Plans for collecting or transforming information, as well as Plans for guiding actions. Although it is not actually necessary, we assume on intuitive grounds that only one Plan is executed at a time, although relatively rapid alternation between Plans may be possible. An organism may—probably does—store many Plans other than the ones it happens to be executing at the moment.

Image. The Image is all the accumulated, organized knowledge that the organism has about itself and its world. The Image consists of a great deal more than imagery, of course. What we have in mind when we use this term is essentially the same kind of private representation that other cognitive theorists have demanded. It includes

---

chological Review, 1958, 65, 151–166. Also, Herbert A. Simon and Allen Newell, Models, their uses and limitations, in L. D. White, ed., *The State of the Social Sciences* (Chicago: University of Chicago Press, 1956), pp. 66–83.

[13] Newell, Shaw, and Simon have also used "plan" to describe a general strategy before the details have been worked out, but they distinguish between such a plan and the program that enables a computer to use planning as one of its problem-solving techniques. See Allen Newell, J. C. Shaw, and Herbert A. Simon, A report on a general problem solving program. *Proceedings of the International Conference on Information Processing*, Paris, 1959 (in press).

Other workers have used the term "machine" rather loosely to include both the Plan and the instrument that executes it. For example, see M. L. Minsky, *Heuristic Aspects of the Artificial Intelligence Problem*, Group Report 34–55, Lincoln Laboratory, Massachusetts Institute of Technology, 17 December 1956, especially Section III.3.

everything the organism has learned—his values as well as his facts—organized by whatever concepts, images, or relations he has been able to master.

In the course of prolonged debates the present authors heard themselves using many other terms to modify "Plan" in rather special ways, but they will not be listed here. New terms will be defined and developed as they are needed in the course of the argument that follows. For the moment, however, we have defined enough to be able to say that the central problem of this book is *to explore the relation between the Image and the Plan.*

Stated so, it may seem to imply some sharp dichotomy between the two, so that it would be meaningful to ask, "Is such-and-such a process exclusively in the Plan or exclusively in the Image?" That the two points of view cannot be used in that way to classify processes into mutually exclusive categories should become apparent from such considerations as these:

—A Plan can be learned and so would be a part of the Image.

—The names that Plans have must comprise a part of the Image for human beings, since it must be part of a person's Image of himself that he is able to execute such-and-such Plans.

—Knowledge must be incorporated into the Plan, since otherwise it could not provide a basis for guiding behavior. Thus, Images can form part of a Plan.

—Changes in the Images can be effected only by executing Plans for gathering, storing, or transforming information.

—Changes in the Plans can be effected only by information drawn from the Images.

—The transformation of descriptions into instructions is, for human beings, a simple verbal trick.

Psychologists who are accustomed to think of their problem as the investigation of relations between Stimulus and Response are apt to view the present undertaking in a parallel way—as an investigation of relations between a subjective stimulus and a subjective response. If that were all we had to say, however, we would scarcely have written a book to say it. Stimulus and response are physiological concepts borrowed from the discussion of reflexes. But we have rejected the classical concept of the reflex arc as the fundamental pattern for the organization of all behavior, and consequently we do not feel a need to extend the classic disjunction between stimulus and response variables into the realm of Images and Plans. To assume that a Plan is a covert response to some inner Image of a stimulus does nothing but parallel objective concepts with subjective equivalents and leaves the reflex arc still master—albeit a rather ghostly master—of the machinery of the mind. We are not likely to overthrow an old master without the help of a new one, so it is to the task of finding a successor that we must turn next.

CHAPTER 2

THE UNIT OF ANALYSIS

Most psychologists take it for granted that a scientific account of the behavior of organisms must begin with the definition of fixed, recognizable, elementary units of behavior—something a psychologist can use as a biologist uses cells, or an astronomer uses stars, or a physicist uses atoms, and so on. Given a simple unit, complicated phenomena are then describable as lawful compounds. That is the essence of the highly successful strategy called "scientific analysis."

The elementary unit that modern, experimental psychologists generally select for their analysis of behavior is the *reflex*. "The isolation of a reflex," B. F. Skinner tells us, "is the demonstration of a predictable uniformity in behavior. In some form or other it is an inevitable part of any science of behavior. . . . A reflex is not, of course, a theory. It is a fact. It is an analytical unit, which makes the investigation of behavior possible." [1] Skinner is quite careful to define a reflex as a unit of behavior that will yield orderly data: "The ap-

---

[1] B. F. Skinner, *The Behavior of Organisms* (New York: Appleton-Century-Crofts, 1938), p. 9.

pearance of smooth curves in dynamic processes marks a unique point in the progressive restriction of a preparation, and it is to this uniquely determined entity that the term reflex may be assigned." [2] This somewhat odd approach to the reflex—in terms of the smoothness of curves—results from Skinner's consistent attempt to define a unit of behavior in terms of behavior itself instead of by reference to concepts drawn from some other branch of science.

Although Skinner's approach absolves the psychologist of certain burdensome responsibilities toward his biological colleagues, the fact remains that the reflex is a concept borrowed originally from physiology and made to seem psychologically substantial largely by the myth of the *reflex arc:* stimulus → receptor → afferent nerve → connective fibers → efferent nerve → effector → response. For many years all those elementary textbooks of psychology that mentioned the nervous system featured the traditional, simplified diagram of the reflex arc in a very prominent position. You may ignore a behaviorist when he tells you that the reflex is a fact, but you can scarcely ignore a physiologist when he draws you a picture of it. You might as well deny the small intestines or sneer at the medulla oblongata as to doubt the reflex arc. Even the most obstinate opponent of physiological explanations in psychology can scarcely forget the bloody tissue from which the reflex—even the reflex-sans-arc—originally grew.

But let us suppose, by a wild and irresponsible flight of fancy, that the physiologists and neurologists suddenly announced that they had been mistaken, that there was no such fact as a reflex arc and that the data on which the theory had been based were actually quite different from what had originally been supposed. What then would psychologists say? Would they persist in talking about reflexes? Has the reflex concept been so tremendously helpful that behaviorists could not afford to give it up, even if its biological basis were demolished?

There is some reason to think that the reflex unit has been vastly overrated and that a good many psychologists would like to get out from under it if they could. The reflex arc may have been helpful in getting psychology started along scientific paths, but the suspicion has been growing in recent years that the reflex idea is too sim-

[2] *Ibid.,* p. 40.

ple, the element too elementary. For the most part, serious students of behavior have had to ignore the problem of units entirely. Or they have had to modify their units so drastically for each new set of data that to speak of them as elementary would be the most unblushing sophistry. After watching psychologists struggle under their burden of conditioning reflexes, Chomsky, the linguist and logician, recently summarized their plight in the following terms:

> The notions of "stimulus," "response," "reinforcement" are relatively well defined with respect to the bar-pressing experiments and others similarly restricted. Before we can extend them to real-life behavior, however, certain difficulties must be faced. We must decide, first of all, whether any physical event to which the organism is capable of reacting is to be called a stimulus on a given occasion, or only one to which the organism in fact reacts; and correspondingly, we must decide whether any part of behavior is to be called a response, or only one connected with stimuli in lawful ways. Questions of this sort pose something of a dilemma for the experimental psychologist. If he accepts the broad definitions, characterizing any physical event impinging on the organism as a stimulus and any part of the organism's behavior as a response, he must conclude that behavior has not been demonstrated to be lawful. In the present state of our knowledge, we must attribute an overwhelming influence on actual behavior to ill-defined factors of attention, set, volition, and caprice. If we accept the narrower definitions, then behavior is lawful by definition (if it consists of responses); but this fact is of limited significance, since most of what the animal does will simply not be considered behavior.[3]

Faced with the choice of being either vague or irrelevant, many psychologists have been restive and ill at ease with their borrowed terms. What went wrong? How was the reflex arc conceived originally, and for what purpose? Can we supplant the reflex arc with some theory of the reflex that is more suited to our current knowledge and interests?

Sir Charles Sherrington and Ivan Petrovitch Pavlov are the two men who are probably most responsible for confirming the psychologist's Image of man as a bundle of S-R reflexes. Yet one may be per-

---

[3] The passage quoted is from page 30 of Chomsky's review of B. F. Skinner, *Verbal Behavior*, in *Language*, 1959, 35, 26–58.

mitted to speculate that neither of them would approve of the way their concepts have been extended by psychologists. In his *Integrative Action of the Nervous System* (1906) Sherrington is particularly explicit in his qualifications and warnings about the reflex. Again and again he states that "the simple reflex is a useful fiction"—useful for the study of the spinal preparation. He expressed considerable doubt that a stretch reflex, of which the knee jerk is the most frequently quoted example, represented his notion of a simple reflex and questioned whether it should be considered a reflex at all. The synapse was invented by Sherrington in order to explain the differences between the observed properties of nerve trunks and the properties that had to be inferred to describe the neural tissue that intervenes between receptor stimulation and effector response. Nerve trunks will transmit signals in either direction. Characteristically, the signals are of an all-or-none type. Reflex action, on the other hand, is unidirectional and the response is characteristically graded according to the intensity of the stimulus. How can these be reconciled? Sherrington resolved the differences by supporting the neuron doctrine: the nervous system is made up of discrete neural units that have the properties of nerve trunks; intercalated between these units are discontinuities which he christened "synapses," and these have the properties unique to reflexes.

In recent years, graded responses have been shown to be a prepotent characteristic not only of synapses but also of all excitable tissue, for example, of the finer arborizations of the nerve cells. The cerebral cortex, man's claim to phylogenetic eminence, "still operates largely by means of connections characteristic of primitive neuropil [which is] the most appropriate mechanism for the maintenance of a continuous or steady state, as contrasted to the transmission of information about such states." [4]

Moreover, additional data have come to light. Today we know that neural and receptor tissues are spontaneously active irrespective of environmental excitation. This spontaneous activity is, of course, altered by environmental events—but the change in spontaneous activity may outlast the direct excitation by hours and even

[4] George Bishop, The natural history of the nerve impulse, *Physiological Reviews*, 1956, 36, 376–399.

days. Furthermore, we know now that the activity of receptors is controlled by efferents leading to them from the central nervous system. As an example, consider the events that control muscular contraction. (Similar, though not identical, mechanisms have also been described for the various sensory systems.) One third of the "motor" nerve fibers that go to muscle actually end in spindles that are the stretch-sensitive receptors. Electrical stimulation of these nerve fibers does not result in contraction of muscle; but the number of signals per unit time that are recorded from the "sensory" nerves coming from the spindles is altered drastically. It is assumed, therefore, that the central nervous mechanism must compare the incoming pattern of signals with the centrally originating "spindle control" signal pattern in order to determine what contribution the muscular contraction has made to the "spindle sensing" pattern. The outcome of this comparison, or *test*, constitutes the stimulus (the psychophysicist's *proximal* stimulus) to which the organism is sensitive. The test represents the conditions which have to be met before the response will occur. The test may occur in the receptor itself (e.g., in the retina) or in a more centrally located neuronal aggregate (as is probably the case for muscle stretch).

It is clear from examples such as this that the neural mechanism involved in reflex action cannot be diagrammed as a simple reflex arc or even as a chain of stimulus-response connections. A much more complex kind of monitoring, or testing, is involved in reflex action than the classical reflex arc makes any provision for. The only conditions imposed upon the stimulus by the classical chain of elements are the criteria implicit in the thresholds of each element; if the distal stimulus is strong enough to surmount the thresholds all along the arc, then the response must occur. In a sense, the threshold is a kind of test, too, a condition that must be met, but it is a test of strength only. And it must have encouraged psychologists to believe that the only meaningful measurement of a reflex was its strength (probability, magnitude, or latency).

The threshold, however, is only one of many different ways that the input can be tested. Moreover, the response of the effector depends upon the outcome of the test and is most conveniently conceived as an effort to modify the outcome of the test. The action is initiated by an "incongruity" between the state of the organism and the state that is being tested for, and the action persists until the incongruity (i.e., the proximal stimulus) is removed. The general pattern of reflex action, therefore, is to test the input energies against some criteria established in the organism, to respond if the result of the test is to show an incongruity, and to continue to respond until the incongruity vanishes, at which time the reflex is terminated. Thus, there is "feedback" from the result of the action to the testing phase, and we are confronted by a recursive loop. The simplest kind of diagram to represent this conception of reflex action—an alternative to the classical reflex arc—would have to look something like Figure 1.

The interpretation toward which the argument moves is one that has been called the "cybernetic hypothesis," namely, that the fundamental building block of the nervous system is the feedback

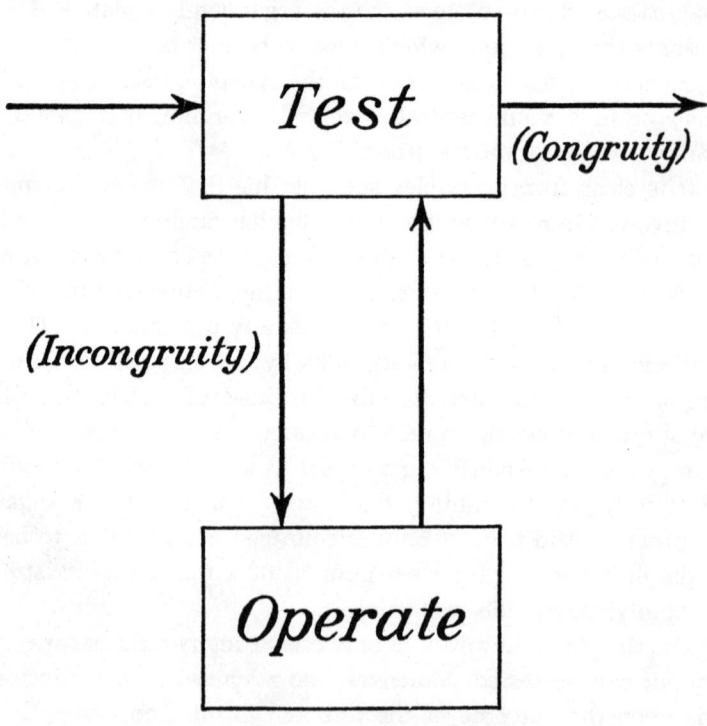

FIGURE 1. *The TOTE unit*

loop.[5] The development of a mathematical theory for servomechanisms, wedded to the physiological accounts of homeostatic mechanisms, has stimulated widespread discussion and speculation about devices closely akin to Figure 1. The argument, therefore, moves toward popular ground.

But what good is this alternative interpretation of the reflex? The psychologist was interested in reflexes because he thought they might provide the units he needed to describe behavior. But simple reflexes have been inadequate. And if reflexes based on afferent-efferent arcs would not turn the trick, why should we hope for better things from reflexes based on feedback loops? It is the reflex itself—not merely the reflex arc—that has failed, and repairing the neurological theory underlying it is not likely to save the day. What do we hope to gain from such a reinterpretation?

Obviously, the reflex is not the unit we should use as the element of behavior: the unit should be the feedback loop itself. If we think of the Test-Operate-Test-Exit unit—for convenience, we shall call it a TOTE unit—as we do of the reflex arc, in purely anatomical terms, it may describe reflexes, but little else. That is to say, the reflex should be recognized as only one of many possible actualizations of a TOTE pattern. The next task is to generalize the TOTE unit so that it will be useful in a majority—hopefully, in all—of the behavioral descriptions we shall need to make.

Consider what the arrows in Figure 1 might represent. What could flow along them from one box to another? We shall discuss three alternatives: energy, information, and control. If we think of *energy*—neural impulses, for example—flowing from one place to another over the arrows, then the arrows must correspond to recognizable physical structures—neurons, in the example chosen. As a diagram of energy flow over discrete pathways, therefore, the TOTE unit described in Figure 1 might represent a simple reflex. Or it might represent a servomechanism.

There is, however, a second level of abstraction that psycholo-

---

[5] Norbert Wiener, *Cybernetics* (New York: Wiley, 1948). For a short review of the early development of this idea, see J. O. Wisdom, The hypothesis of cybernetics, *British Journal for the Philosophy of Science*, 1951, 2, 1–24. For more comprehensive discussion, see W. Sluckin, *Minds and Machines* (London: Penguin, 1954). A little of the cybernetic story is reviewed in the next chapter.

gists usually prefer. We can think of *information* as flowing from one place to another over the arrows. According to the method of measuring information that has been developed by Norbert Wiener and by Claude Shannon, information is transmitted over a channel to the extent that the output of the channel is correlated with the input.[6] We could therefore think of this second level of abstraction as the transmission of correlation over the arrows. In that case, we are concerned not with the particular structures or kinds of energy that are involved in producing the correlation but only with the fact that events at the two ends of the arrow are correlated. The situation is quite familiar to psychologists, for it is exactly what they mean when they draw an arrow leading from Stimulus to Response in their *S-R* diagrams or when they define a reflex as a correlation between *S* and *R* but refuse to talk about the neurological basis for that correlation.

A third level of abstraction, however, is extremely important for the ideas we shall discuss in the pages that follow. It is the notion that what flows over the arrows in Figure 1 is an intangible something called *control*. Or perhaps we should say that the arrow indicates only succession. This concept appears most frequently in the discussion of computing machines, where the control of the machine's operations passes from one instruction to another, successively, as the machine proceeds to execute the list of instructions that comprise the program it has been given. But the idea is certainly not limited to computers. As a simple example drawn from more familiar activities, imagine that you wanted to look up a particular topic in a certain book in order to see what the author had to say about it. You would open the book to the index and find the topic. Following the entry is a string of numbers. As you look up each page reference in turn, your behavior can be described as under the control of that list of numbers, and control is transferred from one number to the next as you proceed through the list. The transfer of control could be symbolized by drawing arrows from one page number to the next, but the arrows

---

[6] A short introduction to these ideas written for psychologists can be found in G. A. Miller, What is information measurement? *American Psychologist*, 1953, 8, 3–11. A fuller account has been given by Fred Attneave, *Applications of Information Theory to Psychology* (New York: Holt, 1959). See also the highly readable account by Colin Cherry, *On Human Communication* (Cambridge: Technology Press, 1957).

would have a meaning quite different from the two meanings mentioned previously. Here we are not concerned with a flow of energy or transmission of information from one page number to the next but merely with the order in which the "instructions" are executed.

At this abstract level of description we are no longer required to think of the test as a simple threshold that some stimulus energy must exceed. The test phase can be regarded as any process for determining that the operational phase is appropriate. For example, to be clear though crude, we do not try to take the square root of "ratiocinate." We may know full well how to extract square roots, but before we can execute that operation we must have digits to work on. The operation of extracting square roots is simply irrelevant when we are dealing with words. In order to ensure that an operation is relevant, a test must be built into it. Unless the test gives the appropriate outcome, control cannot be transferred to the operational phase.

When Figure 1 is used in the discussion of a simple reflex it represents all three levels of description simultaneously. When it is used to describe more complex activities, however, we may want to consider only the transfer of information and control or in many instances only the transfer of control. In all cases, however, the existence of a TOTE should indicate that an organizing, coordinating unit has been established, that a Plan is available.

In the following pages we shall use the TOTE as a general description of the control processes involved; the implications it may have for functional anatomy will remain more or less dormant until Chapter 14, at which point we shall indulge in some neuropsychological speculations. Until then, however, the TOTE will serve as a description at only the third, least concrete, level. In its weakest form, the TOTE asserts simply that the operations an organism performs are constantly guided by the outcomes of various tests.

The present authors feel that the TOTE unit, which incorporates the important notion of feedback, is an explanation of behavior in general, and of reflex action in particular, fundamentally different from the explanation provided by the reflex arc. Consequently, the traditional concepts of stimulus and response must be redefined and reinterpreted to suit their new context. Stimulus and response must be seen as phases of the organized, coordinated act. We might summarize it this way:

> The stimulus is that phase of the forming coordination which represents the conditions which have to be met in bringing it to a successful issue; the response is that phase of one and the same forming coordination which gives the key to meeting these conditions, which serves as instrument in effecting the successful coordination. They are therefore strictly correlative and contemporaneous.[7]

Because stimulus and response are correlative and contemporaneous, the stimulus processes must be thought of not as preceding the response but rather as guiding it to a successful elimination of the incongruity. That is to say, stimulus and response must be considered as aspects of a feedback loop.

The need for some kind of feedback channel in the description of behavior is well recognized by most reflex theorists, but they have introduced it in a peculiar way. For example, it is customary for them to speak of certain consequences of a reflex action as strengthening, or reinforcing, the reflex—such reinforcing consequences of action are a clear example of feedback. Reinforcements are, however, a special kind of feedback that should not be identified with the feedback involved in a TOTE unit. That is to say: (1) a reinforcing feedback must strengthen something, whereas feedback in a TOTE is for the purpose of comparison and testing; (2) a reinforcing feedback is considered to be a stimulus (e.g., pellet of food), whereas feedback in a TOTE may be a stimulus, or information (e.g., knowledge of results), or control (e.g., instructions); and (3) a reinforcing feedback is frequently considered to be valuable, or "drive reducing," to the organism, whereas feedback in a TOTE has no such value (see Chapter 4).

When a TOTE has been executed—the operations performed, the test satisfied, and the exit made—the creature may indeed appear to have attained a more desirable state. It may even be true, on the average, that the TOTE units that are completed successfully in a given situation tend to recur with increased probability, although

---

[7] This passage is from an article by John Dewey entitled, "The Reflex Arc Concept in Psychology," an article as valuable today for its wisdom and insight as it was in 1896.

such a relation would not be necessary. Thus it is possible to discuss a TOTE in the language of reinforcements. Nevertheless, the TOTE involves a much more general conception of feedback. The concept of reinforcement represents an important step forward from reflex arcs toward feedback loops, but bolder strides are needed if behavior theory is to advance beyond the description of simple conditioning experiments.

Perhaps variations in the basic TOTE pattern will prove necessary, so for the purposes of the present discussion we shall continue to regard the diagram in Figure 1 as a hypothesis rather than a fact. The importance of this hypothesis to the general thesis of the book, however, should not be overlooked. It is, in capsule, the account we wish to give of the relation between Image and action. The TOTE represents the basic pattern in which our Plans are cast, the test phase of the TOTE involves the specification of whatever knowledge is necessary for the comparison that is to be made, and the operational phase represents what the organism does about it—and what the organism does may often involve overt, observable actions. Figure 1, therefore, rephrases the problem posed in Chapter 1: How does a Plan relate the organism's Image of itself and its universe to the actions, the responses, the behavior that the organism is seen to generate?

Let us see what we must do in order to expand this proposal into something useful. One of the first difficulties—a small one—is to say more exactly what we mean by the "incongruity" that the test phase is looking for. Why not talk simply about the difference, rather than the incongruity, as providing the proximal stimulus? The answer is not profound: We do not want to bother to distinguish between TOTEs in which the operations are performed only when a difference is detected (and where the operations serve to diminish the difference) and TOTEs in which the operations are released only when no difference is detected. When the diagram is used to describe servomechanisms, for example, it is quite important to distinguish "positive" from "negative" feedback, but, because we are going to be interested primarily in the feedback of control, such questions are not critical. Rather than treat all these varieties as different units of analysis, it seems simpler to treat them all as examples of a more general type of "incongruity-sensitive" mechanism.[8]

A second difficulty—this one rather more important—is the question of how we can integrate this TOTE unit into the sort of hierarchical structure of behavior that we insisted on in Chapter 1. How can the two concepts—feedback and hierarchy—be reconciled? One method of combining feedback components in a hierarchy has been described by D. M. MacKay,[9] who proposed to make the consequences of the operational phase in one component provide the input to the comparator of a second component; MacKay's suggestion leads to a string of such feedback components, each representing a progressively higher degree of abstraction from the external reality. Although MacKay's scheme is quite ingenious, we are persuaded that a somewhat different method of constructing the hierarchy will better serve a psychologist's descriptive purposes. A central notion of the method followed in these pages is that the operational components of TOTE units may themselves be TOTE units. That is to say, the TOTE pattern describes both strategic and tactical units of behavior. Thus the operational phase of a higher-order TOTE might itself consist of a string of other TOTE units, and each of these, in turn, may contain still other strings of TOTEs, and so on. Since this method of retaining the same pattern of description for the higher, more strategic units as for the lower, more tactical units may be confusing on first acquaintance, we shall consider an example.

R. S. Woodworth has pointed out how frequently behavioral activities are organized in two stages.[10] Woodworth refers to them as "two-phase motor units." The first phase is preparatory or mobilizing; the second, effective or consummatory. To jump, you first flex the hips and knees, then extend them forcefully; the crouch prepares for the jump. To grasp an object, the first phase is to open your hand, the second is to close it around the object. You must open your

[8] The notion of an "incongruity-sensitive" mechanism appears to the authors to be related to Festinger's conceptions of "cognitive dissonance," but we have not attempted to explore or develop that possibility. See Leon Festinger, *A Theory of Cognitive Dissonance* (Evanston: Row, Peterson, 1957).
[9] D. M. MacKay, The epistemological problem for automata, in C. E. Shannon and J. McCarthy, eds., *Automata Studies* (Princeton: Princeton University Press, 1956), pp. 235–251.
[10] Robert S. Woodworth, *Dynamics of Behavior* (New York: Holt, 1958), pp. 36 ff.

mouth before you can bite. You must draw back your arm before you can strike, etc. The two phases are quite different movements, yet they are obviously executed as a single unit of action. If stimulation is correct for releasing the action, first the preparatory TOTE unit is executed, and when it has been completed the stimulation is adequate for the consummatory TOTE unit and the action is executed. Many of these two-phase plans are repetitive: the completion of the second phase in turn provides stimuli indicating that the execution of the first phase is again possible, so an alternation between the two phases is set up, as in walking, running, chewing, drinking, sweeping, knitting, etc.

We should note well the construction of a "two-phase" TOTE unit out of two simpler TOTE units. Consider hammering a nail as an

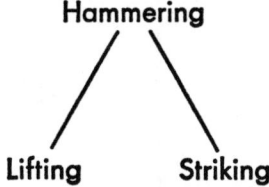

FIGURE 2. *Hammering as a hierarchy*

example. As a Plan, of course, hammering has two phases, lifting the hammer and then striking the nail. We could represent it by a tree, or hierarchy, as in Figure 2. If we ask about details, however, the representation of hammering in Figure 2 as a simple list containing two items is certainly too sketchy. It does not tell us, for one thing, how long to go on hammering. What is the "stop rule"? For this, we must indicate the test phase, as in Figure 3. The diagram in Figure 3 should indicate that when control is transferred to the TOTE unit that we are calling "hammering," the hammering continues until the head of the nail is flush with the surface of the work. When the test indicates that the nail is driven in, control is transferred elsewhere. Now, however, we seem to have lost the hierarchical structure. The hierarchy is recovered when we look at the box labeled "hammer," for there we find two TOTE units, each with its own test, as indicated in Figure 4. When the pair of TOTE units combined in Figure 4 are put inside the operational phase in Figure 3, the result is the hierarchical Plan for hammering nails that is shown in Figure 5.

If this description of hammering is correct, we should expect the sequence of events to run off in this order: Test nail. (Head sticks up.) Test hammer. (Hammer is down.) Lift hammer. Test hammer. (Hammer is up.) Test hammer. (Hammer is up.) Strike nail. Test

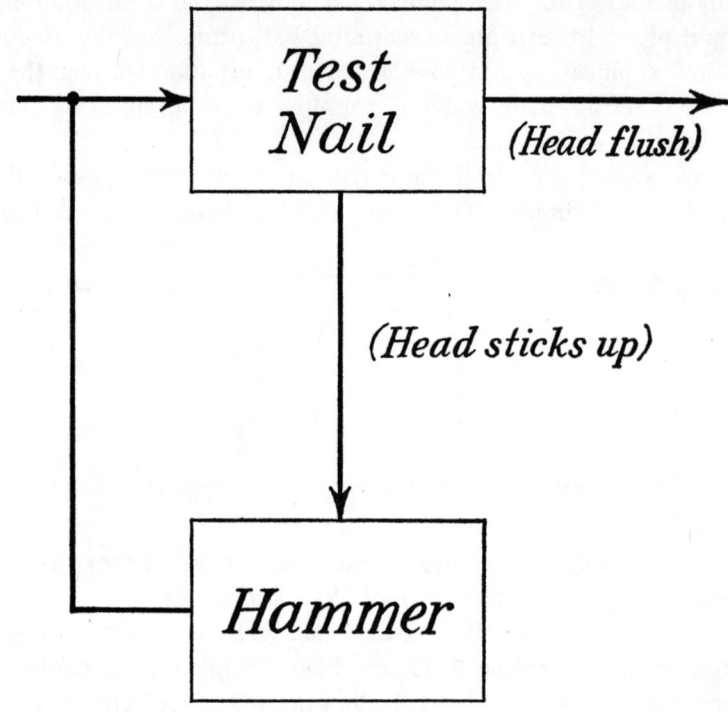

FIGURE 3. *Hammering as a TOTE unit*

hammer. (Hammer is down.) Test nail. (Head sticks up.) Test hammer. And so on, until the test of the nail reveals that its head is flush with the surface of the work, at which point control can be transferred elsewhere. Thus the compound of TOTE units unravels itself simply enough into a coordinated sequence of tests and actions, although the underlying structure that organizes and coordinates the behavior is itself hierarchical, not sequential.

It may seem slightly absurd to analyze the motions involved in

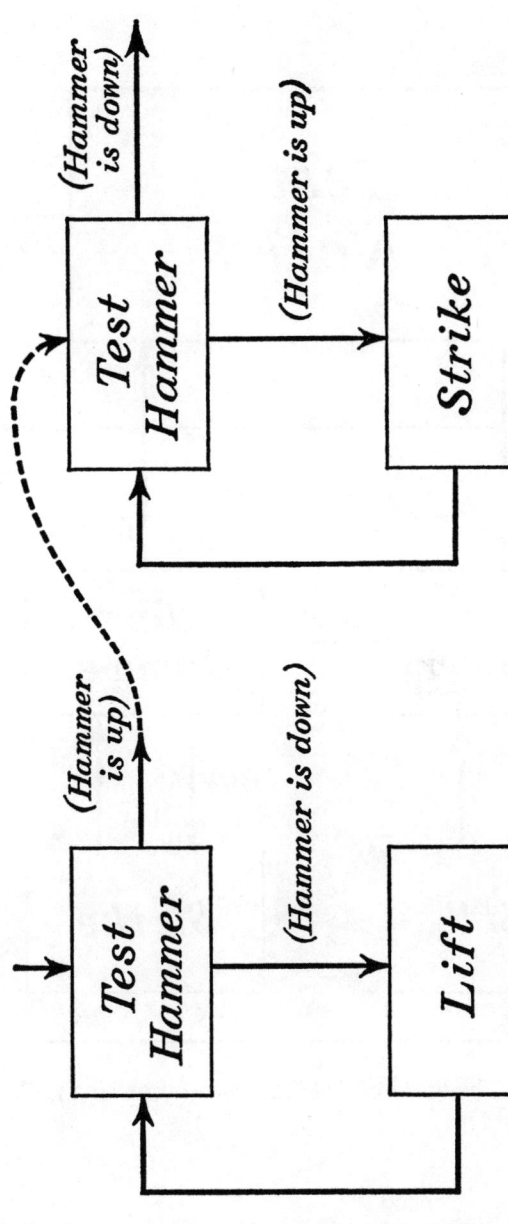

FIGURE 4. Dashed line indicates how two simple TOTE units are connected to form the operational phase of the more complicated TOTE unit in Figure 3.

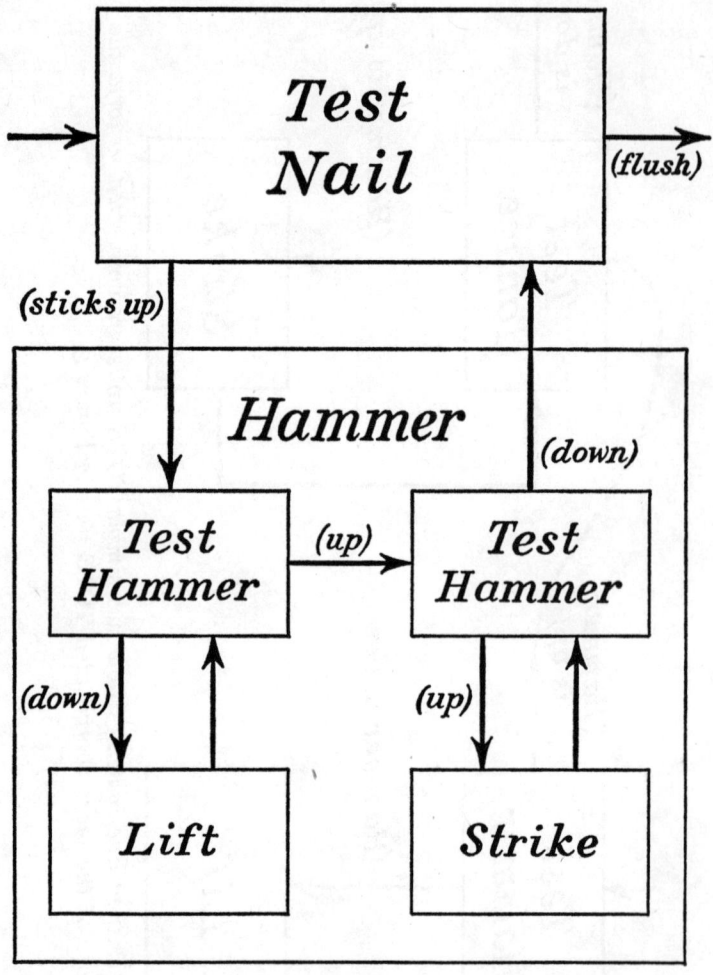

FIGURE 5. *The hierarchical Plan for hammering nails*

hammering a nail in this explicit way, but it is better to amuse a reader than to confuse him. It is merely an illustration of how several simple TOTE units, each with its own test-operate-test loop, can be embedded in the operational phase of a larger unit with its particular test-operate-test loop. Without such an explicit illustration it might not have been immediately obvious how these circles within circles could yield hierarchical trees.

More complicated Plans—Woodworth refers to them as "polyphase motor units"—can be similarly described as TOTE units built up of subplans that are themselves TOTE units. A bird will take off, make a few wing strokes, glide, brake with its wings, thrust its feet forward, and land on the limb. The whole action is initiated as a unit, is controlled by a single Plan, yet is composed of several phases, each involving its own Plan, which may in turn be comprised of subplans, etc.

Note that it is the *operational* phase of the TOTE that is expanded into a list of other TOTE units. If we wish to preserve the TOTE pattern as it is diagrammed in Figure 1, we cannot use it to build up more complicated tests.[11] The tests that are available, therefore, are conceived to be relatively fixed; it is the operational phase that may be quite various and complex. The operational phase may, of course, consist of a list of TOTEs, or it may terminate in efferent activity.[12] If we consider complex Plans—TOTE hierarchies in which the operation of one TOTE is itself a list of TOTE units—then some general properties of such systems become apparent:

[11] The reason that the TOTE of Figure 1 can be expanded only in its operational phase is purely formal and can be appreciated by simple counting: There are four arrows associated with Test; there are two arrows associated with Operate; and there are two arrows associated with TOTE as a unit. Therefore, if the two-arrowed TOTE is used to construct some component of another TOTE, the component it constructs must be the two-arrowed Operate, not the four-arrowed Test. However, rigid restrictions such as these are probably unrealistic and justifiable only in terms of pedagogic simplification. Anyone who has studied the hierarchically organized programs written by Newell, Shaw, and Simon to simulate human problem-solving will recognize how primitive and unelaborated these TOTE hierarchies really are.

[12] If we take seriously the suggested form of the TOTE, the system may be easily trapped into loops. For example, if the subtests in the expansion of an operational phase all pass, but the basic test fails, a loop will exist. In order to avoid loops we might insist that the basic test imply the disjunction of the subtests. A more realistic solution would accept the occurrence of loops as a signal that the Plan was not successful in producing the result for which the basic test was designed; it would then be necessary to provide further machinery for discovering and stopping such loops.

—The hierarchical structure underlying behavior is taken into account in a way that can be simply described with the computer language developed by Newell, Shaw, and Simon for processing lists.

—Planning can be thought of as constructing a list of tests to perform. When we have a clear Image of a desired outcome, we can use it to provide the conditions for which we must test, and those tests, when arranged in sequence, provide a crude strategy for a possible Plan. (Perhaps it would be more helpful to say that the conditions for which we must test *are* an Image of the desired outcome.)

—The operational phase can contain both tests and operations. Therefore the execution of a Plan of any complexity must involve many more tests than actions. This design feature would account for the general degradation of information that occurs whenever a human being is used as a communication channel.

In lower animals it appears that the pattern of their behavior is normally constructed more or less fortuitously by the environment —only man cherishes the illusion of being master of his fate. That is to say, the environment provides stimuli that "release" the next stage of the animal's activity. It is something of a philosophical question as to whether we wish to believe in plans that exist somewhere outside of nervous systems, so perhaps we should say merely that lower animals appear to have more tactics than strategy.

As we ascend the evolutionary scale we find in mammals an increasing complexity in the kind of tests the animals can perform. In man we have a unique capacity for creating and manipulating symbols, and when that versatility is used to assign names to TOTE units, it becomes possible for him to use language in order to rearrange the symbols and to form new Plans. We have every reason to believe that man's verbal abilities are very intimately related to his planning abilities. And, because human Plans are so often verbal, they can be communicated, a fact of crucial importance in the evolution of our social adjustments to one another.

Such matters deserve several separate chapters, but first we shall sketch in some history. A reader familiar with the background out of which such a proposal as the TOTE hierarchy might grow may wish to jump directly to Chapter 4. A reader curious to see the idea in its proper perspective on the intellectual landscape, however, will want to know something about the relevant discussions and experiments that have educated the present authors. Chapter 3 gives some of that material, along with references to books and articles that supply a great deal more.

CHAPTER 3

THE SIMULATION OF PSYCHOLOGICAL PROCESSES

A reflex theorist who is asked to abandon his palpable S's and R's, to surrender his network of S-R connections modeled after a telephone switchboard, and to replace it all by ghostly Images and intangible Plans, is likely to feel he has been asked to walk on air. "How," he grumbles, "can a tough-minded scientist make sense out of such cognitive moonshine?" For years the reflex theorist's stock in trade has been his accusation that the cognitive theorist was at heart a vitalist who could never produce a believable mechanism that would accomplish what he claimed for the living brain. "Everyone recognizes," he would say, "that comparing the brain to a map control room is only a metaphor. If we were to take it seriously, we would have to assume that there is a little man inside the head, a homunculus who can read maps and make decisions."[1] At least since

---

[1] It is amusing that so many psychologists who abhor subjectivism and anthropomorphism unhesitatingly put telephone switchboards inside our heads. In 1943, for example, Clark Hull, in his *Principles of Behavior* (New York: Appleton-Century-Crofts), could take it as self-evident that the brain "acts as a

the time of Descartes, who invented reflex theory as part of his thesis that the body is just a machine, reflex theorists have been winning arguments by insisting on mechanical models for living systems.

Today, suddenly, the argument has lost its force. Now at long last there are machines complicated enough to do everything that cognitive theorists have been talking about. Descartes was impressed by the clockwork figures that jumped out of the shrubbery to startle a stroller; think how much more impressed he would be by a modern electronic computer that spins out calculations at lightning speeds. Leibnitz dreamed of such a machine and tried to describe a thought-calculus it might use to compute answers to problems that require thinking. Today such machines are operating in hundreds of laboratories. The reflex theorist is no longer the only psychologist who can summon up a tangible mechanism to make his claims sound more reasonable. Today a cognitive theorist is also free to become a materialist in good standing—if that is what he wants.

Typical of the new freedom deriving from a deeper conception of what machines can be and do was the discovery that machines can behave purposively. In 1943 Rosenblueth, Wiener, and Bigelow shocked many psychologists by putting their very tough-minded reputations behind the assertion that machines with negative feedback were teleological mechanisms.[2] At that time psychologists generally regarded "teleological" and "unscientific" as synonymous, and it was therefore surprising to realize that machines could strive toward goals, could collect information about the difference between their intentions and their performance and then work to reduce that difference. If entelechy was compatible with mechanism, then

---

kind of automatic switchboard" (p. 18, repeated on p. 384). However, the important adjective, "automatic," is a recent accomplishment. The telephone engineers who had to build and maintain those early switchboards that reflex theorists loved so well were dissatisfied with them because they required a human operator to make the connections. Eventually, of course, the operator was replaced by more elaborate machinery, thus rendering reflex theory scientifically impeccable at last. But in 1892, when Karl Pearson wrote *The Grammar of Science*, he unblushingly provided a "clerk" who carried on the same valuable services in the brain as he would in a central telephone exchange.

[2] Arturo Rosenblueth, Norbert Wiener, and Julian Bigelow, Behavior, purpose, and teleology, *Philosophy of Science*, 1943, 10, 18–24. W. Ross Ashby had also introduced the feedback mechanism as early as 1940 in his paper, Adaptiveness and equilibrium, *Journal of Mental Science*, 1940, 86, 478–483. Priorities are uncertain because the ideas were part of the development of servomechanisms and were subject to security restrictions during the war.

entelechy could be admitted as a respectable concept in psychology. Wiener stated the argument this way:

> It is my thesis that the physical functioning of the living individual and the operation of some of the newer communication machines are precisely parallel in their analogous attempts to control entropy through feedback. Both of them have sensory receptors as one stage of their cycle of operation: that is, in both of them there exists a special apparatus for collecting information from the outer world at low energy levels, and for making it available in the operation of the individual or of the machine. In both cases these external messages are not taken *neat*, but through the internal transforming powers of the apparatus, whether it be alive or dead. The information is then turned into a new form available for the further stages of performance. In both the animal and the machine this performance is made to be effective on the outer world. In both of them, their *performed* action on the outer world, and not merely their *intended* action, is reported back to the central regulatory apparatus.[3]

Such declarations seemed remarkable at first. Given a little time to reflect, however, psychologists realized that these purposive machines were quite familiar, though the language used to discuss them was somewhat new. As early as 1896 the philosopher-psychologist John Dewey had described in much detail the servomechanism involved in reaching toward a candle flame and then jerking away. "The fact is," he said, "that stimulus and response are not distinctions of existence, but teleological distinctions, that is, distinctions of function, or part played, with reference to reaching or maintaining an end."[4] The new terms and explicit analysis supplied by the engineering development were needed, however, before the importance of Dewey's insight could be fully appreciated. Once a teleological mechanism could be built out of metal and glass, psychologists recognized that it was scientifically respectable to admit they had known it all along. They had known, for example, of the homeostatic mechanisms studied by Walter B. Cannon and his associates during the

[3] Norbert Wiener, *The Human Use of Human Beings* (Boston: Houghton Mifflin, 1954), pp. 26–27.
[4] John Dewey, The reflex arc concept in psychology, *Psychological Review*, 1896, 3, 357–370. This remarkable paper, one of the cornerstones of American functional psychology, an anticipation of Gestalt psychology, and a criticism in advance of behaviorism, has been reprinted in Wayne Dennis, ed., *Readings in the History of Psychology* (New York: Appleton-Century-Crofts, 1948).

1920's. They had known about L. T. Troland, who in 1928 introduced the term "retroflex" to name the sensory feedback.[5] They had known about the "circular reflexes" that E. B. Holt revived and elaborated in 1931.[6] And they had known about Edward Tolman, who anticipated the new respectability of teleology by at least two decades and who, in 1939, had described a perfectly respectable feedback mechanism that he called the "schematic sowbug."[7] Even in 1939, however, Tolman could claim no priority, for he had borrowed the central idea from the mechanistic biologist Jacques Loeb. That was something else the psychologists had known all along. Loeb's theory of tropisms was, in 1890, one of the earliest descriptions of a machine that would exhibit purposive, taxic behavior.[8] The idea of the biological servomechanism had been there all along—but the mechanical actualization of the idea in inorganic hardware provided the kind of demonstration that could no longer be ignored. Today we can, almost as a matter of course, propose teleological arrangements such as the TOTE unit discussed in the preceding chapter—the particular realization of the unit in tissue or in metal need not deter us, for we know now that it can be accomplished in a variety of ways.

What is the source of this remarkable increase in confidence that psychologists experience when their ideas can be translated into machinery? Clark Hull has suggested that designing robots is a "prophylaxis against anthropomorphic subjectivism," and he recommends the following to his readers:

> Regard . . . the behaving organism as a completely self-maintaining robot, constructed of materials as unlike ourselves

[5] L. T. Troland, *The Fundamentals of Human Motivation* (New York: Van Nostrand, 1928).

[6] Edwin B. Holt, *Animal Drive and the Learning Process* (New York: Holt, 1931). For the history of the circular reflexes, see Wayne Dennis, A note on the circular response hypothesis, *Psychological Review*, 1954, 61, 334–338. Dennis traces the circular response back to David Hartley in 1749.

[7] E. C. Tolman, Prediction of vicarious trial and error by means of the schematic sowbug, *Psychological Review*, 1939, 46, 318–336.

[8] W. J. Crozier, The study of living organisms, in C. Murchison, ed., *The Foundations of Experimental Psychology* (Worcester: Clark University Press, 1929), pp. 45–127. Another biologist who provided a clear and significant pre-cybernetic account of teleological mechanisms was Alfred J. Lotka. See his *Elements of Physical Biology* (Baltimore: Williams & Wilkins, 1925). (Reissued in 1956 by Dover Press as *Elements of Mathematical Biology*.) Lotka illustrates his argument by the operation of a mechanical beetle that was able to avoid falling off table edges; and he expresses his scorn for thinkers who call a system teleological only so long as they are ignorant of its workings.

as may be. In doing this it is not necessary to attempt the solution of the detailed engineering problems connected with the design of such a creature. It is a wholesome and revealing exercise, however, to consider the various general problems in behavior dynamics which must be solved in the design of a truly self-maintaining robot. . . . The temptation to introduce an entelechy, soul, spirit, or daemon into a robot is slight; it is relatively easy to realize that *the introduction of an entelechy would not really solve the problem of design of a robot because there would still remain the problem of designing the entelechy itself, which is the core of the original problem all over again.* The robot approach thus aids us in avoiding the very natural but childish tendency to choose easy though false solutions to our problems, by removing all excuses for not facing them squarely and without evasion.[9]

Passages such as this suggest that nothing less than the construction of a teleological machine would convince an experimental psychologist that there is not something occult implied by the terms "goal," "purpose," "expectation," "entelechy."

Surely there is something more to a psychologist's feeling of materialistic satisfaction and confidence than just his triumph over subjectivism. Machines are not the only way he has of facing his problems "squarely and without evasion." Indeed, psychologists are most likely to construct machines for just those functions whose objective character is least in doubt, where the threat of subjectivism is

[9] Hull, *Principles of Behavior*, pp. 27–28. This passage expresses Hull's distaste for nineteenth-century vitalism in general, and particularly for that purposeful, organizing, vital principle that Hans Driesch named "entelechy." In the twentieth century it has become clear that Driesch was wrong, but not for the reason Hull gives. Hull thought that the vitalistic distinction between animals and robots failed because animals, being nothing but machines, could not operate purposefully. In fact, however, the distinction failed because *both* organisms and machines can demonstrate the operation of a purposeful entelechy. Designing an entelechy is no trick at all for an electrical engineer. In spite of this resounding failure, however, vitalism is not dead. It has merely retreated. In order to find something distinctive about biological systems, the modern vitalists have retreated from purpose to memory, an alternative first suggested by Henri Bergson. The current contention is that the stability of genetic and personal memory is—according to the laws of quantum mechanics—incompatible with the microscopic sizes of the gene and the synapse. Therefore, the stability of memory requires some nonphysical explanation. For a sophisticated defense of the idea that maintaining information in an organism is not, in general, accomplished by mechanistic means, see Walter M. Elsasser, *The Physical Foundation of Biology* (New York: Pergamon, 1958). According to Elsasser's view, a self-maintaining robot that behaved like an organism would prove nothing unless its component parts were reduced to the extremely small size characteristic of biological systems.

most remote. The conditioned reflex, for example, is seldom considered an example of "anthropomorphic subjectivism," yet numerous machines have been designed and built to demonstrate the phenomenon of conditioning or of conditioning aided by the law of effect.[10] They were not designed to perform any mentalistic function but merely to display the rather mechanical fact that a new connection was being formed.

It seems to the present authors that the attempts to simulate psychological processes with machines are motivated in large measure by the desire to test—or to demonstrate—the designer's understanding of the theory he espouses. History suggests that man can create almost anything he can visualize clearly. The creation of a model is proof of the clarity of the vision. If you understand how a thing works well enough to build your own, then your understanding must be nearly perfect.

The germ of wisdom behind this intuition was made explicit by the mathematician A. M. Turing in 1937.[11] The import of Turing's work for psychologists was that if they could describe exactly and unambiguously anything that a living organism did, then a computing machine could be built that would exhibit the same behavior with sufficient exactitude to confuse the observer. The existence of the machine would be the test of the accuracy of the description.

One consequence of taking Turing's theorem seriously is that it directs attention toward the electronic computer as the right kind

---

[10] In 1946 E. G. Boring, in Mind and mechanism, *American Journal of Psychology*, 1946, 59, 173–192, listed the following attempts to design robots that would learn: J. M. Stephens, A mechanical explanation of the law of effect, *American Journal of Psychology*, 1929, 41, 422–431; A. Walton, Conditioning illustrated by an automatic mechanical device, *American Journal of Psychology*, 1930, 42, 110 f.; H. D. Baernstein and C. L. Hull, A mechanical model of the conditioned reflex, *Journal of General Psychology*, 1931, 5, 99–106; R. G. Kreuger and C. L. Hull, An electrochemical parallel to the conditioned reflex, *Journal of General Psychology*, 1931, 5, 262–269; G. K. Bennett and L. B. Ward, A model of the synthesis of conditioned reflexes, *American Journal of Psychology*, 1933, 45, 339–342; D. G. Ellson, A mechanical synthesis of trial-and-error learning, *Journal of General Psychol.*, 1935, 13, 212–218; H. Bradner, A new mechanical "learner," *Journal of General Psychology*, 1937, 17, 414–419; T. Ross, The synthesis of intelligence—its implications, *Psychological Review*, 1938, 45, 185–189. The frequency with which these toys were described in the journals (and no one can guess how many more vanished unreported) bears eloquent testimony to the importance psychologists attach to having a credible mechanism to support their theoretical speculations.

[11] An excellent introduction to Turing machines will be found in Martin Davis, *Computability and Unsolvability* (New York: McGraw-Hill, 1958).

of machine to simulate human behavior. But many psychologists, impressed by the haphazard unpredictability of behavior generally, feel intuitively that models based on random processes offer better prospects than the computers do, and so the two kinds of machines, deterministic and stochastic, seem to compete with each other for the psychologist's attention. Kochen and Galanter, however, argue that computer models are more appropriate than stochastic models for describing human choice behavior:

> Ignoring the question of whether or not a "conscious" plan guides the decision-making procedure at each trial, it is assumed that the choices are made according to a plan. Such a plan shall be called a *strategy*. It differs mainly in degree from a relatively "stochastic decision-making procedure," as might be observed in the behavior of rats in a T-maze. The latter type of behavior seems best described by certain kinds of stochastic processes, whereas a computerlike mechanism in which random elements play a secondary role seems a more fruitful model for "planned" behavior.[12]

Although the work on stochastic models is being actively pursued by mathematical psychologists, it will not be reviewed here; since we are concerned here primarily with planned behavior, we shall concentrate on deterministic automata.

Another thing that Turing's theorem did—or should have done—was to focus attention on the adequacy of the description of behavior. A machine cannot be expected to simulate something that has never been described—it can be held responsible only for those aspects of behavior that an observer has recorded. No simulation is complete and no simulation preserves all the characteristics of behavior. If in building a machine to simulate the behavior of a moth flying toward a light we use wheels so that the machine rolls rather than flies, the simulation is considered adequate up to transformations of locomotion. In a sense, we say that we do not care how the beast gets there so long as its trajectory is "equivalent" to that of

[12] Manfred Kochen and Eugene H. Galanter, The acquisition and utilization of information in problem solving and thinking, *Information and Control*, 1958, 1, 267–288. Of course, an electronic computer can be used to study stochastic models as well as deterministic ones; see, for example, Saul Gorn, On the mechanical stimulation of habit-forming and learning, *Information and Control*, 1959, 2, 226–259.

the moth. But even that is acceptable only when we allow a shift from three to two dimensions of movement.

A simulation is invariant with the behavior being simulated only up to some group of allowable transformations. The simulator and his critics must, for example, agree in advance on the aspects of the behavior that are to remain the same from organism to machine. This agreement is normally established by requiring the machine to simulate, not the behavior per se, but the psychologist's *record* of the behavior. A theorist is, therefore, at the mercy of the person who decides what aspects of the behavior are worth recording and simulating.

The extent to which an organism and a machine can be interchanged without altering specified aspects of the situation is the extent to which the simulation is successful. A successful model does not have to *look* like the organism it simulates—the fact that clever modelers can make a mechanical mouse look like a mouse, or a mechanical moth look like a turtle, is mere window dressing. A woman who broke a valuable vase took the pieces to a potter, asked him to make an "exact duplicate"—and was rightfully distressed when he duplicated every chip and shard.

The situation is most familiar, perhaps, in the concept of synonymy. We say that "bachelor" and "unmarried man" are synonymous because they are interchangeable in (nearly) all contexts without alteration of the truth value of the propositions in which they occur. In that case, it is the truth value that must remain invariant. In the case of a successful model, the thing that must remain invariant is the aspect of the organism's behavior that the experimenter chose to record.

Since it is necessary to simulate only the record of the animal's behavior, not the animal itself, the big, fast digital computers that began to evolve after World War II could be used—they did not need to scurry around the room like a rat in a maze or resemble the three pints of brain matter they were supposed to imitate. The computer did not even need to observe the same time scale. The computer's task was merely to simulate—to compute—those aspects of the experimental situation that students of human behavior were interested in. A theorist could embody his ideas in a program of instructions, the program could be stored in the "memory" of the computer, and when "stimuli" were presented the computer would, like an organism, operate upon the input information according to the instructions it had been given in order to generate a "response." In principle, it sounds very simple.

For several years, however, there was a good deal more talk than work. Writing the kind of complicated programs that are necessary in order to simulate a human being requires a tremendous investment of time and ingenuity. While the computers and the programming art were expanding, the theorists discussed how best to use them, eventually, for simulation. The first direction these discussions took was toward neurological, rather than psychological, simulation. This direction seemed especially promising because of a long list of analogies: the open-or-shut relay was analogous to the all-or-none neuron, the electrical pulses in the computer were analogous to the neural impulses, the mercury delay lines were analogous to the reverberating circuits in the nervous system, the memory circuits of the computer were analogous to the association areas of the brain, and so on and on. The neurological direction also seemed promising because McCulloch and Pitts had invented a formal representation of neural nets and used it to establish that any function that could be described logically, strictly, and unambiguously in a finite number of words could be realized by such nets.[13] That is to say, they showed that their neural nets comprised a Turing machine. This formalization made possible some very sophisticated analyses of neurological functions and properties even before they were simulated by computers. The speculations about neural nets were widely publicized and seem to have had a stimulating effect on neurology and neurophysiology. We have every reason to expect great strides forward in this field. It is not, however, the kind of theory we are interested in here.

Our present interest is in the use of computers as automata to

[13] Warren S. McCulloch and Walter Pitts, A logical calculus of the ideas immanent in nervous activity, *Bulletin of Mathematical Biophysics*, 1943, 5, 115–133. For some of the earlier work, see Nicholas Rashevsky, *Mathematical Biophysics* (Chicago: University of Chicago Press, 1938). For some of the more recent work, see M. L. Minsky, *Neural-Analog Networks and the Brain-Model Problem*, Ph.D. thesis, Princeton University, 1954; see also the several selections in C. E. Shannon and J. McCarthy, eds., *Automata Studies* (Princeton: Princeton University Press, 1956). And for perspective, see John von Neumann, *The Computer and the Brain* (New Haven: Yale University Press, 1958).

illustrate the operation of various *psychological* theories. Efforts in this direction lagged somewhat behind the neurological and seem to have been of at least two different kinds. Some of the psychological theorizing aimed the computer at the Image, and some of it aimed the computer at the Plan. Not until late in the 1950's did these two lines grow together.

Consider the Image-inspired theories first. One of the early attempts to use computer simulation in order to understand psychological (rather than neurological) processes was made by the British psychologist Kenneth Craik, who was convinced that thought depends on images. But how was a computer to have an image? His answer was that an image is a form of symbol and that thought consists of building and modifying such symbols by processing the information from the sense organs; to the extent that a computer symbolizes and processes information, it is thinking. He says:

> My hypothesis then is that thought models, or parallels, reality—that its essential feature is not "the mind," "the self," "sense-data," nor propositions but symbolism, and that this symbolism is largely of the same kind as that which is familiar to us in mechanical devices which aid thought and calculation.[14]

In the terms we have introduced here, Craik was struggling with the problem of how the Image could be represented in a computer.

Craik's untimely death prevented him from following up these ideas, and the work that pursued the problem of image formation and recognition by computers was largely cast in neurological rather than psychological terms.[15] However, Donald M. MacKay picked up the

---

[14] K. J. W. Craik, *The Nature of Explanation* (Cambridge: Cambridge University Press, 1943), p. 57.

[15] Some of the relevant contributions to a neurological theory of perception were: W. Pitts and W. S. McCulloch, How we know universals: The perception of auditory and visual forms, *Bulletin of Mathematical Biophysics*, 1947, 9, 127–147; D. O. Hebb, *The Organization of Behavior* (New York: Wiley, 1949); W. A. Clark and B. G. Farley, Generalization of pattern recognition in a self-organizing system, *Proceedings of the Western Joint Computer Conference*, Los Angeles, March 1955, pp. 86–91; O. G. Selfridge, Pattern recognition and modern computers, *ibid.*, pp. 91–93; G. P. Dinneen, Programming pattern recognition, *ibid.*, pp. 94–100; N. Rochester, J. H. Holland, L. H. Haibt, and W. L. Duda, Test on a cell assembly theory of the action of the brain, using a large digital computer, *IRE Transactions on Information Theory*, 1956, Vol. PGIT-2, No. 3, 80–93; P. M. Milner, The cell assembly: Mark II, *Psychological Review*, 1957, 64, 242–252; F. Rosenblatt, The perceptron: A probabilistic model for information storage and organization in the brain, *Psychological Review*, 1958, 65, 386–408. This list is far from complete. The fact that we are in this book more interested in the Plan

argument and carried it a step further when he pointed out that an Image could be constructed in a machine if the machine were able to remember the reactions it required to imitate its input.[16] The act of replication might be guided by feedback—the difference between the incoming configuration and the internal replication would represent an error signal for the machine to reduce. These acts of replication would then provide a basic "vocabulary" in terms of which the machine could describe its own experience (a notion not completely unlike Hebb's neurological "phase sequences").

These theories, clever as they were, did not seem to come to grips with the problem of motivation. It remained for Galanter and Gerstenhaber, in 1956, to point out the importance of motivation and to propose a theory for determining which Images would serve as models for thinking. Different evaluations do indeed modify a person's Image of his problem and so lead to different forms of behavior.[17]

Of all the work on machine imagery, however, the most impressive is that by Gelernter and Rochester.[18] They have programmed a computer to prove theorems in plane geometry and equipped the machine to draw diagrams experimentally, much as a student does. The diagrams simplify tremendously the process of searching for a proof. A more persuasive demonstration that Tolman's analogy to "a map control room" need not involve a homunculus to read the maps could hardly be imagined.

Psychologists seem to have been somewhat slower to recognize that the same kind of problems of pattern and organization exist at the behavioral level as at the level of the Image. Perhaps it was the in-

---

than in the Image deprives us of an excuse to summarize these valuable and interesting contributions to perceptual theory, but we mention them as part of the accumulating evidence that computer simulation will play an increasingly important role in the future development of both neurological and psychological theory.

[16] D. M. MacKay, Mindlike behavior in artefacts, *British Journal for the Philosophy of Science*, 1951, 2, 105–121.

[17] Eugene Galanter and Murray Gerstenhaber, On thought: The extrinsic theory, *Psychological Review*, 1956, 63, 218–227. Eugene Galanter and W. A. S. Smith, Some experiments on a simple thought-problem, *American Journal of Psychology*, 1958, 71, 359–366.

[18] H. L. Gelernter and N. Rochester, Intelligent behavior in problem-solving machines, *IBM Journal of Research and Development*, 1958, 2, 336–345. H. L. Gelernter, Realization of a geometry proving machine. *Proceedings of the International Conference on Information Processing*, Paris, 1959 (in press).

terminable discussion of "trial-and-error" processes that fostered a general belief that relatively simple stochastic models would suffice as theories. In 1949 Miller and Frick tried to complicate this simple picture by using Markov processes to explain the sequential organization of behavior.[19] Their work represented a relatively obvious generalization of Claude Shannon's suggestion that Markov processes could be used to explain the sequential organization of messages.[20] Surely, sequential organization of behavior could nowhere be more important than for communication, so it seemed that if Markovian machines would generate grammatical English, they would be adequate for simulating all other forms of behavior as well. The actual creation of such a machine, however, was prohibited by the fantastically large number of internal states that would be required in the machine for even the crudest approximations to actual behavior. The crux of the problem was not clear, however, until Noam Chomsky proved that any machine that tries to generate all the grammatical strings of words by proceeding, as a Markovian machine would, from left to right, one word at a time in strict order, will need to have an infinite number of internal states.[21] Since the point of a theory is simplification, machines with infinitely many parameters cannot be considered seriously. The only alternative seems to be one that respects the hierarchical structure of the sequence—the kind of "parsing" machine that we have already mentioned in Chapter 1.

One reason that linguists have been motivated to express their description of language in terms congenial to communication theory and to modern computers has been their interest in the possibility of mechanical translation. The development of communication theory since 1948 has revolutionized our thinking in a dozen different

[19] George A. Miller and Frederick C. Frick, Statistical behavioristics and sequences of responses, *Psychological Review*, 1949, 56, 311–324. See also F. C. Frick and G. A. Miller, A statistical description of operant conditioning, *American Journal of Psychology*, 1951, 64, 20–36, and G. A. Miller, Finite Markov processes in psychology, *Psychometrika*, 1952, 17, 149–167.

[20] Claude E. Shannon, A mathematical theory of communication, *Bell System Technical Journal*, 1948, 27, 379–423. Actually, Markov himself had used his ideas to describe written texts.

[21] Noam Chomsky, Three models for the description of language, *IRE Transactions on Information Theory*, 1956, Vol. IT-2, 113–124. However, the difficulties involved in applying stochastic theory to sequences of responses that are patterned in a hierarchy of units had been noted earlier by John B. Carroll, *The Study of Language* (Cambridge: Harvard University Press, 1953, p. 107).

fields, ranging all the way from electrical engineering to the social sciences.[22] Most of the implications of that work lie outside the scope of the present book, but the attempt to use computers to translate messages from one language into another is particularly relevant to this discussion.[23] The first step in this direction, of course, is to use a computer as an automatic dictionary, to exploit its high speeds to accomplish the humdrum task of searching through the vocabulary to find the possible equivalents in the target language. But word-for-word substitutions, even between closely related languages, do not produce grammatical or even intelligible translations. The machine must know something about the grammar as well as the vocabulary of the languages it is translating. Or, more precisely, it must have a set of instructions for deciding among alternative translations, for recognizing idioms, for rearranging the order of the words, for detaching or supplying affixes to roots, etc. In principle, there is no reason we cannot store a two-language dictionary and several hundred coded rules of grammar in a computer and get a usable output. But in practice, the actual coding of the dictionary and the efficient phrasing of the rules pose many tedious and perplexing puzzles. They will probably be overcome, but at the present writing, mechanical translation is still not proceeding as a routine business anywhere in the United States.

The current state of the world makes translation an important problem for the survival of our society, and we must hope the linguists and their programmers will soon succeed. Even without success, however, there are certain lessons that we can draw from their experience that have enlightening implications for psychologists and linguists.

In the first place, the very large amount of information that has to be encoded for the computer has comprised, until very recently, one of the major bottlenecks in the implementation of the scheme. There just is not enough room in a computer for it to contain a full

[22] Cf. George A. Miller, *Language and Communication* (New York: McGraw-Hill, 1951).
[23] An introduction to the problem can be found in W. N. Locke and A. D. Boothe, eds., *Machine Translation of Languages* (New York: Wiley, 1955). There is a journal devoted exclusively to the subject: *Mechanical Translation*, Massachusetts Institute of Technology, Cambridge, Mass. But see also R. A. Brower, ed., *On Translation* (Cambridge: Harvard University Press, 1959).

vocabulary and still be able to retrieve items from the memory as rapidly as they would be needed for, say, ordinary speech rates. In the terms of our present discussion, the Image of the average, well-educated European or American adult must contain an amazing amount of knowledge all organized for fast access to attention. In some respects, apparently, our brains are still a great deal more complicated than the biggest computer ever built.

In the second place, it becomes obvious that there are two very different attitudes one can take toward the job. In one attitude, the programmer says, "I want to make it work any way I can, but the simpler it is, the better." In the other attitude, he says, "I want to make the computer do it the same way people do it, even though it may not look like the most efficient method." As citizens we should applaud the former attitude, but as psychologists, linguists, neurologists—as students of the human being—we are bound to be more interested in the latter. It has been suggested that the attempt to discover an efficient way for the computer to do the task should be called a problem in "artificial intelligence," whereas the attempt to imitate the human being should be called a problem in "simulation." To date, little effort has been made to approach the translation problem with the intent of simulating a human translator.

And, finally, there is nothing but a distressingly vague criterion for determining when the computer has succeeded and when it has failed.[24] A translation is multi-dimensional, and who can say how much better one dimension must be in order to counterbalance an inferiority in some other dimension? Probably the evaluation should be based upon the comparison of the machine's output with a professional translator's output, but exactly how the comparison is to be made is quite difficult to say. In the most successful branches of science we have learned how to measure the discrepancies between our observations and our theories, but with the kind of simulations now possible, criteria for the goodness of fit have yet to be devised.

Mechanical translation illustrates a general class of non-numerical problems toward which the computer has been directed. The inspiration for the work did not arise from an attempt to understand

[24] George A. Miller and J. G. Beebe-Center, Some psychological methods for evaluating the quality of translations, *Mechanical Translation*, 1956, 3, 73–80.

or develop any new theories in neurology or psychology, but from the translation problem itself and from a desire to see just how good our computers really are. It has been principally the computer engineers, plus a few mathematicians, who have tried to make computers play chess,[25] or prove theorems in logic,[26] or wrestle with some branch of mathematics.[27] Inasmuch as most of the efforts have been on problems of "artificial intelligence" rather than in the simulation of human beings, they contribute little but context to the psychological problem. However, the tasks that the engineers and mathematicians have selected to explore on the computer are, in some sense not easily defined, about the right "size" for present-day machines to tackle. The Image that a computer must have in order to play chess, or to do problems in the propositional calculus, is quite restricted and reasonably determinate, and therefore does not overload the computer. Yet at the same time these tasks are large and complicated enough to be interesting and to enable a machine to surprise us by its successes.[28] They are good problems. But what is needed, from the psychologist's point of view, is an attempt to *simulate* the human chess-player or logician, not just to replace him or defeat him.

The first intensive effort to meet this need was the work of Newell, Shaw, and Simon, who have advanced the business of

[25] Some of the publications on this task, whose attractiveness is not solely a matter of showmanship, are C. E. Shannon, Programming a computer for playing chess, *Philosophical Magazine*, 1950, 41, 256–275; A. Newell, The chess machine, an example of dealing with a complex task by adaptation, *Proceedings of the Western Joint Computer Conference*, Los Angeles, March 1955, pp. 101–108; J. Kister, P. Stein, S. Ulam, W. Walden, and M. Wells, Experiments in chess, *Journal of the Association for Computing Machinery*, 1957, 4, 174–177; A. Bernstein and M. deV. Roberts, Computer versus chess player, *Scientific American*, June 1958, 198, 96–105. A. Newell, J. C. Shaw, and H. A. Simon, Chess-playing programs and the problem of complexity, *IBM Journal of Research and Development*, 1958, 2, 320–335. See also A. L. Samuel, Some studies in machine learning using the game of checkers, *IBM Journal of Research and Development*, 1959, 3, 210–229.
[26] Seven centuries of work on mechanical methods to solve problems in logic are reviewed by Martin Gardner, *Logic Machines and Diagrams* (New York: McGraw-Hill, 1958).
[27] Cf. Gelernter and Rochester, *op. cit.*, and Allen Newell, J. C. Shaw, and Herbert A. Simon, *Report on a general problem solving program*, Proceedings of the International Conference on Information Processing (Paris, 1959, in press).
[28] For a broad, imaginative, though highly condensed survey of the artificial intelligence problem, see M. L. Minsky, *Heuristic Aspects of the Artificial Intelligence Problem*, Group Report 34–55, Lincoln Laboratory, Massachusetts Institute of Technology, 17 December 1956. Minsky's psychology is generally quite sophisticated.

psychological simulation further and with greater success than anyone else.[29] Later, particularly in Chapter 13, we discuss their ideas in more detail. For the present, however, we shall comment simply that they have created an information-processing language that enables them to use the computer in a non-numerical manner. Their language systematically exploits a hierarchical (list structure) system of organization that is uniquely suitable for writing heuristic programs for problem solving, programs that enable a computer to simulate the information processing done by human subjects who are given the same task to solve.[30] Newell, Shaw, and Simon have used their techniques to simulate human problem solving in logic, chess, and trigonometry and have evolved a set of principles, applicable to a wide variety of situations, that they feel are characteristic of the ways human beings solve problems in general. Their accomplishments have influenced the present authors in many ways—not merely in terms of their specific solutions to innumerable technical problems but generally by their demonstration that what so many had so long described was finally coming to pass.

It is impressive to see, and to experience, the increase in confidence that comes from the concrete actualization of an abstract idea—the kind of confidence a reflex theorist must have felt in the 1930's when he saw a machine that could be conditioned like a dog. Today, however, that confidence is no longer reserved exclusively for reflex theorists. Perhaps some of the more fanciful conjectures of the "mentalists" should now be seriously reconsidered. Psychologists have been issued a new license to conjecture. What will they do with it? Will the new ideas be incorporated into existing theory? Or will it be easier to begin afresh?

A major impetus behind the writing of this book has been the conviction that these new ideas *are* compatible with, and provide extensions of, familiar and established psychological principles. In

[29] Cf. footnotes 10, 12, 13 in Chapter 1.
[30] Since the development by Newell, Shaw, and Simon of their information-processing language (IPL), two other new programming languages have been created around the idea of list structures: At the Massachusetts Institute of Technology, John McCarthy has developed LISP, and at International Business Machines, H. L. Gelernter has developed FLPL. At the time this is written, however, neither of these newer programming languages has been described in publications.

the pages that follow the attempt will be made to show what these principles are and how they can be revised and elaborated in the light of recent developments in our understanding of man viewed as a system for processing information.

intention - the uncompleted parts of a Plan whose execution has already begun (61)

CHAPTER 4

VALUES, INTENTIONS, AND THE EXECUTION OF PLANS

All acts have in common the character of being intended or willed. But one act is distinguishable from another by the content of it, the expected result of it, which is here spoken of as its intent. There is no obvious way in which we can say what act it is which is thought of or is done except by specifying this intent of it.[1]

In this passage from his Carus Lectures, C. I. Lewis reminds us that the acts people perform cannot be characterized simply by specifying the time-order of their parts—in the way we might describe the motions of a billiard ball or a falling stone. The term "intent" is Lewis's way of trying to catch this elusive and unique feature of the behavior of living systems. In speaking in these terms he is like any ordinary person who tries to say what makes his actions meaningful—but he is quite unlike most experimental psychologists.

[1] Clarence Irving Lewis, *An Analysis of Knowledge and Valuation* (La Salle, Ill.: Open Court, 1946), p. 367.

Intention went out of style as a psychological concept when reflex theory and its derivatives became the foundation for our scientific theories of behavior. Only rarely in the past twenty years has the concept been used outside the clinic as a technical term in a psychological explanation. And most of the explicit uses that have occurred can probably be traced to the influence of Kurt Lewin.[2]

Lewin used the concept of intention in order to combat an overly simple theory that actions are always strengthened whenever they are successful. (He uses the example of someone who intends to mail a letter. The first mailbox he passes reminds him of the action. He drops the letter in. Thereafter, the mailboxes he passes leave him altogether cold. He does not even notice them. Now, according to Lewin, the intention to mail the letter created a positive *valence* on the mailbox, which attracted the person's attention to it. When the occasion arose and the intentional act was consummated, the valence vanished and further mailboxes were ignored. According to classical theory, dropping the letter into the mailbox should have the effect of strengthening the association between mailboxes and the response of reaching into the pocket for a letter to be mailed. The poor fellow should have made abortive responses toward three or four mailboxes before the strength of the association had diminished. Instead of accumulating habit strength, however, the fact is he had no further interest in mailboxes. Therefore, reasoned Lewin, the simpler theory is inadequate and a more complex representation of a life space, complete with valences created by intentions, is required.)

The present authors are in fundamental agreement with Lewin. Intention does pose an interesting and important problem for psychology. And we agree that the associationistic doctrine described above can never provide an adequate explanation. But Lewin goes on to draw an interesting analogy that we want to reject. An intention, he says, creates a quasi-need. Just as hunger gives food a positive valence, so does the intention to mail the letter give the mailbox a positive valence. Just as eating reduces the positive valence of food, so does mailing the letter reduce the quasi-need and remove the

[2] Kurt Lewin, Intention, will and need, in David Rapaport, *Organization and Pathology of Thought* (New York: Columbia University Press, 1951), Chapter 5. A summary can be found in W. D. Ellis, *A Source Book of Gestalt Psychology* (New York: Humanities Press, 1938).

positive valence from mailboxes. For Lewin, there is a complete parallel between the dynamics of intentions and the dynamics of any other kind of motivated behavior. It is this dynamic property of an intention that we feel is confusing, and we wish to reformulate it.

There are simpler alternatives. What does it mean when an ordinary man has an ordinary intention? It means that he has begun the execution of a Plan and that this intended action is a part of it. "I intend to see Jones when I get there" means that I am already committed to the execution of a Plan for traveling and that a part of this Plan involves seeing Jones. "Do you intend to see Smith, too?" asks about other parts of the Plan. "Yes" would be a clear reply. "No" is a little ambiguous but probably means that it is part of my Plan to avoid Smith. "I don't know" means that that part of the Plan has not yet been developed in detail and that when it is developed it either may or may not include Smith. People are reasonably precise in their use of "intent" in ordinary conversation. And they do not use it to mean that something is temporarily valuable or that they have any particular needs, either real or quasi. The term is used to refer to *the uncompleted parts of a Plan whose execution has already begun.*[3]

Criminal lawyers are constantly troubled over the distinction between intention and motivation. For example, Jones hires Smith to kill someone. Smith commits the murder, but he is caught and confesses that he was hired to do it. Question: Is Smith guilty? If we consider only the motives involved, the employer is guilty because he was motivated to kill, but the gunman is not guilty because his motive was merely to earn money (which is certainly a commendable motive in a capitalistic society). But if we consider their intentions, then both parties are equally guilty, for both of them knowingly undertook to execute a Plan culminating in murder. The legal confusions arise when the lawyer begins to argue that Smith could not have intended to murder because he had no motive. Only a motive, he says will create an intention. Lewin and his associates would further confuse the issue by arguing that an intention will create a

---

[3] In common speech, an additional requirement seems to be that the Plan be conscious. The present authors are willing to tolerate "unconscious intentions." This seems to be the position of E. C. Tolman, Psychology vs. immediate experience, *Philosophy of Science*, 1935, 2, 356–380. It is, of course, a basic Freudian concept. See also G. E. M. Anscombe, *Intention* (Oxford: Blackwell, 1958).

motive. The present authors take the position that a motive is comprised of two independent parts: value and intention. A value refers to an Image, whereas an intention refers to a Plan.

Presumably, a normal, adult human being has constant access to a tremendous variety of Plans that he might execute if he chose to do so. He has acquired a skill for swinging golf clubs, in the kitchen there is a book with a recipe for making a cake, he knows how to get to Chicago, etc. As long as he is not using them, these various available Plans form no part of his intentions. But as soon as the order to execute a particular Plan has been given, he begins to speak of its incompleted parts (insofar as he knows them) as things he intends to do.

Therein resides a crucial difference between a chain of actions and a Plan of action. When a chain is initiated with no internal representation of the complete course of action, the later parts of the chain are not intended. When a Plan is initiated, the intent to execute the later parts of it is clear.

But where then are values? An evaluation is a form of empirical knowledge and so helps to form the person's Image. But have values no special influence on our Plans? If not, why should any Plan ever be executed? To answer the second question first, Plans are executed because people are alive. This is not a facetious statement, for so long as people are behaving, *some* Plan or other must be executed. The question thus moves from *why* Plans are executed to a concern for *which* Plans are executed. And to cope with this problem of choice we do indeed need some valuational concepts.

Just as the operational phase of a Plan may lead to action, so the test phase of a Plan may draw extensively upon an Image. Thus, the evaluations a person has learned are available for use in the test phases of the Plan; we assume that every test phase in every TOTE unit can have some evaluation function associated with it. Ordinarily, the operational phase of a TOTE should increase the value of the situation as indicated by the test phase. But that is by no means a necessary condition for executing the TOTE. When a Plan is complex —made up of a hierarchy of subparts—it may be that some of the parts have negative values associated with them. That is to say, in order to achieve a positive result it may be necessary to do something that, by itself, has a negative evaluation. When this happens, a person who is executing the Plan can rightly be described as first intending, then carrying out, actions that he considers to be undesirable.

An intended operation that will someday provide the anticipated positive value for an extensive Plan of action may be delayed almost indefinitely while a person continues to execute preparatory subplans leading to outcomes with negative evaluations. Such actions obviously occur repeatedly in the lives of adult human beings—civilized society would scarcely be possible without them—yet they are unusually difficult to understand in terms of simple hedonism or simple reinforcement theory or any other psychological theory that makes no allowance for cognitive structure, for an Image and a Plan.

It seems reasonable to think of the test phases of the more strategic portions of a Plan as associated with overriding evaluations. Thus, a hierarchy of TOTE units may also represent a hierarchy of values. At the root of the hierarchy we can imagine that there is a kind of prototest that, when satisfied, carries a larger positive evaluation than could be counteracted by any accumulation of negative values, or costs, from the TOTE units in more tactical positions. Of course, when we choose a Plan and begin to execute it we may be unaware of some of the detailed tactics that will be needed to carry it through; necessarily, therefore, we would be unaware of all the values associated with those unforeseen tactics until the Plan was well along in its execution. If the negative values accumulate until they outweigh any conceivable positive value associated with the prototest, we may discontinue the execution of the Plan. When, for example, we walk out of the dentist's office before we have been in the dental chair, some change in values must be inferred. (Note, however, that the *intention* may be invariant under these value transformations. The intention to see a dentist vanishes only when a new Plan is executed—it does not gradually lose strength as the desire to see the dentist declines.)

When we say, "I need a mailbox in order to mail this letter," the word "need" should not be taken as expressing a dynamic or evaluative property associated, either temporarily or permanently, with mailboxes. Mailing the letter may be part of an utterly hateful business—any values, positive, negative, or neutral, can be attributed to the letter or to the mailbox—yet the simple mechanical fact would remain true, namely, that Solomon himself cannot put a letter in a mailbox if he does not have a mailbox. It is important to distinguish such mechanical "needs" from dynamic or evaluative needs. Lewin was clearly aware of this problem, yet he did not resolve it. He says quite explicitly that the value of an object is not identical with its valence. The example he cites concerns a sum of gold that might represent a great value for one person without tempting him to steal it, but for another person it might have a strong valence prompting him to steal. Having thus clearly seen the difference between values and valences, however, he drops the matter with the comment that sometimes they are related and sometimes they are independent. If the concept of valence is replaced, as we propose, by the concept of specific criteria that must be met before the execution of a Plan can continue, then there is no reason to expect that objects satisfying the criteria will always be valuable or that they will always satisfy needs. They may, or again, they may not.

The reader will, we hope, forgive us our banalities, for sometimes the obvious is hard to see. The fundamental, underlying banality, of course, is the fact that once a biological machine starts to run, it keeps running twenty-four hours a day until it dies. The dynamic "motor" that pushes our behavior along its planned grooves is not located in our intentions, or our Plans, or our decisions to execute Plans—it is located in the nature of life itself. As William James says so clearly, the stream of thought can never stop flowing. We are often given our choice among several different Plans, but the rejection of one necessarily implies the execution of some other. In sleep we are about as planless as we can get.

In this renunciation of the dynamic properties of Plans,[4] how-

[4] In discussing this point with some of our colleagues we have encountered the reaction that we have not really renounced dynamic properties in the Plan, but rather that we have actually explained them. If so, it is certainly an odd definition of "dynamic." The "explanation" is simply that, so long as it stays alive, the psychobiological machine must continue to execute the successive steps in some Plan. It is our impression that this is not what most psychologists have meant when they used the term "dynamic." As we understand it, "dynamic" is usually taken to mean that the organism is striving toward some state or object that, when achieved, will reduce unpleasant tensions, etc. These "states," "goals," "tensions," if they exist at all, must be represented in the Image, not in the Plan. Hence we persist in speaking of our position as a "renunciation of the dynamic properties of Plans."

ever, we should not lose sight of the fact that something important does happen to a Plan when the decision is made to execute it. It is taken out of dead storage and placed in control of a segment of our information-processing capacity. It is brought into the focus of attention, and as we begin to execute it we take on a number of menial but necessary tasks having to do with gathering data and remembering how far in the Plan we have progressed at any given instant, etc. Usually the Plan will be competing with other Plans also in the process of execution, and considerable thought may be required in order to use the behavioral stream for advancing several Plans simultaneously.

The parts of a Plan that is being executed have special access to consciousness and special ways of being remembered that are necessary for coordinating parts of different Plans and for coordinating with the Plans of other people. When we have decided to execute some particular Plan, it is probably put into some special state or place where it can be remembered while it is being executed. Particularly if it is a transient, temporary kind of Plan that will be used today and never again, we need some special place to store it. The special place may be on a sheet of paper. Or (who knows?) it may be somewhere in the frontal lobes of the brain. Without committing ourselves to any specific machinery, therefore, we should like to speak of the memory we use for the execution of our Plans as a kind of quick-access, "working memory." There may be several Plans, or several parts of a single Plan, all stored in working memory at the same time. In particular, when one Plan is interrupted by the requirements of some other Plan, we must be able to remember the interrupted Plan in order to resume its execution when the opportunity arises. When a Plan has been transferred into the working memory we recognize the special status of its incompleted parts by calling them "intentions."

The recall and resumption of interrupted tasks have, largely as a result of Lewin's interest, received some attention in the psychological laboratory. The studies are well known, as is Lewin's interpretation in terms of tension systems that are reduced when the task is successfully completed. Since both Lewin's tension system and our working memory are carefully considered explanations, they both account for most of the observed phenomena and it is difficult to find clear points of contrast between them. (This difficulty is enhanced by a wonderfully free and easy interpretation by Lewin of "tension system.") But there are a few points on which the two theories can be compared, and we shall concentrate on these.

First, we assume it is a well-known fact that interrupted tasks tend to be resumed and tend to be well remembered. However, the tasks must be a little complicated. Simple, repetitious, continuous tasks—marking crosses on a sheet of paper, stringing beads, etc.—will not usually be resumed and do not stand out in the subject's memory when he is later asked what tasks he performed. This observation seems eminently reasonable from either Lewin's or our point of view. For the present authors, the argument would be that such tasks require little or no record of what has been and what remains to be accomplished, and hence they have no special representation in the subject's working memory. For Lewin, the argument was that such tasks cannot be interrupted, they can only be halted. Therefore, interruption does not serve to continue or prolong a tension system. So far, the two views do not quarrel with each other. Moreover, it is recognized that even these continuous tasks can be interrupted if the subject is told in advance that the task calls for a given amount of activity. If he is told, for example, that his task is to put thirty beads on a string, he can be interrupted before he reaches that number. Both views still agree, since we predict that he will remember the task because he had to count and remember a number in order to keep his place, and Lewin predicts the same result because the task is now interruptable. But suppose that the subject is given a pile of beads to string, told he must put *all* of them on the string, but not told any specific number. Now the predictions will be different. We say there should be no tendency to resume or recall the task, since memory function is performed externally by the pile of beads, not by the subject. The Lewinian view would predict that since a tension system would remain undischarged because the task was interrupted, the bead-stringing should be more quickly resumed and more frequently recalled. We do not have experimental data with which to settle the point, but it appears to us to be a point on which data might help. We are at least encouraged to see that our view is not just a rephrasing of Lewin's, since a fairly clear disagreement can be formulated.

Second, suppose a person intends to write letters to five different people. He assembles the writing materials and begins, but he is interrupted before he finishes. The question is, will it make a difference in his tendency to resume the task if he is interrupted in the middle of a letter rather than between letters? In our view, it would make a difference. An interruption between letters leaves him with no memory problem, so the interrupted Plan is not assigned any special place in his working memory where it might remind him to finish the job. We are not clear what the correct prediction would have been for Lewin. On the one hand, each letter is a separate task with its own tension system to be discharged, so he would predict as we do. But, on the other hand, there might be very little tendency to resume under either condition, because the completion of a task "similar" to the interrupted one (the completion of the first three letters) is supposed to provide a "substitute consummation" to reduce the tension systems associated with the other letters.

In our terms, writing letters would be called a "flexible" Plan, because its parts can be performed in any order. That is to say, it does not matter in which order the letters are written. Usually, there is more working memory involved in keeping track of inflexible Plans, because such Plans tend to become more elaborate and specific; we therefore would make a general prediction that, so long as external memory is not used, a task that requires an inflexible Plan will be resumed and recalled more frequently after interruptions.

Third, in one experiment subjects were told on half the interrupted tasks that the tasks would be resumed and on the other half that they would not be resumed. This advance information made very little difference in their tendency to recall interrupted tasks better. It was on the basis of this experiment that Zeigarnik concluded that the possibility of resumption had no effect on recall. However, an equally valid conclusion might be that verbal instructions given at the time of interruption cannot change the extent to which working memory has already been devoted to the execution of the Plan. But further experiments could be helpful in settling the difference.

Finally, "It is often observed," Lewin wrote,[5] "that even making a written note of an intention is conducive to forgetting it, though according to the association theory it should reinforce the coupling between the referent and the goal-presentation. Making a note is somehow a consummation, a discharge." This observation takes on particular significance for us, of course, since in our view the use of external memory devices ordinarily lightens the load on our personal memories. The forgetting, if our observation is valid, would not be the result of a consummation or a discharge of tension, but rather the result of freeing our working memory capacity for other planning activities.

It was a general observation in Zeigarnik's studies that adults did not participate as enthusiastically as the children and that they did not show as strong a tendency to recall the interrupted tasks. It seems probable to us that an adult has several Plans of his own whose execution must be temporarily suspended during the experiment and that he might be reluctant to lose track of them for these little laboratory games. Also, it seems probable to us that an adult would have learned how to make use of external memory devices for his Plans whenever possible, and so might not use his internal working memory in the same way a child would.

These considerations have, perhaps, drifted rather far into the details of a particular line of research. And the present authors may seem a bit too intolerant of Professor Lewin, a man who has contributed so much to advance our understanding of the psychology of the will. The excuse is that Lewin in his early work came very close to saying some of the same things this book is trying to say. His papers offer a challenge—both in theory and in observations. On the majority of points the present interpretation agrees with his predictions, but the disagreements in theory have been emphasized in the hope of stimulating their resolution in the laboratory.

If an intention is, as here described, the unfinished part of a Plan that is being executed, how could anyone forget what he intends to do? Forgetting intentions is a commonplace occurrence, of course, and several psychologists have offered explanations. It is generally assumed that forgetting an intention is not the same as forgetting a

[5] Rapaport, *op. cit.*, p. 111.

telephone number, although perhaps the same mechanism may occasionally be responsible. Usually, however, forgetting an intention appears to have some active quality to it that is not involved in the kind of forgetting Ebbinghaus studied. The classic work that emphasizes an active component in forgetting intentions, of course, is Freud's *Psychopathology of Everyday Life*. Freud's emphasis, naturally, was on the dynamic or evaluative aspects of such forgetting, on the repression of the intended act by other psychic forces that opposed it in some way.

The most obvious thing to say about a forgotten intention is that the Plan that gave it life was not completed. The question that is basic to all others, therefore, is why one Plan was abandoned and another pursued instead. If we try to translate Freud's dynamic explanation into the language of this essay, we must say that Plans are abandoned when their execution begins to produce changes in the Image that are not as valuable as we had expected. (This would be consistent with the Freudian view, but it is not the only possible explanation.) The diagnostic value of a forgotten intention is that it so often underscores a change in Plan that might otherwise have gone unnoticed. And the change in Plan, in turn, provides a clue to aspects of the Image that might not ordinarily be accessible to introspection. We could, of course, examine the conditions that cause us to be unaware of the fact that we have changed our Plans, but presumably the conditions would be essentially those that psychoanalysts tell us produce repression. Thus we accept the notion that dynamic changes in the Image—especially in the evaluative aspects of the Image—exert close control over the Plans we try to execute. Altering the planner's Image is a major dynamic mechanism for altering his Plan, and thus for altering his behavior. Social psychologists who have considered the problems of persuasion have generally agreed that the best techniques involve some change in the audience's concepts or values. But we are here (as throughout most of this book) concerned more with the *execution* than with the *formation* of Plans.

We can easily imagine other, nondynamic conditions that might lead one to abandon a Plan and thus to forget an intention. The working memory may go awry, especially when the execution of the task has been interrupted for some reason. To take an extreme example, the man whose appointment book is destroyed through no fault of his own will have lost track of numerous Plans, both pleasant and painful. Remembering the Plan is most difficult when we try to do it without external crutches, when the Plan is new or transient, and when the Plan is complicated. If the Plan is written down in detail, if it is one we follow repeatedly, or if several consecutive subplans are involved, then our working memory has an easier task. We therefore assume that intentions would be forgotten more frequently in the former situations than in the latter, *ceteris paribus*, for purely mechanical reasons that Ebbinghaus would understand as well as we do.

Presumably we are constantly revising our Plans after we begin to execute them. Ordinarily we do not make any special note of these changes, but merely execute the new Plan as quickly as possible. But a special problem arises with shared Plans. When you have made known your intentions, other people may depend upon you to carry them out. Thereafter, changes in your Plans must take into account what has been said. You may change the Plan for any of a dozen reasons and then forget to incorporate into your new Plan a subplan for communicating to your friend about the change. Forgetting to tell somebody that you have changed your intentions is a very different process from forgetting your intentions.

Still another nondynamic reason for forgetting an intention might be that some preparatory step in the Plan leading up to the intended act proved to be impossible. An applied mathematician may intend to solve a problem by first inverting a matrix and them computing certain quantities, but he discovers that the particular matrix does not have an inverse. He will forget his intention to compute the quantities, but not because he has repressed it or found it potentially dangerous, etc. No doubt many intentions must be forgotten because we are not bright enough or strong enough to execute the Plans in which they were embedded. Not all Plans are feasible.

Two general consequences of the present argument are worth brief comment before closing the chapter. First, more research is needed on the way people use external aids as memory devices—to record their Plans, their intentions, and their progress in executing their Plans. In our enthusiasm for memorizing nonsense syllables we have overlooked the importance of some of these ancillary kinds of memory. Memory for intentions should not be the private property of clinicians.

Second, what we call an "effort of will" seems to be in large measure a kind of emphatic inner speech. Much, probably most, of our planning goes on in terms of words. When we make a special effort the inner speech gets louder, more dominating. This inner shouting is not some irrelevant epiphenomenon; in a very real sense it *is* the Plan that is running our information-processing equipment. As psychologists we should listen to it more carefully.

C. I. Lewis says only what is plainly open to common sense in the following comment:

> Knowledge, action, and evaluation are essentially connected. The primary and pervasive significance of knowledge lies in its guidance of action: knowing is for the sake of doing. And action, obviously, is rooted in evaluation. For a being which did not assign comparative values, deliberate action would be pointless; and for one which did not know, it would be impossible. Conversely, only an active being could have knowledge, and only such a being could assign values to anything beyond his own feelings. A creature which did not enter into the process of reality to alter in some part the future content of it, could apprehend a world only in the sense of intuitive or esthetic contemplation; and such contemplation would not possess the significance of knowledge but only that of enjoying and suffering.[6]

In this short paragraph Lewis puts the problem of the present discussion. It is so obvious that knowing is for the sake of doing and that doing is rooted in valuing—but how? How in the name of all that is psychological should we put the mind, the heart, and the body together? Does a Plan supply the pattern for that essential connection of knowledge, evaluation, and action? Certainly any psychology that provides less—that allows a reflex being to behave at random, or leaves it lost in thought or overwhelmed by blind passion—can never be completely satisfactory.

[6] Lewis, *op. cit.*, p. 1.

CHAPTER 5

INSTINCTS

What are instincts? Probably no concept in psychology has had a more checkered career than this one, the favorite explanation for all behavior during one generation and the favorite theoretical scapegoat during the next.

Some definitions of instinct have emphasized its conative, striving, goal-directed, motivational aspects. Unfortunately, however, the driven quality of instinctual behavior always seems to vanish when the behavior is analyzed closely. For example, a young salmon has an instinct to go down river to the sea. One could say that he is driven by an instinct to reach salt water. But when the facts are examined more critically it turns out that the salmon has a photokinetic and phototropic response to the sunlight that strikes him in the shallow water when his skin pigment is thin. Of course, one might persist that the fish is driven to avoid sunburn, but that concept seems completely superfluous. Statements about the "dynamic" aspects of instincts almost always conceal ignorance of the physiological processes involved.

Other definitions of instinct stress the inherited, unlearned, innate character of instinctive behavior. Animals isolated from their kind at birth demonstrate characteristic patterns of activity that they could not have acquired through learning or imitation. But is it the *behavior*, the specific pattern of muscular coordinations, that is unlearned? The difficulties with this definition are well known to anyone who has tried conscientiously to decide which parts of an animal's behavior were learned and which parts were inherited. In rats, for example, one might expect to find that copulation is an instinctive kind of behavior. And in some sense it is. Yet the grossness of the copulatory behavior of a rat who has not had grooming experience demonstrates clearly that some practice of these instinctual responses is necessary. After struggling mightily with this fractionation of behavior into the innate versus the acquired, many psychologists have abandoned the concept of instinct entirely. As Frank Beach once noted, the more carefully any particular species of animal is studied, the less one hears about instincts in that species.

The position of the present authors is that the study of instinct would be much less confusing if we said it was the *Plan*, not the behavior, that is inherited. The small nugget of gold that has encouraged psychologists to retain the concept of instinct in spite of its notorious difficulties can be preserved, we think, by defining an instinct as an inherited, inflexible, involuntary Plan. When we say a Plan is *involuntary*, we mean that it cannot be changed depending upon its consequences for the organism. When we say a Plan is *inflexible*, we mean that the component parts of the Plan cannot be rearranged or reordered. And when we say a Plan is *inherited*, we mean that the Plan does not have to be learned or discovered; the actions involved may be learned or unlearned, but the Plan that provides the underlying structure to the actions is innate. In the purest case of instincts, perhaps, the entire performance from general strategy down through particular tactics to each individual twitch of a muscle could be programmed in advance, but if such an instinct exists, we have never heard of it.

In recent years, particularly in Europe, there has been a revival of interest in the problem of instinct. The new field of ethology has made available a rapidly growing collection of detailed observations against which any interpretation of instinct can be tested. The present authors have not read all of this material, but we have surveyed the more accessible secondary sources in order to determine whether contemporary research is producing the kind of results that the concept of inherited Plans had led us to expect. The outcome of that survey was encouraging and some of the major points are worth summarizing here.[1]

First, of course, we discovered that ethologists have much to say about the stimulus control of behavior, about the recognition by the animal of the conditions appropriate for executing a Plan. Most ethologists use a term invented by Konrad Lorenz—the *innate releasing mechanism*—to describe the fact that a Plan is not executed until certain conditions are met. Many ingenious studies have been conducted in order to determine exactly what perceptual pattern is necessary for the release of a particular reaction. Those studies indicate that the test phase of a TOTE unit is innately associated with the appropriate operate phase.

The phenomenon that has been called "imprinting" provides an interesting illustration of the relation between the test phase and the operational phase of an innate Plan. A gosling should follow its mother. The operational phase of this Plan, the walking, can be built into the gosling in advance. But until it has been hatched a gosling cannot know what its mother looks like. Therefore the test phase cannot be completely established until later. The "follow that" Plan of the gosling initially has no built-in test to characterize an appropriate "that." The "that" is defined at a critical period during the gosling's development when it first sees a moving object. This first large moving object that a gosling normally sees is the goose, so the Plan develops in an adaptive way. If the first large moving object the gosling sees happens to be an ethologist, however, some amusing consequences can result. But the important point is that the gosling must have, somewhere in its little Image, a picture of mother. Only then can it test to see if a particular object is the object to be followed or not.

Second, we were impressed by Tinbergen's attempt to integrate the ethological research on instinctual behavior in terms of a hier-

---

[1] A thorough review of the history of the ideas and observations that comprise ethology is available in W. H. Thorpe's *Learning and Instinct in Animals* (Cambridge: Harvard University Press, 1956).

archy.[2] A hierarchy is such an important aspect of what we have been calling a Plan that we could not help but feel encouraged. For readers who have not looked at Tinbergen's interesting book lately we can mention briefly one of his favorite examples, the reproductive behavior of the male stickleback. The stickleback is a small and very aggressive fish. Its reproductive instinct includes several different kinds of behavior. The instinct is triggered by an increase in length of the days, which leads the stickleback to migrate to shallow water. There he selects his own territory, and visual stimulation releases a typical pattern of behavior. He settles in, starts to build a nest, shows certain bodily changes, begins to react to strangers by fighting, etc. Thus, under the large heading of "reproductive instinct," Tinbergen lists four subheads: fighting, nest-building, mating, and caring for the young. Which one of these four will occur at any particular time depends upon the environmental conditions at that time. If another male stickleback invades the territory, the fighting pattern will be released. But there are several varieties of fighting: chasing, biting, threatening, etc. The type that is released depends upon the actions of the invading male. Or, if no other stickleback is present and the male is building the nest, there are several different actions he may make depending upon temporary conditions: digging, testing materials, boring, gluing, etc. In this way Tinbergen develops and elaborates his hierarchical description into ever smaller, more discrete units.

The instinctive hierarchy is usually described by ethologists in terms of units called "consummatory acts." A consummatory act is characterized, so they say, by a thoroughly stereotyped motor pattern. In the case of the reproductive instinct of the male stickleback, the consummatory acts in fighting are chasing, biting, threatening, fleeing, etc. The consummatory acts of mating include the zigzag dance, leading the female to the nest, showing the entrance, quivering, fertilizing the eggs, etc. These are acts that can be recognized easily from direct observation of the animal's behavior. And they usually have a "self-exhausting" character—they "satisfy" the animal, or

---

[2] N. Tinbergen, *The Study of Instinct* (Oxford: Oxford University Press, 1951), Chapter V. We refer here exclusively to Tinbergen's behavioral descriptions, not his hierarchical system of neural centers.

change the conditions that initiated them. These consummatory acts would seem to correspond to the inflexible Plans we have been looking for.

Tinbergen is explicit, moreover, that there is a hierarchical organization within each consummatory act. The consummatory act is much more complex than a reflex or a tropism; it is a coordinated activity of several parts of the animal's body, which can in turn be analyzed into movements of muscle groups and then, finally, into contractions of individual muscles. At the higher levels of the hierarchy the various components of the instinct can be rearranged rather flexibly depending upon the particular environmental circumstances that prevail. Tinbergen interprets this to mean that the instinctual hierarchy becomes progressively less flexible as it approaches the level of actual behavior:

> Now it seems that the degree of variability depends entirely on the level considered. The centres of the higher levels do control purposive behavior which is adaptive with regard to the mechanisms it employs to attain the end. The lower levels, however, give rise to increasingly simple and more stereotyped movements, until at the level of the consummatory act we have to do with an entirely rigid component, the fixed pattern, and a more or less variable component, the taxis, the variability of which, however, is entirely dependent on changes in the outer world.[3]

In comparing Tinbergen's hierarchical description with the hierarchical organization that we refer to here as a Plan, one is struck by the fact that the higher levels in his description are not sequential, but merely classificatory. Not until Tinbergen's description reaches the level of the consummatory acts does it take on the hierarchically organized sequence characteristic of a Plan. Thus we are led to think of relatively discrete, stereotyped, innate Plans for organizing actions into a consummatory act, but those acts are themselves ordered in time by some other kind of mechanism. The alternative mechanism may be either *chaining*, if the consequences of one act provide the situation needed to release the next, or *concatenation*, if the next act is released by events that were not regularly caused by the preceding act. Concatenations are flexible, chains are inflexible, and, although

[3] *Ibid.*, p. 110.

Plans may be flexible, innate Plans are not flexible. Thus the larger units, which are simply concatenated, appear to be variable, flexible, interchangeable in order, but the smaller units, which are chains and Plans, appear to be rigid, fixed, and inflexible.

It is always difficult, of course, to distinguish behavior based on a Plan from behavior based on a chain, but a simple concatenation is usually easy to distinguish. However, organisms are often so well adapted to their natural environments that a concatenation may give the appearance of purposive, intentional behavior—as if the environment itself could serve as part of the animal's memory. It is almost as if the Plan were not in the organism alone, but in the total constellation of organism and environment together. How far one is willing to extend the concept of a Plan beyond the boundaries of an organism seems to be a matter of metaphysical predilections. We shall try to confine our use of the term to Plans that either are, have been, or could be known to the organism, so that we shall not speak of concatenated behavior as part of a Plan even when it is highly adaptive. Nevertheless, the physical continuity of the environment itself can provide a kind of integration of instinctive acts. For example, when a stickleback's nest-building is interrupted by a fight, he can return to it later and take up where he left off, because the nest "remembers" where the interruption occurred. Or, to phrase it differently, the sight of the partially built nest "releases" the next step in building the nest. Thus the kind of flexibility that an animal achieves in the higher, more "strategic" levels is, though adaptive, still of a reactive, concatenated character quite different from the kind of flexibility that can be achieved by an intelligent human being.

A third and final point about instinctive Plans that becomes evident when one reads the ethological reports is that even the simplest animals are often very clever about carrying on several Plans simultaneously, both in isolation and together. Of course, if one considers each of the consummatory acts in Tinbergen's hierarchy of the reproductive instinct to represent a different Plan, then the immediately preceding discussion of concatenations can be taken as a description of one way to carry on several Plans at once. But some further examples may be interesting.

The digger wasp provides a carefully analyzed illustration.

According to Tinbergen's account of Baerends's research, the female, when about to lay an egg, digs a hole, kills or paralyzes a caterpillar, carries the caterpillar to the hole, deposits an egg on it and stows it away in the hole. When the egg hatches and the larva begins to consume its food, she brings some moth larvae. Then she may bring six or seven caterpillars, after which she closes the hole and leaves it forever. Now, this Plan for laying an egg is relatively simple and the releasers can be patiently discovered for each part of it. But an interesting feature is that the digger wasp does not work on just one hole at a time. Usually there are two or even three holes, each in a different phase of development. The state of each of the various holes releases in her the action appropriate for that hole, or, as one might say, the environment helps her to remember what the next step in the adaptive concatenation must be.

Another example is the behavior of the worker bee in the hive. The worker responds largely to proprioceptive tests, or releasers, and does whatever is appropriate for the situation as it is perceived. A cell that has been started by one bee can be continued by any other bee. Thus the hive follows a kind of public plan, to which each bee, even the queen, contributes its part by the execution of the individual Plans. In this example, a number of individual Plans are coordinated, through the releaser type of mechanism, into one larger, shared plan for the hive. An even more common instance of coordinating separate Plans into one social plan must occur whenever two animals come together for mating. The public plans of animals, however, are more properly called "adaptive concatenations" rather than Plans.

The more one considers the virtues of releasers the more respect one feels for the flexibility they permit in the adaptations of a relatively simple biological system. The range, variety, and complexity of the tests that can be used to release the consummatory acts increase as we climb the phylogenetic scale. For example, the mating behavior of chimpanzees is guided by releasers so complex that they can attain sophistication only through demonstration. As yet, however, the organization of these more complicated patterns of instinctive behavior in mammals has received relatively little study.

The description of instincts that seems to be currently accepted by ethologists has many features that are congenial to the thesis of this book. Their work emphasizes that there are configurations, Gestalten, on the behavioral side of the organism as well as on the perceptual side—an emphasis that is essential for any description of instinct based on Plans rather than on chains or mere concatenations of reflexes.

MOTOR SKILLS AND HABITS

Consider for a moment the family record player. It is a machine with a routine, or program, that it follows whenever it is properly triggered. The machine has a routine for changing records. Whenever the appropriate stimulus conditions are present—for example, when the arm is near enough to the spindle or when a particular button is pushed—the routine for changing the record is executed. There is even a "sense organ" that discriminates between ten-inch and twelve-inch records, and there are effectors that push the next record into place and lower the tone arm gently into the groove of the record. The entire performance is obviously involuntary, for no matter how we curse the machine for failing to play the record we want, we will not alter its sequence of operations. The routine for changing records is built into the machine, locked in, and it never guides the actions of any other machine.

However, the record that is played by the machine is also a program. It is a program that controls the small movements of the stylus and, simultaneously, the larger and audible movements of the diaphragm of the loudspeaker. But the record is a *communicable* program. It can be played on any one of a large class of different machines. Machines that can use communicable programs, that can share them with other similar machines, are obviously more flexible than those that cannot. The fixed cycle of the record changer makes it far less flexible than the phonograph stylus, which can follow an indefinite number of different patterns of movement. Communicability is an extremely important property that a program—or a Plan—can have. Communicable programs are not limited to the mechanical world; the chromosome is an example of a communicable program in biological form. At the behavioral level, of course, communicable Plans play the central role in our educational processes.

Habits and skills are Plans that were originally voluntary but that have become relatively inflexible, involuntary, automatic. Once the Plan that controls a sequence of skilled actions becomes fixed through overlearning, it will function in much the same way as an innate Plan in instinctive behavior. The description of the conditions under which various skilled components will be triggered, or released, is much the same in both cases. The new problem that we must consider when we move from instincts to habits and skills concerns how learned Plans become automatized.

When an adult human being sets out to acquire some new skill, he usually begins with a communicable program of instructions. Another person, either verbally or by exemplification, communicates more or less schematically what he is supposed to do. But just having the basic strategy in verbal form does not mean that the learner can correctly develop and elaborate the tactics on the first try to execute the Plan. For example, when a man learns to fly an airplane he begins by getting a communicable Plan from his instructor.[1] The Plan— or a rough, symbolic outline of its strategy—is communicated through some such message as this:

[1] California tends to bring out unusual behavior, so the authors were not completely surprised when one member began to disappear in the late afternoons to learn to fly. When challenged, he explained that he was, in fact, conducting research on a problem of concern to us all: how movements are integrated into larger units to comprise a smoothly running Plan of action. What had seemed to be neglect of duty turned out to be selfless devotion to the common cause. In the course of his explanations a number of examples were discussed that helped to shape the writing of this chapter.

To land this plane you must level off at an altitude of about ten feet. Then, after you have descended to about two feet, pull back on the elevators and touch down as you approach stalling speed. You must remember that at touch-down the control surfaces are less sensitive, and any gust may increase your airspeed. That may start the plane flying again, so be prepared to take corrective measures with the throttle and elevators. And if there is a cross-wind, lower the wing on the windward side, holding the plane parallel to the runway with the opposite rudder.

That is the strategy for landing airplanes. When skillfully elaborated and executed it will serve to get pilot and craft safely back to earth. It is a short paragraph and could be memorized in a few minutes, but it is doubtful whether the person who memorized it could land a plane, even under ideal weather conditions. In fact, it seems likely that someone could learn all the individual acts that are required in order to execute the Plan and still be unable to land successfully. The separate motions, the separate parts of the Plan, must be fused together to form a skilled performance. Given the description of what he is supposed to do, the student still faces the major task of learning how to do it.

There is a kind of complementarity between the teacher and the student. It is easy for the teacher to describe the general strategy, but difficult for him to communicate the detailed tactics that should be used. For the student, on the other hand, each of the muscular movements involved can be made in isolation, but it is difficult for him to combine those tactical details into a larger motor unit, into a feedback mechanism that will effortlessly guide his movements to reduce the differences between his intended and his actual performance. In order to be able to execute the Plan by a smooth, controlled motor unit, the aspiring aviator must find many small, intercalated acts not specified in the instructor's original description of the Plan. The general strategy provided by the teacher says nothing about the activities of individual muscle groups—the instructor "knows" these intercalated acts because he knows how to fly, but they are locked in, implicit, tacit, rather than explicit and communicable. Thus, we get a picture of the instructor working from the strategic toward the tactical in his efforts to communicate the Plan, while the student is working from the tactical toward the strategic in his efforts to carry it out.

Even when an instructor does recognize a possible intercalated act, it may actually be better pedagogy to let the student invent his own idiosyncratic tactics for carrying the Plan into his muscles.

> On take-off the throttle should be opened slowly so that rudder-control can be introduced smoothly to overcome the tendency of the plane to turn as a result of increased torque. Open the throttle continuously so that it is completed by the time you count to five; when you reach three start to apply some right rudder.

The instruction to count is an attempt to provide a more detailed integration of the successive parts of the Plan and it is bad teaching. The student is, or feels, terribly tense and terribly busy. Telling him to count to five is almost certain to interfere with his performance of other parts of the Plan. Counting might work for some people, but for the entire sample that we studied it was a dismal failure—he found a trick of his own that he liked far better. As he pushed the throttle forward to the panel he kept one finger of the hand on the throttle extended, and when the extended finger hit the panel he began to apply the right rudder. This simple device provided the feedback that enabled him to convert a sequence of discrete acts into a coordinated unit of behavior.

Since a learner must discover these little tricks that can connect the successive parts into a smoothly running skill, it might appear that he is merely *chaining* one activity to the next, not building a hierarchical Plan. But if the skill is simply a chain of reflexes, each one hooked to the next, then it is difficult to understand why, in the preceding example, the instructor's method of chaining was not satisfactory. Unless there is some over-all pattern to the skill, a pattern that the instructor sees one way and the student sees differently, why would one intercalation, *ceteris paribus*, be better or worse than another?

What would happen if all the details of a sequence were worked out by the coach and imposed with rigid insistence on the learner? If skills were nothing but chains of reflexes, a detailed account of the correct sequence should be an efficient way to teach them. Probably the most intensive effort to specify exactly what a person must do with each movement is the work of "motion study" experts. On an assembly line in a factory there may be a task that consists of, let us say, assembling three washers on a bolt. The analysis of this task into "micromotions" will specify the exact time at which each hand should move and the operation it should perform. For the left hand, the instructions may read "Carry assembly to bin," "Release assembly," "Reach for bolt," etc., while at the same time the right hand is instructed to "Reach for lock washer," "Select and grasp washer," "Carry washer to bolt," etc. For each of these motions a fixed duration is specified. This is about as near as anyone can come to writing programs for people that are as detailed as the programs we write for computing machines.

The description of the task can be transformed in various ways in an attempt to find a sequence of motions that achieves the result most efficiently, with fewest movements and in least time. The men who make this kind of analysis have developed certain general rules about how sequences of action can be formed to run off smoothly and rapidly. For example, the two hands should begin and complete their movements at exactly the same time. Motions of the arms should be opposite and symmetrical. There must be a fixed position for all tools and materials. And on and on. Following these rules, motion-study engineers are able to develop chains of responses that can be executed with nearly maximal efficiency. But, unfortunately, workers may not acquire the strategies possessed by the engineers—they frequently object to being so tightly regimented and seem to feel that the boss is trying to exploit them unfairly.

When people have time to develop the skill themselves, that is to say, when they form a Plan to guide the gross actions—even an inefficient Plan—they find for themselves the interposed elements that produce the skill. Finding these elements is essentially a test of the adequacy of the strategy. Once a strategy has been developed, alternative modes of action become possible, and we say that the person "understands" the job that he is to do.

In most natural situations, the development of skills involves the construction of a hierarchy of behavioral units, each unit guided by its own Plan. This fact is seldom recognized in the motion-study analysis, which is rather puzzling because the hierarchical character of skills was pointed out explicitly by Bryan and Harter at least as early as 1897, when they demonstrated the successive levels of skill involved in telegraphy.[2] In 1908 Book wired a typewriter to record the time of occurrence of successive key-strokes and then collected data while people learned the "touch method" of typing. People first memorized the positions of the different letters on the keyboard. Then they would go through several discrete steps: look at the next letter in the material that was to be copied, locate this letter in their image of the keyboard, feel around on the actual keyboard for the key corresponding to the remembered position, strike the key, and look to see if it was correct. After a few hours of practice these components of the Plan began to fit together into skilled movements, and the learner had acquired dependable "letter habits." Further speed resulted when they began to anticipate the next letter and build up small subroutines to deal with familiar sequences like -ing and the. By then dependable "word habits" were developing. Finally, the experienced typist read the text several words ahead of the letters he was typing at the moment, so that one could say he had developed "phrase habits." He learns, one might say, to put feedback loops around larger and larger segments of his behavior. This sequence of stages in the acquisition of typing skill is familiar to anyone who has gone through it, who has watched the units at one level of skill come smoothly together to form units at a higher level, until eventually a skilled typist can concentrate on the message and let the muscles take care of the execution of details.

Typewriting, however, is a rather special case. The final components, the key movements, are very discrete and atomic. Probably most of the skills we have to acquire are much more fluid in their execution, but these are correspondingly more difficult for a psychologist to collect data on.

We have assumed that the human being who is acquiring a new skill is aware of the strategy that he is attempting to follow. At least, he is aware of it in the sense that he can talk about it or point to ex-

[2] For a short but representative summary, see R. S. Woodworth and H. Schlosberg, *Experimental Psychology* (New York: Holt, rev. ed., 1954), pp. 809–813.

amples of it. It is quite possible, of course, to build up skills without verbalizing the strategy, the way a baby learns.

Almost no one—including physicists, engineers, bicycle manufacturers—can communicate the strategy whereby a cyclist keeps his balance. The underlying principle would not really be much help even if they did know how to express it: "Adjust the curvature of your bicycle's path in proportion to the ratio of your unbalance over the square of your speed." It is almost impossible to understand, much less to do. "Turn your handle bars in the direction you are falling," we tell the beginner, and he accepts it blindly, not understanding then or later why it works. Many teachers impart no rule at all, but perform their service by running along beside the bicycle, holding it up until the beginner "gets the idea."[3] It is not necessary, fortunately, to know explicitly the rules that must be observed by a skillful performer—if it were, few of us would ever be able to sit up in our cradles. Sometimes we can help a learner do the right thing for the wrong reason, as when we tell a skier to make a left turn by imagining that he is putting his right hand in his left pocket or when we tell a golfer to keep his eye on the ball. But for the most part we must rely upon inarticulate guiding and demonstrating until the pupil "catches on" or "gets a feel for it."

Animals acquire skills, of course, without memorizing verbal descriptions of what they are supposed to do. When we train an animal to execute a series of responses in order to attain a valued outcome, the strategy is not carried in the animal's memory. Only the experimenter needs to know the total Plan. The animal is required merely to build up the smooth transitions that chain one action to the next. That was probably the goal of the motion-study experts.

For example, if we wish to train an animal to press a lever in order to get a ball, then to push the ball into a funnel, and after that to return to the food magazine to be fed, we could build up the chain in many different ways. Any of the components could be taught at any time. Then when they are put together the consequences of one

[3] The bicycle is borrowed from Michael Polanyi, *Personal Knowledge* (Chicago: University of Chicago Press, 1958). Chapter 4 in that remarkable book emphasizes the importance of our inarticulate skills for all branches of knowledge and the extent to which we blindly accept a frame of reference that we cannot justify when we acquire a skill.

action become the occasion for the next action, and each new segment is released as it becomes appropriate. Probably we would choose to build up the chain of responses backwards, starting first with the approach to the food tray, then with the ball down the funnel, etc. Many psychologists are quite skillful at training animals to perform such long and elaborate stunts. But we would argue that the animals seldom acquire the total Plan; the strategy is in the trainer, or in his mechanical substitute, the experimental equipment. The animal has learned a number of different components that enable it to perform as though it had a larger Plan. The critical test occurs when some particular outcome in the long chain fails to occur on schedule. The animal will not continue with the next step. Tolman and his students have argued that rats are capable of mastering a total Plan as well as its component parts, but a rat's skills in this direction are difficult to demonstrate in a laboratory situation.[4] In any case, rats are so vastly inferior to human beings in their ability to remember elaborate Plans that it is difficult to see why psychologists have felt that valid generalizations about cognitive structure could be extended from rats to men. A central feature of the difference, of course, is that men have language to communicate their Plans from expert to novice and from one generation to the next.

The verbal Plans with which a beginner tackles a new job—the look-remember-hunt-hit-check Plan for typing, or the move-right-rudder-when-extended-finger-touches-panel Plan for taking off—get turned over to the muscles that carry them out when the skill is acquired.[5] The verbal form of the Plan is a learner's crutch which is

[4] The evidence indicates that rats, and probably most other inarticulate creatures, are much more proficient in mastering Plans when the Images that support them can be spatially organized. The well-known observation by Karl Lashley in his *Brain Mechanisms and Intelligence* (Chicago: University of Chicago Press, 1929) that rats that had learned a maze could still negotiate it even though Lashley had, by surgical operations, made it impossible for them to use the customary sequence of movements must mean that new motor tactics could be substituted into the same general strategy; certainly the maze skill was not a learned chain of movements. When the organization cannot be represented spatially, however, as in Hunter's temporal maze (see W. S. Hunter, The temporal maze and kinaesthetic sensory processes in the white rat, *Psychobiology*, 1920, 2, 1–17), the rat has great difficulty. Cf. Donald T. Campbell, Operational delineation of "what is learned" via the transposition experiment, *Psychological Review*, 1954, 61, 167–174.

[5] For a discussion of the integration and symbolization of overlearned responses, see George Mandler, Response factors in human learning, *Psychological Review*, 1954, 61, 235–244.

later discarded when he learns to walk alone. The entire pattern of movements, guided continually by perceptual feedback, can then be represented in other Plans as if it were a unitary, independent act. The same procedure of welding these new units together to form still larger skilled units may repeat at the higher level, until eventually the typist is planning whole paragraphs or the aviator is planning whole trips, secure that when the time comes to execute the Plan the subdivisions will be prepared to carry out orders in a rapid, efficient manner.

The verbalized strategies of a beginner may achieve the same result as the involuntary, habitual strategies of an expert, so there is a sense in which we recognize that they are the "same" Plan. But the beginner's plan is carried out in a way that is voluntary, flexible, and communicable, whereas the expert's version of the Plan is involuntary, inflexible, and, usually, locked in. One can say that the development of skill frees the verbal planner to work with larger units of the Plan.

The implication of this attitude toward skills and habits is that man is assumed to be capable of building up his own "instincts." Lower animals come with strategies wired in; man wires them in deliberately to serve his own purposes. And when the Plan is highly overlearned, it becomes almost as involuntary, as resistant to change depending upon its outcome, as if it were innate. Take a skilled typist, who for years has triggered off a muscular pattern for striking t, then h, and finally e whenever he wants to write "the." Offer him money to type a page with the word "the" always transcribed as "hte," then watch him work. Probably he will not be able to do it. If he does, he will do it by slowing down, by trying to reinstate letter habits instead of word and phrase habits, thus abandoning his usual Plan for typing. If you put pressure on him to work fast in order to earn the money, he will certainly not be able to inhibit his usual Plan of action. Your money is quite safe. But one word of caution: Do not let the offer stand too long, for habits are not completely resistant to change. If you take the time, you can replace them with new habits. Let him practice enough and he will build up the action unit needed to win your money.

A good typist has constructed a set of inflexible strategies with most of the properties of instincts, a fact that nonpsychologists often recognize when they speak of habitual actions as "instinctive." The human being is frequently the victim of releasers for his skilled acts, just as the lower animal is for his instinctive acts. A trained athlete, for example, waits for the starting gun before he begins to execute his Plan for running the race. But he does not have his starting completely under volitional control, for otherwise he would never make a false start, or "jump the gun." The human being's advantage lies in the fact that his releasers are more complicated and that, moreover, he can usually determine the conditions under which a releasing stimulus will be presented, whereas in the case of the animal's instinctive act the trigger is usually simple and is provided by an environment that is not under the animal's control.

The construction of integrated strategies for skilled acts through long practice and repetition has a further consequence for the kind of planning that the adult human can do. The construction of these subplans enables a person to deal "digitally" with an "analogue" process.[6] The input to an aviator, for example, is usually of a continuously varying sort, and the response he is supposed to make is often proportional to the magnitude of the input. It would seem that the good flier must function as an analogue device, a servomechanism. The beginner cannot do so, of course, because his Plans are formulated verbally, symbolically, digitally and he has not yet learned how to translate these into the continuous, proportionate movements he is required to make. Once the subplan is mastered and turned over to his muscles, however, it can operate as if it were a subprogram in an analogue computer. But note that this program, which looks so contin-

[6] In the language of computing machines, an analogue device is one in which the magnitudes involved in the computations are represented by physical quantities proportional to those magnitudes, e.g., by a voltage, a duration, an angle of rotation, etc. Thus, continuous variation in the input to the machine will result in a correspondingly continuous variation in the magnitude of the processes that represent it inside the machine and in the output of the machine. A digital computer, on the other hand, represents the magnitudes with which it works by symbols corresponding to discretely different states of the machine, e.g., by a relay that is closed or open, or a dial that can assume any one of ten positions, etc. Thus there is no simple resemblance between the input to a digital computer and the processes that represent that input inside the machine. If you multiply by writing the numbers on paper, you are using a digital procedure. If you multiply by using a slide rule, you are using an analogue procedure. See John von Neumann, *The Computer and the Brain* (New Haven: Yale University Press, 1958).

uous and appropriately analogue at the lower levels in the hierarchy, is itself a relatively stable unit that can be represented by a single symbol at the higher levels in the hierarchy. That is to say, planning at the higher levels looks like the sort of information-processing we see in digital computers, whereas the execution of the Plan at the lowest levels looks like the sort of process we see in analogue computers. The development of a skill has an effect similar to providing a digital-to-analogue converter on the output of a digital computing machine. (It may also be true that the perceptual mechanism provides an analogue-to-digital input for the higher mental processes, but we shall not explore that possibility here.) When an action unit has become highly skilled it can be executed directly without being first expressed in a digital, or verbal, form, and even without focal awareness.[7]

A reader who resents such crudely mechanistic analogies and hypotheses has the authors's sympathy, but it is difficult to know how to express more accurately the difference between the strategic and tactical levels of skilled and habitual Plans. The argument could, of course, be phrased in neurological terms that might sound a bit less offensive. The cerebellum, for example, which has been considered the regulator and integrator of voluntary movements, may play the role of the digital-to-analogue converter. In a discussion of the cerebellum as a feedback mechanism, T. C. Ruch commented that "slowness of voluntary movement is characteristic of cerebellar patients and of normal individuals executing unpracticed movements."[8] The problem for most theories of the neural basis of skilled movements is that the skilled movements run off so very rapidly that there is little time for proprioceptive feedback from one movement before another must occur. Any simple conception in terms of feedback, or error-correcting, circuits must cope with the relatively slow transmission rates that are possible over neural paths. Ruch suggests that "a time-tension pattern of muscle contraction" is instituted, projecting into

[7] Pavlov's well-known distinction between a first signal system, concerned with directly perceived stimuli, and a second signal system, devoted to verbal elaborations, seems, insofar as we understand it, to parallel the present distinction between analogue and digital systems. See Brian Simon, ed., *Psychology in the Soviet Union* (Stanford: Stanford University Press, 1957).

[8] T. C. Ruch, Motor systems, in S. S. Stevens, ed., *Handbook of Experimental Psychology* (New York: Wiley, 1951), Chapter 5, p. 204.

the future, and then he notes that for such "planning movements" the nervous system would have to have some way, presently unknown, of storing impulses for fixed delays.

> The cerebral-cerebellar circuit may represent not so much an error-correcting device as a part of a mechanism by which an instantaneous order can be extended forward in time. Such a circuit, though uninformed as to the consequences, could, so to speak, "rough-in" a movement and thus reduce the troublesome transients involved in the correction of movement by output-informed feedbacks.[9]

These suggestions correspond remarkably well to the kind of hierarchical Plans we have been considering here, particularly if we can consider Ruch's "instantaneous order" as an instruction generated by a digital device and issued to an analogue device for the execution of planned movements. A Plan, either stored in or transferred to the cerebellum, would provide the roughed-in movement in advance of its actual execution.

With proper scientific caution, Ruch comments that such analogies between neural systems and servo systems are "essentially allegorical." Yet it is difficult to see how we can get along without them. The first thing we must know about any machine we might want to study is that it really *is* a machine, and the second is a shrewd guess as to what it is supposed to do. Given that much guidance, it is then possible to analyze in proper scientific spirit how the parts work to accomplish their purpose. But without a guess to guide him, the scientist may waste his beautifully precise descriptions on irrelevant aspects of the problem. It is in that spirit that one ventures a guess that the cerebellum is a machine to provide analogue Plans for regulating and integrating muscular coordinations, that is to say, that the cerebellum is a critical component in a digital-to-analogue converter on the output of the neural system for processing information.

In the chapters that follow there will be little discussion of the analogue levels of action until Chapter 14. It will be assumed that skills and habits can be represented digitally as a sort of motor vocabulary. It may be well, therefore, to summarize what we have said

[9] *Ibid.*, p. 205.

about instincts and skills: Both skills and instincts are on-going patterns of action, directed toward the environmental conditions that activate and guide them and organized hierarchically into action units with more than one level of complexity. The authors contend that these characteristics cannot be understood in terms of a theory of behavior based solely on chains of reflexes or simple S-R connections; some theoretical machinery at least as elaborate as the TOTE hierarchies envisioned here would seem to be indispensable.

We turn now to more complicated behaviors in which the manipulation of symbols, especially verbal symbols, becomes a critically important, though often covert, component.

CHAPTER 7

THE INTEGRATION OF PLANS

Most people in our culture try to carry on several Plans at the same time. Mrs. Jones has a recurrent Plan for keeping her house running that she revises and executes daily. She also has a nonrecurrent Plan to visit her sister in Baltimore. And she is collaborating in a shared Plan to get her neighbor elected sheriff. With all of these Plans (and more) running at one time, her problem is to perform those acts that simultaneously advance the greatest number of them. Thus, Mrs. Jones may decide to drive to town, get her hair done before she leaves to see her sister, pick up the election posters at the print shop, and buy the week's groceries. One trip to town serves to advance three Plans at once.

Psychologists recognize that people do things because several "motives" are working together, and they have discussed the phenomenon in terms of "summation" and the "multiple causation of behavior," etc. But they have done very little to advance our understanding of it beyond the level any intelligent layman must achieve in order to get through a modern day in a modern city. How do we coordinate several Plans into the single stream of behavior that we have available? How do we judge whether some new Plan is compatible with what we are already doing or whether it will be impossible to assimilate it into our other Plans? How are our multiple Plans related to the multiple roles we must play in society? How does the ability to reconcile and coordinate different Plans develop in children? How can we learn to relate all our Plans to the hands of the clock?

It would help a great deal if we had a general language specially designed for talking about Plans.[1] Such a language would, presumably, give us a convenient notation for such aspects as flexibility of Plans, the substitution of subplans, conditional and preparatory subplans, etc. For example, it does not particularly matter in what order Mrs. Jones chooses to run her errands when she gets to town. The three subplans can be permuted in order, and so we say that this part of her Plan is flexible. But she cannot permute the order of these with the subplan for driving to town, or for driving home. That part of the Plan is inflexible. Some subplans are executed solely for the purpose of creating the conditions under which another subplan is relevant. Such preparatory or mobilizing subplans cannot be freely moved about with respect to the other subplans that they anticipate. Another important dimension of freedom that should be analyzed is the interchangeability of subplans. Mrs. Jones can drive to town over a variety of equivalent routes. The variety is limited only by the condition that they terminate when one of her three alternative destinations is reached, since only then would the next part of her Plan become relevant. Given a satisfactory Plan and a statement of the flexibility and substitutability of its subplans, we should then be able to generate many alternative Plans that are also satisfactory. And we should like to have ways for deciding which combinations of Plans are most efficient (in some appropriately loose sense of "efficient").

[1] The information-processing languages developed by Newell, Shaw, and Simon are one solution, of course, but what we are thinking of here would be a more abstract and general sort of calculus—something that would deal with instructions at about the same level of generality as that on which propositional logic deals with descriptive statements. We have given a small amount of thought to the problem, but are not persuaded that anything less complex than a computer language could be developed. The reader who would like to pursue the question further can find a rich source of data and ideas in Roger G. Barker and Herbert F. Wright, *Midwest and Its Children* (Evanston: Row, Peterson, 1954).

It is not always obvious, especially to the person concerned, whether or not two Plans are compatible. We once knew a very intelligent man who spent years trying to write an introductory physics text in the form of a novel so that more people would read it. A great deal of work went into his project before he was able to convince himself that the Plan for writing a physics text could not be coordinated with the Plan for writing a novel. Or, again, for years physicists assumed that the position and the velocity of a particle could be measured simultaneously to any required degree of accuracy. The man who discovered that the Plans for making these two measurements simultaneously were incompatible produced a revolution in our conception of the physical universe. The discovery that two Plans are incompatible may require great intelligence and may completely revise the Image.

We see, therefore, that a person who is caught between conflicting Plans is in a somewhat different situation from the person caught between conflicting motives. He is almost necessarily unaware that his Plans conflict, whereas he may be painfully conscious of his incompatible desires. There is almost certain to be a large penumbra of confusion surrounding the incompatible Plans; the person seems to be deliberately frustrating himself, but cannot discover why. He knows something is wrong, but cannot discover what it is. The two Plans may be isolated from one another in such a way that it never occurs to the person to contrast one with the other. In severe cases the result may be a "dual personality."

The problem of conflicting Plans is most difficult when the two Plans are quite pervasive and the total abandonment of either one of them is impossible. This kind of conflict is common among neurotic patients. A frequent example is provided by the person who has accepted two Plans of life, one from his mother and the other from his father. Either Plan might be executed separately, and often both Plans can be executed simultaneously. But it may happen that the pattern supplied by the mother conflicts with that supplied by the father. For example, the mother may give a Plan that requires personal independence, whereas the father supplies a Plan that demands he be authoritarian. When he tries to execute both of these Plans simultaneously he cannot discover any acts that advance them both at the same time.

Indecision, vacillation, or inaction may be the result, so that neither Plan is executed. Or he may struggle to free himself from one Plan or the other, to identify with one parent or the other. If the person tries to free himself from the maternal pattern, his rejection of maternal love may cause a crisis in character: ethical guilt. If he tries to abandon the Plan supplied by his father, his rejection of the paternal edict may cause a crisis in conduct: moral guilt. In any situation where a successful Plan suddenly becomes useless, the reluctant desertion of that Plan is accompanied by strong emotions. But more about this in Chapter 8.

It should be noted in passing that the task of integrating several Plans into a single stream of behavior must be accomplished by the same organism that is forming and executing the several different Plans. If successive Plans are merely concatenated by chance happenings in the person's environment, there is no problem. But if he coordinates them intelligently, there must be some kind of mechanism for doing it. And, presumably, that mechanism will itself be of the same general form—a TOTE hierarchy—that we have described already. The new feature, however, is that the "objects" that this coordinating TOTE hierarchy tests and operates upon are themselves TOTE hierarchies. That is to say, we must have Plans that operate upon Plans, as well as Plans that operate upon information to guide motor behavior. This fact introduces a degree of complexity that we shall try to discuss in later chapters.

The problem of coordinating several Plans into a single stream of action is difficult enough, but consider how much more difficult things can become when several people try to work together, when they try to execute a public plan based upon some public image. A public plan exists whenever a group of people try to cooperate to attain a result that they would not be willing or able to achieve alone. Each member takes upon himself the performance of some fragment of the public plan and incorporates that fragment into his individual, personal Plans. If the public plan is, for instance, to build new swings on the community playground, then Jones must agree to get the materials and have them delivered, Smith must agree to clear away the old swings, Brown must agree to put up the new swings, and Cohen must agree to collect contributions from the neighbors to pay for it. Taken separately, none of these activities would make much sense. Only as part of a larger, shared plan do they have any meaning.

Of course, each of the four men involved in the shared plan may get helpers and subdivide his part of the plan even further. In this way we would find that the community had constructed a "tree," a hierarchy of plans analogous to the hierarchical Plans we have discussed in single individuals. At the trunk of the tree are a few people who plan the strategy for the entire group. At the tips of the limbs are the many workers who carry out the tactics of their own subplans. We Americans spend a great deal of our time coordinating and participating in just this kind of social planning.

As soon as "social planning" is mentioned, of course, a host of associations rush to mind. There is, for example, the traditional debate over the role of the government as a source of social plans. Should the state lay out our social plans for us in five-year installments, or should we trust that some natural equilibrium will result from the interaction of our private Plans? In a simple situation a planner may be able to get all the alternatives in hand and collect enough information to make intelligent decisions. But when the situation begins to become at all complex—long before anything so formidable as a government is considered—the human planners will find their tasks impossible. In large organizations, therefore, it is unavoidable that much of the apparent direction is an unplanned resultant of innumerable individual Plans.

Some shared plans are temporary, one-shot affairs, whereas others are recurrent and relatively enduring. The plan to put new swings on the playground is nonrecurrent; it will be discarded as soon as it has been executed. On the other hand, most business organizations perform the same task over and over, repeatedly. A manufacturer continually buys raw materials, converts them into a finished product, and tries to sell the product at a profit. The plan is not discarded after it is once successfully performed. There is a consequent permanence to the various subplans of these on-going enterprises, and people have time to acquire special skills and special knowledge about particular parts of the enterprise. The division of labor and of responsibility that is possible and efficient under these circumstances defines a set of social *roles*. The concept of role is indispensable to the sociologist and the social psychologist when they attempt to understand relatively complicated kinds of human conduct. We will not survey role theory here, but merely comment in passing that a person's role in any group should be defined in terms of the Plans that he is expected to execute in that group. ("Role" is one of those wonderful concepts apparently able to tolerate any number of alternative definitions, so one more should cause no trouble.) Each of us plays numerous roles in different groups, and the majority of the Plans we individually execute have their origins in our social commitments.

Social planning provides an interesting area to study the nature of plans and their execution. In the first place, social plans are interesting because they are the source of so much of our individual activity. And, in the second place, shared plans are such simon-pure examples. That is to say, human institutions exist primarily for the purpose of executing plans that their members, as individuals, would be unable or unwilling to execute. When the plans that form their *raison d'être* are taken away—finished, frustrated, outlawed, outgrown, completed, whatever—the group may disband. Sometimes they may hold reunions to swim in an ocean of emotion, but then they have become social groups with corresponding changes in the plans they execute. But many planless groups disappear and are never heard from again. In this respect groups are like computers, 90 percent plan and 10 percent image. Individuals, on the other hand are about 75 percent Image and 25 percent Plan.[2]

Still a third source of interest in shared plans is their easy accessibility. A shared plan must be communicated to the members of the group and hence it can also be communicated to a scientific observer. In dealing with the privately planned actions of an individual there may be constant uncertainty about the Plan that he is following, since he may be unable or unwilling to disclose it. In the social context, however, the Plan that must be executed by an individual is often prescribed in great detail because an attempt has been made to obtain optimal, not just satisfactory, performance from him. In that case a variety of interesting problems can arise.

[2] These percentages are reliable to no decimal places, based as they are on no figures more quantitative than a figure of speech.

Finally, public plans are interesting because they are often so terribly important. They are important for the social units that execute them. Survival may hang in the balance. And they are important to the individuals who participate in their execution, since they determine many of the particular opportunities, accomplishments, and frustrations that will shape the person's life.

The present authors are convinced that one of the most significant arenas for the development and exploitation of a science of human planning is provided by the shared plans incorporated in nearly every human institution. Indeed, we think we perceive the development of such a science in the field of business administration. March and Simon have viewed this work through opinions that are attractive to us.[3] In the event that anyone should mistakenly assume that the science of administration will be a simple, obvious system based on two or three axioms and intelligible to every successful businessman, we invite him to examine the list of 206 variables, all relevant and important, that March and Simon require. In so complex a wonderland we are grateful to be able to refer to the work of others.

The integration and coordination of plans, both individually and socially, is an important aspect of the general problem of planning. We should not leave the topic without first pointing out the significance of clocks and calendars for coordination. Both space and time enter into our Plans in pervasive ways.[4] Spatial considerations are obviously important because activities that we intend to pursue so often have characteristic places where they are feasible and/or relevant. Temporal considerations are slightly more subtle, perhaps. If we had only a single Plan to consider, there might be little need to worry about time; the execution of the Plan could take whatever length of time it required. But when Plans compete, it is our time that they compete for. We must establish rules concerning priorities, rules about when a Plan can be pursued and how long before it must be dropped, either temporarily or permanently, for the execution of a

[3] James G. March and Herbert A. Simon, *Organizations* (New York: Wiley, 1958). We should warn the reader that what we speak of here as a Plan is referred to by March and Simon as a program, and what they refer to as planning is only a part of what we would include in the complete process of constructing, coordinating, and executing Plans.

[4] See Edward T. Hall, *The Silent Language* (New York: Doubleday, 1959), for a comparison of our uses of time and space with their uses in other cultures.

more important Plan. When we attempt to coordinate our Plans with the Plans of others, the clock comes into its own as the petty dictator of our lives. Criteria of space and time must therefore be built into the test phases of almost every Plan to determine where and when any Plan will be relevant and feasible. Time and space, clocks and keys, become dimensions of everything we do.

Americans, we are told, are the most diligent servants of time.

> The American never questions the fact that time should be planned and future events fitted into a schedule. He thinks that people should look forward to the future and not dwell too much on the past. His future is not very far ahead of him. Results must be obtained in the foreseeable future—one or two years, or, at the most, five or ten. Promises to meet deadlines and appointments are taken very seriously. There are real penalties for being late and for not keeping commitments in time. From this it can be surmised that the American thinks it is natural to quantify time. To fail to do so is unthinkable. The American specifies how much time it will require to do everything.[5]

Such is the verdict of an anthropologist. These words should remind us that planning may be a purely American characteristic, not a universally human one. But, useful as such warnings are, we have decided to ignore this one. Planning is a function we have seen span whatever boundaries separate Americans from the digger wasp and the computing machine. It is not the fact that Americans plan that makes them different from their fellow men. It is the way Americans plan and, particularly, the respect Americans show for their shared plans that distinguish them from men who live in other cultures. In its broader aspects, we would argue, planning is not an American idiosyncracy. It is an indispensable aspect of the human mind.

Nonetheless, a cautious reader should not overlook the American origins of this book on the psychology of Plans.

---

[5] *Ibid.*, pp. 172–173. Essentially the same opinion of the temporal aspects of American life was reached by Kurt Lewin (see *Resolving Social Conflicts* [New York: Harper, 1948], pp. 13–14) and by Florence Kluckhohn (see Dominant and variant value orientations, in C. Kluckhohn, H. A. Murray, and D. M. Schneider, *Personality in Nature, Society, and Culture*, 2nd edition [New York: Knopf, 1955], Chapter 21, pp. 342–357).

CHAPTER 8

RELINQUISHING THE PLAN

The discussion of public plans in the preceding chapter ignores rather flagrantly a crucial problem of good administration: How do you persuade people to give up a segment of their lives in order to execute the common plan? Regular cash payments have proved to be a satisfactory method in our culture, but even that will usually not suffice to make a person execute the public plan with all the enthusiasm and intelligence he would lavish upon a Plan of his own. The problem of persuasion (or, in other contexts, seduction) has long fascinated some of our greatest psychologists.

In view of the difficulties so commonly encountered in persuading other people to execute our plans, it is quite significant to note that there is one situation where another person becomes fanatically intent on doing what we tell him. He becomes so cooperative, in fact, that it is a full-time job just to keep him from hurting himself in our interests. The situation is, of course, hypnosis.

One of the seven wonders of psychology is that so striking a phenomenon as hypnosis has been neglected. Some psychologists literally do not believe in it, but consider it a hoax, an act put on by a cooperative stooge. The majority of psychologists admit that hypnosis is an actual phenomenon, but they have not worked with it and do not quite trust anyone who has. Unfortunately, in spite of its remarkable effects, few psychologists have any very good idea what hypnosis is or what to use it for. Two of the present authors have shared this suspicious attitude, and thus arrive at the task of writing on the subject with an embarrassing lack of firsthand experience. It is important to say at the outset, therefore, that considerable reliance has been placed on the excellence of a recent review by Weitzenhoffer.[1] His monograph defines the topic for the purposes of the present discussion.

Let us begin with a flat-footed announcement of what the source of hypnotic phenomena must be and then proceed to examine some of the reported phenomena in detail. The present conception of hypnosis is quite simple. It is based on a naïve faith that the subject means what he says when he tells us that he surrenders his will to the hypnotist. Is there any reason to doubt him? It is just as good a theory as any of the others that have been proposed.

The trouble with such a theory, of course, is that no one knows what the will is, so we are scarcely any better off than before. The only effect is to shift the focus of the difficulty. Now the trouble is not that we lack a good theory of hypnosis, but that we lack a good theory of the will. And that is the point at which the arguments of the present book become relevant.

Suppose that under ordinary conditions a waking person is constantly constructing and revising more or less coherent Plans for his own behavior. Suppose that some of these Plans are visualized, some are felt kinesthetically, etc., but the more elaborate voluntary Plans involve a self-conscious exploitation of language. Inner speech is the kind of stuff our wills are made of. When we will to do something, we may imagine doing it and we repeat our verbal command to ourselves, subvocally, as we concentrate on the task. It is a familiar fact, emphasized by nearly all behavioristic psychologists since J. B. Watson, that most of our planned activity is represented subjectively

[1] André M. Weitzenhoffer, *General Techniques of Hypnotism* (New York: Grune and Stratton, 1957).

as listening to ourselves talk. The hypnotized person is not really doing anything different, with this exception: the voice he listens to for his Plan is not his own, but the hypnotist's. The subject gives up his inner speech to the hypnotist.

It is not sufficient to say merely that a hypnotized subject is listening to Plans formulated for him by the hypnotist. Any person watching the pair of them at work would also be listening to the same Plans but would not feel the same compulsion to carry them out. What is the difference between normal listening and hypnotized listening?

It is assumed that a waking person hears the suggested Plans and then either incorporates them or rejects them in the planning he is doing for himself. But a hypnotized subject has stopped making his own Plans, and therefore there can be no question of coordination, no possible translation from the hypnotist's version to his own. The hypnotist's version of the Plan is the only one he has, and so he executes it. The basic assumption here, as in other chapters, is that he must execute *some* Plan all the time. Of course, the subject is capable of elaborating the Plan that the hypnotist gives him, just as he would normally supply the tactics to elaborate some strategy of his own. But the hypnotist's Plan takes precedence over any Plans of his own.

So the question becomes: How does a person stop making Plans for himself? This is something each of us accomplishes every night of our lives when we fall asleep. Stopping is not always easy, as anyone who has suffered from insomnia will attest, but most of us manage to do it without too much difficulty. It would be natural to suppose that the same procedure would work when a person wanted to turn off his own inner speech in order to become hypnotized. He would try to create the same conditions under which he usually falls asleep. He would make the room dark and quiet. He would sit or lie down in a relaxed, comfortable position. (These conditions which we consider necessary for sleep are not universally required. It would be interesting to see if cultural differences in sleeping habits were correlated with differences in the induction of hypnosis.) The person might try to stop thinking about his own Plans by giving his innerspeech machine something dull and stupid to do, like counting sheep or concentrating on some small detail. He would try to discourage himself from thinking fitfully of what is going to happen next, what people will think of him, how long he has been here, where he is in relation to other objects in the room, etc. He would, in short, try to relax and stop talking to himself. And that is exactly what the standard hypnotic procedures ask him to do. In hypnosis, however, he does not fall asleep, because he finds that there is a substitute Plan provided by the operator's voice, and so the operator's Plans begin to be played out on the subject's nervous system as though they were his own.

An alternative procedure for inducing hypnosis is for the operator to give the subject difficult and conflicting instructions at a fairly rapid rate, so that the subject's own planner becomes confused. Instead of coasting to a halt, it becomes overloaded and quits. In this crisis the Plans offered by the hypnotist may be accepted as a welcome relief from confusion. This technique, however, requires more skill than do the standard methods.

Undoubtedly there is more to the process of inducing hypnosis than this description includes, otherwise every student who became confused or fell asleep during a lecture would find himself hypnotized. In order to substitute his voice for the person's own, a hypnotist must provide Plans, not just comments or descriptive statements, and these Plans should be coordinated as well as possible with the subject's perceptions and movements in order to facilitate the illusion that they are coming from within, rather than from another person. Many of the tricks that good hypnotists use can be understood in this light.

It should be fairly obvious by now that speech plays a critical role in this conception of hypnosis and that it might be quite disturbing to these ideas if a subject in a deep trance were fluent verbally. On this interesting point the present authors are handicapped by inexperience and must rely on Weitzenhoffer. First, in describing what a hypnotized person looks like he says:

> The subject has a strong *disinclination to talk*. It is often necessary to address him several times before obtaining an answer. Sometimes it is necessary to order him to answer questions. Even then the subject often favors nods and shakes of the head over words. When conversation of a sort has been es-

tablished, the subject is usually found to show a lack of spontaneity and initiative. His speech tends to be low in volume and rather flat and expressionless, he mumbles his answers and must be ordered to speak louder and more distinctly. At other times the speech of the subject can be best described as "thick."[2]

Later, in discussing the various phenomena that can be demonstrated under hypnosis, Weitzenhoffer raises the problem of enabling a hypnotized subject to talk without awakening. He says:

> Many hypnotized subjects will readily answer questions, repeat suggestions and even hold complex conversations, without coming out of the trance. However, some wake up or their trance state lightens considerably, the minute they are made to talk. This often can be prevented by the simple expedient of giving suggestions, prior to making the subject talk, to the effect that, although he is deeply asleep, he will be able to hear your voice distinctly, to talk to you without awakening and to answer all of your questions. Then ask him a few simple questions such as his age, his name, etc., and give further suggestions to the effect that he can do this without waking. This procedure is particularly important of course in therapeutic work, where anxiety-provoking questions must be asked sooner or later. It is then that the subject or patient is most likely to become dehypnotized. In therapy a much longer period should be spent asking relatively innocuous questions, and slowly moving to anxiety-provoking questions.[3]

The fact that many hypnotized subjects hold complex conversations is puzzling, although various *ad hoc* explanations could be devised. If the present view has any merit, the subject's speech poses an important problem for further study. Is it possible for him to use language in a planning function while he is in the trance? On the whole, these descriptions are approximately what one would expect if the subject had turned off his inner speech when he stopped making his own Plans. Moreover, it seems likely that the subject's lack of facial expressions is also a symptom of his reluctance to communicate.

Obviously, a hypnotized subject does not relinquish all his capacity for planning. It is still necessary for him to supply tactics for

[2] *Ibid.*, p. 211.
[3] *Ibid.*, p. 353.

executing the strategy laid down by the hypnotist. If his cessation of planning were to extend to the point where he could not even work out the step-by-step details of the hypnotist's Plans, then we would expect to find him in a state of stupor, or torpor, from which he could not be stirred. Indeed, such states have been observed and are called variously "animal hypnotism," the "Braid effect," the "plenary trance," etc. Differences among these various states of immobilization are subtle and will not be discussed here. It is sufficient to know that immobilization can occur, as though the termination of self-planning were really complete. It should also be noted that some subjects do not respond by acting out suggestions when they are hypnotized, but still have very strong and vivid hallucinations which they observe more or less passively. Those subjects who sit passively would seem to require fewer resources for self-planning than subjects who begin to act as if their hallucinations were true perceptions.

It is generally recognized that hypnotic subjects differ widely in the degree of hypnotism they can achieve. Several scaling procedures have been developed for measuring the depth of hypnosis, and they seem to have fairly high reliability. It is necessary to give some account of these different levels in terms of the point of view taken here.

In order to account for the levels of hypnosis, let us assume that there are several different kinds of Plans that are normally executed in the waking state and that these can, with some small degree of independence, be given up individually. Most important, of course, is the kind of planning by inner speech that sets the voluntary strategy for so much that we do. It is the capture of this planning function that marks the passage of a subject into a trance state. But there must be still other planning functions that are performed more or less automatically as a kind of "housekeeping." They are, so to speak, parts of every Plan we make, and they serve to settle various details once and for all without the necessity for fresh decisions on each new Plan. These general-purpose routines will become clearer from a few samples.

The normally awake person must have a more or less involuntary mechanism that takes care of his bodily posture, his tonus, his orientation in space. If the Plan containing these instructions were terminated, the subject would simply collapse. Since the tendency for subjects to collapse when they are told to relax is so great, the hypnotist must give them a special command not to fall out of their chairs. He says, in short, what the person would say to himself: keep the posture-plan working.

Another kind of Plan that will normally be executed more or less automatically is the tagging of our experience with verbal labels and the storing of it in memory. The labels serve the same function as do addresses in a calculating machine. When the label is recalled it is possible to go to that address and find the record of the experience. Now, it is possible to cripple this part of the machinery in two obvious ways, one in terms of storage and the other in terms of retrieval procedures. The amnesias that are so easily produced in hypnosis, and which frequently occur spontaneously in deep trances, would seem to involve the suspension of those Plans that are necessary in order to store or retrieve information.

Some of the most dramatic effects in hypnosis, however, would seem to result from the suspension of "stop-rules." Any device that is supposed to follow literally a given program of instructions must be told under what conditions it should begin and under what conditions it should give up. A waking person who finds some planned action impossible will quickly stop and devise an alternative Plan. A hypnotized subject cannot do this and so may struggle with increasing tension, single-mindedly intent on executing the only Plan the hypnotist has provided. One of the most common stop-rules, no doubt, concerns how much pain we are willing to tolerate before we abandon a particularly painful Plan. Presumably, the TOTE units must normally include somewhere in their test phase an implicit rule saying, "If the pain exceeds an amount X, stop and transfer control to Y." We think the anesthesias that are so familiar a feature of hypnosis can be understood as a result of the omission of these tests when the subject is no longer constructing his own Plans.

In this connection it may be relevant to recall an incident related by a psychologist who had recently gone through basic training in the Army. He was told to run, so he and the other trainees began running. After going on as long as he could he finally stopped, puffing, "I can't go on any more." At this point he was ordered to continue running until he was told to stop or until he fell on his face. If he fell, there was a doctor who would immediately take care of him. And so he began running again. After a short period he lost all voluntary control. He looked down and saw somebody's legs pumping away under him and was mildly surprised to notice that they were attached to his own body. He had learned that his "physiological limit" was a good deal further on than he would voluntarily have set it. And he had learned that it was safe to relinquish to his officers the task of determining what was humanly possible.

What we accept as the limits of human endurance are usually well on the safe side of irreversible tissue damage. Under hypnosis, when the stop-for-pain rule can be relaxed or even eliminated, it is possible to bear children, endure surgery, etc., without any apparent pain. The change in the stop-rule, plus the amnesia for the painful situation, provide all the psychological protection that can be derived from any anesthetic.

It is also likely that stop-rules can be changed in the opposite direction, as well. The suggestions that the subject cannot move certain parts of his body would seem to be exactly the reverse of the suggestions that he can continue to move them after he would normally have stopped.

Still another kind of ancillary Plan that can be suspended involves perceptual reality-testing. There has been much written by psychologists about how a person can tell his perceptual images from his imaginative images. By and large, criteria of vividness have not proved satisfactory.[4] The basic difference between the two types of images concerns the conditions under which they will change. The imaginative image can be altered by an act of will, by creating a Plan for changing the image into something else and then executing the Plan. Such subjective Plans normally have remarkably little effect on perceptual images. However, perceptual images can usually be modified by moving or adjusting the receptor organs themselves. Thus it seems likely that as children we must all learn a set of subplans for testing the plasticity of our images, for distinguishing between imagination and perception. These are normally included as part of

---

[4] See, for example, C. W. Perky, An experimental study of imagination, *American Journal of Psychology*, 1910, 21, 422–452. She demonstrated rather conclusively that images cannot be distinguished from perceptions on purely introspective grounds.

the test phase of all our TOTE units. In hypnosis, however, these reality-testing Plans can be temporarily suspended so that the subject has vivid hallucinations which he is unwilling to admit are not true perceptions. This stage of visual hallucinations should accompany the blank stare (eye movements not used to test the image) that is so characteristic of the deep hypnotic trance.

Perhaps grammatical habits should also be put among the ancillary Plans. That is to say, the rules of formation and transformation of sentences may be so thoroughly habitual that they can be retained even when the subject has given up his usual, spontaneous inner speech and is using his grammatical habits merely to implement and elaborate Plans provided by a hypnotist. Grammatical skills are discussed more fully in Chapter 11.

A variety of other hypnotic phenomena seem to us to be intelligible in these terms, for example: (1) When a hypnotist stops talking to his subject we should expect to see the subject lapse into quiet immobility, or fall asleep, or become dehypnotized. (2) Posthypnotic suggestions are Plans—made well in advance for the subject by the hypnotist and carried unconsciously until the time when the test phase is satisfied and the Plan is executed. (3) Since the subject is awake, we would expect his brain waves to be like those of waking people. (4) The subject must trust the hypnotist, but no kind of love or transference situation is necessary to establish the phenomenon. (5) Any drugs that would interfere with speech should make a person easier to hypnotize, which seems to be the case. Thus we can proceed through a list of phenomena that are characteristic of hypnosis without finding any that seem to contradict the relatively simple hypothesis we have advanced.

The major implication of this conception of hypnosis is not so much the explanation provided for hypnotic phenomena as it is the intimate connections that are implied among volition, inner speech, and normal, waking consciousness. It is not too improbable, we feel, that consciousness is in some essential way the capacity to make one's own Plans and that volition is the capacity to execute them. If so, then language, by extending man's ability to Plan, must tremendously expand his consciousness of himself and his world over that available to, for instance, a chimpanzee.

One virtue of this account is that it makes it obvious why a person cannot be hypnotized "against his will" and why he can be unhypnotized so quickly when the hypnotist tells him to be. Is there any way to gain similar control over him when he is unwilling? Is there some way that a person's resistance could be overcome, that he could be forced to relinquish the planning function to another person? The question calls to mind the notorious "brain-washing," or "thought control," procedures that have been used with military and political prisoners. The first step, presumably, would be to make the person stop planning for himself. This might be achieved by deliberately frustrating every self-made Plan that he tries to execute, even the Plans dealing with his most personal bodily functions. The object is to make him believe that only the Plans originating from his captor can be executed. He may be set the task of confessing, but given no inkling of what it is that he must confess. Whatever he confesses will be wrong, or insufficient. Through all of this frustration of every self-made Plan, however, the prisoner hears repeatedly a strong, clear Plan offered by the thought reformer and corresponding to the reformer's own ideology. Destroying one Plan is only the prelude to building up another. Of course, a prisoner may be more than willing to adopt the new Plan in order to avoid the terror and humiliation of his imprisonment, but if he does not have an Image that will support the elaboration of the new Plan, his willingness is of no avail. Along with the surrender of his planning function, therefore, the subject must develop a new set of concepts. These, too, are presented endlessly in ways he cannot ignore.

It is amazing that such methods could ever fail, that man who can be controlled so completely by other people when he is willing should be so stubborn when he is unwilling. Until psychologists achieve a clear understanding of what "willingness" consists of, however, amazement can be the only appropriate attitude. Whatever else, it is clear that to find oneself without any Plan at all is a serious matter. Interpreted literally, it is impossible, for *complete* planlessness must be equivalent to death. For example, there are well-documented cases of primitive people who have violated some taboo, have been isolated by their tribe, and have died shortly thereafter. It does not seem to be an exaggeration to say these people die of planlessness. If such a diagnosis seems extravagant, at least it enables us to understand what a physician is talking about when he says a patient died because "he lost his will to live." Deep sleep, anesthesia, concussion, the plenary trance of hypnosis—these are probably as close to complete planlessness as we can ever get. The catatonic who sits immobile is a man without action, but he is not a man without Plans. His immobility is itself a part of the Plan he is executing.

Nevertheless, patients do come to the psychiatrist with the complaint that they are unable to decide what to do, that they feel completely planless. This is one of the two large categories of trouble that will make people seek medical help for their psychological ills. When a person becomes acutely mentally ill his presenting complaints are almost always one of two kinds: Either (1) he cannot choose between two or more Plans whose execution would call for incompatible actions; such problems were discussed in Chapter 7. Or (2) the Plans that have guided his actions until recently are no longer relevant or feasible; some particular facet of his life has become planless.

How can it happen that someone finds himself suddenly without any Plans for dealing with an important segment of his life? Such a symptom might be a result of brain damage produced, say, by a series of small strokes. But if, as is usually the case, the person's brain is apparently undamaged, we must look for more psychological origins. Perhaps the complexities and ambiguities involved in the situation are too great for him to understand or to tolerate, and his planning mechanism turns itself off before it produces anything that could be executed. Perhaps he was living largely on borrowed Plans —Plans determined by a loved one, by children, by the boss—and the source of these Plans is suddenly withdrawn. Or perhaps he completed the execution of his Plans, the job is done, and he is ready to die but can only retire. Or perhaps some haphazard stroke of fortune exploded him out of his usual rut and thrust him suddenly into a situation for which he is totally unprepared, where his previous Plans are completely useless.

The person who makes his life's Plans in terms of concrete and specific objectives, in terms of "goals," invites the disaster of planlessness. If the goal is well defined—to earn a million dollars, to unify the Armed Services, to climb Mt. Whatever—he may be frustrated by success and left with no Plan for the remainder of his life. Or he may be frustrated by failure, by the exhaustion of every possible Plan he can devise without the attainment of the goal. It is not necessary, however, to organize one's Plans in terms of frozen and brittle terminal states. Unlike good problems in science or mathematics, successful living is not a "well-defined problem," and attempts to convert it into a well-defined problem by selecting explicit goals and subgoals can be an empty deception. As Gordon Allport has pointed out, it is better to plan toward a kind of continual "becoming" than toward a final goal.[5] The problem is to sustain life, to formulate enduring Plans, not to terminate living and planning as if they were tasks that had to be finished. This simple point has been overlooked by many psychologists who seem to take it for granted that all behavior must be oriented toward explicit goals.

Given that a person finds himself planless, for whatever reasons, what are his reactions? Whenever an enduring Plan—a Plan that has guided action for any prolonged period of the person's life—becomes useless, irrelevant, or not feasible, some characteristic reactions ensue: they are pathological only in the extreme case. Plans that are intended to span long periods of time build up large "investments" of special habits and skills, investments that might be lost if the Plan is never executed again. Moreover, the realization that an enduring Plan must be changed at a strategic level can cause a considerable upheaval in the person's Image as well as in his Plans. A rule that most people seem to learn, probably when they are very young, is: When in the execution of a Plan it is discovered that an intended subplan is not relevant or is not feasible, the smallest possible substitutions of alternative tactical subplans are to be attempted first, and the change in strategy is to be postponed as long as possible. Whatever the mechanism, if the person becomes planless rather suddenly, marked mood swings are apt to occur: the person is said to become "emotional." The activation appears to result directly from the suddenness in the alteration of Plans; the interpretation of the increase in "emotion," that is, the way the person feels, appears more related to the extent to which the Plans are pruned, that is, whether only tactics are affected or entire strategies have to be abandoned.

[5] Gordon W. Allport, *Becoming: Basic Considerations for a Psychology of Personality* (New Haven: Yale University Press, 1955).

One possible reaction is to reinstate the old Plan in spite of the fact that it is no longer relevant or feasible, to continue to develop it, transform it, and execute it despite its inadequacy. In its most extreme form, this is the paranoid reaction. The person may go through a brief stage where the irrelevance of his Plan is crystal clear to him. Then the paranoid transformation sets in. This transformation changes whatever part of the Image might interfere with the execution of the Plan. Paranoid reactions, if the Plans are not obviously socially destructive and are not too obviously irrelevant, may go undetected for years. A paranoid person may even be able to persuade others that his Plans are feasible, so that he is aided in their execution.

A second possibility is to hang on to as much of the general strategy as possible and consider making revisions only in the tactical branches of the Plan. The person may attempt to "act out" some early situation, letting present persons symbolize earlier ones and attempting to impose on them the same strategy used earlier, except for necessary modifications of tactics. In more severe forms, the process may be characterized as schizophrenic. A sudden extensive abandoning of tactics, that is, the pruning of a plan, seems to produce emotional excitation that, in the absence of alternative tactics, is felt by the person as depression. According to Sullivan's scheme, for example, a patient regresses to earlier and simpler (parataxic and protaxic) modes of interaction and during this part of the process may show symptoms of agitation (unplanned action), as in agitated depression or in hebephrenia.[6] When the process has stabilized and the patient has not developed new tactics, he is said to suffer from a chronic depression, or, if the regressive process has gone far enough, he may be classified as a "simple schizophrenic." The seriousness and intensity of the acute episode probably depends upon how rapidly the tactics are abandoned.

A third possibility is to give up the strategy, but to hold on to the tactics. Various habitual acts, once an important part of the total Plan, or of the person's "style of life," may have become unconscious, involuntary. When the larger Plan is dropped, these frag-

[6] H. S. Sullivan, *The Interpersonal Theory of Psychiatry* (New York: Norton, 1953).

ments, should they survive, may now be inappropriate. In extreme instances they would constitute the stuff that compulsions and obsessions are made of. The patient may have a very difficult time getting rid of them or formulating his new Plans in such a way that the old tactics are once more relevant and useful. The survival of autonomous islands of involuntary Plans may well form a part of the clinical picture of hysteria and, when very marked, of catatonia. Both hysteria and catatonia are characterized by habitual, ritualistic patterns of behavior that substitute for the development of new, useful Plans.

For whatever reason, whether it be a threat to a person's Image or intrinsic to the wholesale abandonment of large segments of Plans, the more or less sudden realization that an enduring Plan must be changed at a strategic level is accompanied by a great deal of emotional excitation. When this excitation can find no focus in either the Image or in action, the person experiences "anxiety." The patient may then develop Plans to cope with the anxiety (defense mechanisms) instead of developing new Plans to cope with reality.

Can the execution of a given Plan acquire some value in and of itself? Considerable argument has led the present authors tentatively to the position that psychological theory will be simpler if values are restricted to the domain of knowledge, to the Image instead of the Plan. How, then, can we account for the person's feeling of "commitment," to use an existentialist term? How can we explain his suffering when an enduring Plan must be abandoned? Giving up the Plan must affect the person's Image of himself in ways that are difficult for him to accept. Or, to express the same notion somewhat differently, the Plan itself may be, and usually is, represented in the Image. The person's knowledge of himself includes the fact that he is capable of executing the Plan. Insofar as the Plan itself is symbolized in the Image, its representation can have some positive (or negative) value associated with it. In fact, some such assignment of values to the symbols in the Image that represent Plans would probably be an aid in the decision to transfer some familiar Plan to a new situation, a decision that forms a crucial part of thinking and of problem-solving generally.

CHAPTER 9

NONDYNAMIC ASPECTS OF PERSONALITY

Psychologists who devote their intellectual lives to the search for significant dimensions of difference—let us dub them "clinicians" for short—have not given much attention to the differences in the ways people make Plans. This neglect may have been inherited from their experimental colleagues. The first experimenters were dedicated to the analysis of the Image, and their favorite weapon was an inner eye called "introspection." Next, the behaviorists expanded the science by focusing attention on the movements of an organism, rather than on its ideas. But Image and behavior became competitors, and therefore it was not recognized that both are important and that they need to be linked by the sort of planning function described in these pages. On both sides of the argument the experimenters were searching for invariances that would characterize a generalized mind, or the basic laws of behavior—the kind of differences among people that a clinician loves were just experimental errors in the laboratory. The Image is a relatively stable structure; red is red and circles are circular, even when tilted, etc. And behavior is controllable; when a response is properly under the control of a reinforcing stimulus, you cannot detect the differences among men, rats, birds, and fish. The principal differences one finds when one examines the Image or the behavior of different people involve their values and reinforcements. Consequently, the clinician has been forced to concentrate his attention on the dynamic aspects of psychology, since only there does he find the kind of variation from one person to the next that is essential if we are to understand personality.

But is this restriction to the Image or to behavior necessary? In the present context, of course, the question is purely rhetorical. There is still another domain, the Plan, where people differ greatly and significantly from one another, where the differences cannot easily be attributed to evaluative origins, and where we can find a rich source of clinical insights. Some psychologists have come very close to this domain when they have discussed personality in terms of "style," but it is not clear that all differences in style should be reduced to differences in the kinds of Plans people use. In any event, the study of style has not prospered—it has been a less fruitful topic than, for example, needs, values, drives, valences, etc. One difficulty, no doubt, is that the variations are so great that psychologists have not known how to catch them in their clinical and psychometric nets. Whereas the Image is, values excepted, discouragingly stable among members of similar cultures, the Plan is so variable that it almost defies description. A clinician wants people to be different, but not *that* different.

Popular speech recognizes differences in values by such sayings as, "One man's meat is another man's poison," "There is no accounting for tastes," etc. We may even accuse each other of basic differences in our Images with such comments as, "His ideas are weird," "He doesn't speak our language," etc. But individuality is perhaps more often captured by such phrases as, "John would have handled it differently," "Bill would have done it like this," "You never know what he will try next," "They never give up," etc. These phrases relate to differences in the way people tackle a problem and carry it through. In order to follow up this lead we might look at some of the obvious ways in which Plans can differ, then try to see if we recognize these differences among the people we know.

Source. Because Plans are communicable it is possible to imitate others, to accept their Plans, instead of using your own. David Riesman has laid particular stress on this aspect of character and has described those who act on their own Plans as "inner-directed," those who act on borrowed Plans as "other-directed." We shall not compete with *The Lonely Crowd* by trying to elaborate the difference in these pages. It is worth noting, however, that men and women show characteristic differences in the ways they prefer to tackle problems: whereas men when given the chance tend to produce an analytic or abstract Plan for solving the problem, women more often begin by seeking help from others.[1]

Span. Some Plans incorporate events that are expected to occur months, years, even centuries in the future, others are limited to the next few seconds or minutes. There are large differences in the temporal scope of planning that will occur in different cultures, but even within a single culture there are characteristic differences between individuals in the extent to which they worry about remote events. Whereas one person may make elaborate Plans for the financial security of his grandchildren, another may be unwilling to develop Plans that extend much beyond his evening meal.

Detail. Some people sketch in only the general strategy of their Plans before they begin to execute them; others will not decide to execute any Plan until they have elaborated the smallest tactics with a fine pen. How meticulous you are is probably a highly stable feature of your planning. If you must have every detail worked out, you are what is usually referred to as a compulsive person. Of course, the nature of the Plan itself and also the value of the Image which the Plan's execution will affect are both considerations in determining how far one should go in "debugging" a Plan before it is executed, and it might be possible experimentally to isolate some of these factors that determine Plan complexity.[2]

---

[1] G. Alexander Milton, Five studies of the relation between sex-role identification and achievement in problem solving. (Technical Report 3, contract Nonr 609(20), NR 150–166.) Departments of Industrial Administration and Psychology, Yale University, 1958.

[2] A study by Walter Gruen, Behavioral correlates of some dimensions of the cognitive field, *Journal of Personality*, 1959, 27, 169–186, illustrates the kind of thing that can be done. People were given a Rorschach ink-blot test and they were required to learn the correct path through a long and complicated stylus maze. During the initial stages of learning the maze, the people who had given many

Flexibility. A Plan is flexible if the order of execution of its parts can be easily interchanged without affecting the feasibility of the Plan. The degree to which a person would favor flexible Plans is probably related to the amount of detail he characteristically demands, but the correlation is worth some empirical verification. The flexible planner might tend to think of lists of things he had to do; the inflexible planner would have his time planned like a sequence of cause-effect relations. The former could rearrange his lists to suit his opportunities, but the latter would be unable to strike while the iron was hot and would generally require considerable "lead-time" before he could incorporate any alternative subplans. The person who characteristically devises inflexible Plans and then refuses to interrupt them is usually referred to as a rigid person.[3]

Speed. Some people Plan more rapidly than others. No doubt intelligence is involved here to a large extent, but that is not all there is to it. Two people of equal intelligence might work out Plans in equivalent detail for coping with the same anticipated situation, yet one may arrive at his Plan immediately, constructing it almost as rapidly as he can describe it, whereas the other must spend hours with pencil and paper. Planning is a skill, and as with all skilled acts, some people are quicker than others.[4]

Coordination. Some people seem to keep each Plan in a separate

---

"whole responses" on the Rorschach were best able to organize sequences of correct moves in the maze into larger units. As the learning progressed, however, the people who had given many "formal responses" (no mention of movement or color, only form) and "large detail responses" on the Rorschach mastered the maze perfectly in the shortest time. Although a projective test provides a special approach to the study of personality, and although maze-learning is a reasonable test of planning only by the grace of reasonable assumption, nevertheless, Gruen's results encourage the present authors to believe that a person's interest in detail —both in his Images and his Plans—could be studied objectively.

[3] One way to approach this aspect of personality has been illustrated by A. S. Luchins, Mechanization in problem solving, *Psychological Monographs*, 1942, No. 248. Subjects who had discovered a satisfactory Plan for solving a series of water-measuring problems differed in their ability to change it when an easier Plan became possible. Compare the review of this work and of other studies of individual differences in problem solving: Donald W. Taylor and Olga W. McNemar, Problem solving and thinking, in C. P. Stone (ed.), *Annual Review of Psychology* (Palo Alto, Annual Reviews, 1955, Vol. 6, pp. 455–482).

[4] Although it may not be directly relevant, a study by F. L. Wells, Instruction time in certain multiple-choice tests; Cases XCVI–CII, *Journal of Genetic Psychology*, 1950, 267–281, illustrates one way this aspect might be studied. By recording how long each subject wanted to study the instructions before he started taking an ability test, Wells found consistent individual differences that could not be explained in terms of differences in general ability.

compartment, to execute each Plan independently of all the others. They make three trips to town in one afternoon, each trip connected with the execution of a different Plan. Again, one suspects that low intelligence may have something to do with the isolation of one Plan from another, but intelligence is not the whole story. It would be instructive to know whether the person who has trouble coordinating his own Plans is also the person who has trouble coordinating his Plans with those of other people.

Retrieval. The kind of working memory that people prefer to use when they are executing a Plan seems to represent a characteristic difference. One person will insist on writing things down, running his life from a calendar pad, whereas another person will keep in his own head everything he intends to do. Also, some people will become very upset if they lose track of how far they have progressed in the execution of some Plan, but others seem almost irresponsible, or "flighty," in their willingness to let one Plan drop absent-mindedly as they pursue another.

Openness. Some people are very cagey about announcing what their Plans are, whereas others feel quite free to describe them to anybody who inquires (and, unfortunately, even to those who do not inquire). An additional complication arises, of course, if we consider the fact that some people freely describe Plans they will never execute.

Stop-orders. A rich source of individual differences is connected with the location and kind of stop-orders a person will insert into his Plans. A little more than the familiar notions of persistence and satiation [5] is involved, however, because one person may give up because time is gone, another because no one agrees with him, another because he wants to avoid hurting himself, etc. Here we come very close to some of the dynamic properties of the Image that will, usually unconsciously, determine what kind of outcomes will terminate the execution of the Plan. Notice, incidentally, that perseverance is not necessarily correlated with compulsiveness in the context of the present discussions.

[5] See, for example, the review by Kurt Lewin, Behavior and development as a function of the total situation, in L. Carmichael, ed., *Manual of Child Psychology* (New York: Wiley, 1946), especially pp. 824 ff.

This list could be extended quite a bit further, no doubt, but these should be sufficient to suggest what kind of differences in Plans one could look for in a study of personality. Professional students of personality could probably tidy up these ideas and organize them in ways more appropriate to the work that has been done in this field. The present authors are inclined to say that what they are describing here are personality traits and that the theory of personality developed by Gordon Allport is as close to what we have in mind as anything else we are familiar with.[6] In order to test the validity of this association, the reader is invited to take a sample of trait names and to see how many of them can be characterized in terms of Plans. The authors have tried this exercise and have concluded that it is very easy to make the translation from trait name to some aspect of planning in most cases, but they may be too prejudiced to judge the matter objectively. In any case, many trait names have very dynamic connotations. For example, "dominance" can be either a need to control one's environment or the trait of communicating one's Plans to other people. "Order" can be considered as a need for cleanliness, neatness, balance, precision, or it can be described as the extensive use of environmental memory. And so on.

The sort of trait theory—if that is what it should be called—to which a student of Plans could subscribe would have to be shorn of these dynamic, evaluative overtones. Values are properly a part of the Image system, as has been repeatedly argued in these pages. This distinction would lead to a less evaluative kind of trait system than clinicians are accustomed to. And the traits would not be simple differences in the amount of some otherwise undefined facet of personality, but would be attributable to, or derivable from, different structural aspects of the person's Plans. The structure of Plans would then be able to stand as part of the description of a personality on an equal footing with the current descriptions of need structure.

[6] Gordon W. Allport, *Personality: A Psychological Interpretation* (New York: Holt, 1937). It should be apparent, however, that there is no necessary connection between an interest in Plans and Allport's trait theory of personality. Henry Chauncey, of the Educational Testing Service in Princeton, New Jersey, has shown us an interesting personality test, the Myers-Briggs Type Indicator, that explores (among other things) the extent to which people like to plan their activities in advance; the test was designed to get at basic personality differences, similar to those proposed by C. G. Jung, one of which is the extent to which plans are used.

Neither one is more fundamental or more important than the other.

Having wandered this far afield, the present authors will go a step farther and point out that differences in Plans would seem to characterize different cultures as well as different personalities. There does not seem to be any sizeable body of anthropological literature that one might consider an adequate basis for analysis, but casual observations by anthropologists and sociologists indicate that the differences are there waiting to be described. A Persian businessman, we are told, runs his affairs in a planless state that would drive any American to distraction. He will order machinery before he knows how he can pay for it, and he will pay for it before he makes any plans for how to use it. An Arab will say that the future is known only to God and that it would be impertinent to plan how it will happen. A Navajo is bound to the present and cannot consider promises of future benefits as anything worth planning for. Latin Americans will assume that other people will enforce stop-rules for them and that in matters of passion they do not have to control themselves. And so on.

Although anthropologists have not made any more systematic studies of planning than have psychologists, anthropologists have had something to say about different attitudes toward time. The American takes his elaborate system of timekeeping for granted, assumes everyone must conceive of time as he does, and cannot understand why people in other cultures are so unconcerned about keeping appointments, finishing the jobs they start, confining certain activities to certain hours of the day, etc. Time is much less important in other cultures than it is in ours, and plans are made and executed in a much more leisurely, informal way. It seems to us possible that planning is one of the most important points of contact between those two equally extravagant concepts, culture and personality.

The fact that Americans place so high a value on the faithful execution of shared plans may be part and parcel of that "stress of modern life" we hear so much about. Our insistence on this point may be producing many character disorders, disturbances that would not arise in another culture. Or, more likely, other cultures may be better able to tolerate a person whose style of planning is unusual or who fails to complete the execution of shared plans.

CHAPTER 10

PLANS FOR REMEMBERING

The usual approach to the study of memorization is to ask how the material is engraved on the nervous system, how the connections between the parts of it become learned, or imprinted, or strengthened, or conditioned. The usual answers have to do with the amount of practice, with the beneficent consequences of success, with the facilitating or inhibiting effects arising from similarity among parts of the materials or between these materials and others, with the meaningfulness or other sources of transfer of previous learning, and so on.[1] No one who knew the experimental data would question that all these factors are important in determining how fast and how well a person will be able to commit a particular string of symbols to memory. The reason for returning to this well-cultivated plot and trying to crowd in another crop is that an important aspect of the memorizing process seems to have been largely ignored. It has been ignored because the traditions of, first, behaviorism and, later, opera-

[1] The field of psychological research that we have in mind is reviewed in John A. McGeoch and Arthur L. Irion, *The Psychology of Human Learning* (New York: Longmans Green, ed. 2, 1952).

tionism tended to prevent psychologists from speculating about symbolic processes inside the memorizer and encouraged an organization of the field in terms of what the experimenter, rather than the memorizer, was doing. Since the present authors have here thrown operational and behavioral caution to the winds, they are free to speculate about what the learner is doing and to ignore (for the moment) what the experimenter is up to. It is the learner, not the experimenter, who must be explained. Let us focus attention on him, on his task, and on his efforts to cope with it.

Ordinarily the simplest way to find out what a person is doing is to ask him. But psychologists have become very chary about asking people what they are doing because, they usually say, people really do not know what they are doing and it is just a waste of time to believe what they tell you. This skepticism may indeed be justified in many cases, especially those dealing with emotions and motivations. But it seems foolish to refuse to listen to the person under any circumstances. What he says is not always wrong. More often what he says would provide a valuable clue if only we were able to understand what it meant.

If you ask a man who has just memorized his first list of nonsense syllables to tell you what he did in order to master the list, he will have quite a lot to say. And he will usually be eager to say it. In fact, the only part of the task that has any interest or appeal to most subjects concerns the discovery and use of a technique for solving the problem. He will say that he was trying to connect things up and make sense of them. Of course, you knew that he had to connect them up, but how did he make sense out of the carefully chosen nonsense he was given? Well, it wasn't easy, but he did it. Now, that first nonsense syllable, BOF, was just plain remembered the way it came, but the second one reminded him of "XAJerate," the third one turned into "MIBery," and the fourth turned from ZYQ to "not sick." So he had a kind of sentence, "BOF exagrates his misery because he is not sick," instead of the cryptic BOF, XAJ, MIB, ZYQ, and he could imagine a hypochondriac named BOF who continually complained about his health. That MIBery-misery association wasn't too good, however, because for two or three trials through the list he remembered MIS instead of MIB. But he finally worked it out by thinking of "mibery" as a new word meaning "false misery." The fleeting thought that ZYQ was a strange way to spell "sick" was just amusing enough to fix the fourth syllable. Now the fifth and sixth syllables went together, too. . . . And so the subject chatters on, spinning out long descriptions of the various ideas, images, associations, and connections that occurred to him during the learning. Is it nothing but chatter? Or is this the sort of data that psychologists ought to study most carefully? Data about the number of trials required to reach this or that criterion set by the experimenter may be far less valuable for understanding what memorization is all about.

The attitude of most experimental psychologists toward these associative links that a memorizer spends so much of his time looking for is illustrated by the following comment:

> Such aids in memorizing are naturally regarded with much favor by O, but E would like to be rid of them. They make the learning task less uniform and introduce variability and unreliability into the quantitative results. Besides, E wants to study the formation of new associations, not O's clever utilization of old ones.[2]

Is there some way to interpret this comment so that it does not mean that the experimenter has no interest in what his subject is trying to do? It would appear that the present authors hold a minority opinion, for they believe that it is better to try to find out what a person is doing than to assume he is doing what you want to study.

The principal reason this kind of report looks so hopeless to a psychologist is that every subject tells a different story. The associations seem to be entirely random, or certainly idiosyncratic, and how can anyone make a science out of things no two of which behave the same way? It is much easier to think in terms of an average subject with normal, but unspecified, associations. It may even be better to do so, because introspections are notoriously unreliable and because there is no assurance that these elaborate translations and groupings and associations by the memorizer are really any help at all. We would expect the properly cautious student of human learning to

[2] Robert S. Woodworth and Harold Schlosberg, *Experimental Psychology* (New York: Holt, rev. ed., 1954), p. 708.

tell us something like this: "The most parsimonious theory of human learning is that the continued repetition of a correct response, followed by reinforcement or confirmation, builds up the excitatory potential for that correct response while all other response tendencies are inhibited or extinguished. All the talk the subject gives us is just that—talk. It really has nothing to do with the more fundamental, probably unconscious process of laying down a good, solid memory trace that will lead reliably from the stimuli to the desired responses." Now, although this approach may be parsiminous, it has since 1885 made rote memorization one of the dreariest chapters—psychophysics not excepted—in experimental psychology. The alternative approach may be hopelessly complicated, but at least it is more interesting.

A memorizer's task in the psychological laboratory is to learn how to produce a particular sequence of noises that he would never make ordinarily, that have no significance, and that will be of no use to him later. Rote serial memorization is a complicated, tricky thing to learn to do, and when it is mastered it represents a rather special skill. The argument here is that such a skill could not run itself off successfully unless it were guided in its execution by a Plan of the sort we have been discussing. What the subject is telling us when he reports all the wild and improbable connections he had to use is the way in which he developed a Plan to control his performance during the test period.

Now, it would be extremely easy at this point for us to become confused between two different kinds of Plans that are involved in rote memorization. On the one hand, the subject is attempting to construct a Plan that will, when executed, generate the nonsense syllables in the correct order. But at the same time he must adopt a Plan to guide his memorizing, he must choose a strategy for constructing the Plan for recall. There are a variety of ways open to the subject for memorizing. One is to translate the nonsense syllables into words, then to organize the words into sentences and/or images, even, if necessary, to organize the sentences and images into a story if the length of the list demands such higher-order planning. Another Plan the person can use is sheer drill without any translation, perhaps aided by rhythmic grouping, until the list rolls out as the letters of the alphabet do. Or he can play tricks with imagery—imagining each syllable at a different location in the room, then simply looking there and "reading" it when it is needed, etc. There are a variety of such strategies for learning, and they should be investigated. But it is the impression of the present authors that the average person, when confronted with a list of nonsense syllables for the first time, will do something similar to the performance described above.

Unless a person has some kind of Plan for learning, nothing happens. Subjects have read nonsense syllables hundreds of times and learned almost nothing about them if they were not aware that they would later be tested for recall. In order to get the list memorized, a subject must have that mysterious something called an "intent to learn." Given the intention, the act follows by a steady, slow heave of the will. This proposition has provoked a certain amount of exploration by memory psychologists. The data that have been collected are extensive and various, and only fools would attempt a simple generalization about them. The simple generalization of the present authors is this: An intention to learn means that the subject executes a Plan to form a Plan to guide recall. (See Chapter 4 for a discussion of intention.) The intention does not "stamp in" or "strengthen" the associations—it merely signifies that the person will search for associations that he already has.

A subject may, of course, form fragments of a Plan for memorizing more or less absent-mindedly and incidentally, without anticipating that they may become useful to him later, and in that case he will learn without intending to. The important thing is to have a Plan to execute for generating the recall responses; ordinarily, but not invariably, that Plan will not be achieved without intent to learn, that is to say, without executing a *metaplan* for constructing a Plan that will guide recall. If you ask a person what words are suggested to him by various nonsense syllables, and if you let him arrange those words into sentences, all as part of some unexplained game but without any suggestion that recall will be tested, if you encourage him by other tricks to do all the things he would do in forming a Plan for recall, then you will find that he has inadvertently learned a great deal of the material without intent to learn. (Without glancing back, try to recall the four nonsense syllables used in the example at the beginning of this chapter.) For example, if you ask a person merely to notice whether the numbers on a list suggest anything to him—birth dates, street addresses, telephone numbers—he will recall the numbers later just as well as he would have if you had instructed him to memorize them intentionally.[3] It is the execution of the Plan, not just the intent to execute it, that is important.

The study of learning Plans should tell us something about how people form Plans in general. The natural, naïve, first-impulse kind of response to the nonsense syllables is to translate them into words. This suggests that a natural element of nonrecurrent Plans—new or temporary, as opposed to instinctive or habitual Plans—are words and phrases, a suggestion that supports our speculations about the general importance of words in our Plans. Moreover, people tend to master the material in chunks organized as units. This fact tends to become obscured by the mechanical methods of presentation used in most experiments on rote learning, because such methods do not enable the subject to spend his time as he wishes.

If we listen carefully to the memorizer's explanation of how he reproduces a list of nonsense syllables in the correct order, we note that the translation into words is only the first step in his campaign. The second is to group the words into phrases, then, if necessary, to group the phrases into stories or bizarre episodes. This procedure results in a hierarchical organization of the list. The list turns out to have, say, four parts, each of which has its own smaller parts, each of which, perhaps, consists of words that suggest the nonsense syllables. When this hierarchical structure is complete—when the Plan for recitation is constructed—the subject is able to recite the syllables in their correct order.[4] There would seem to be no fundamental difference between the way his recitation is guided by a hierarchical

[3] Irving J. Saltzman, Comparisons of incidental and intentional learning with different orienting tasks, *American Journal of Psychology*, 1956, 69, 274–277.
[4] The importance of a hierarchical organization in serial memorization has been pointed out in three articles by George A. Miller: The magical number seven, plus or minus two, *Psychological Review*, 1956, 63, 81–97; Information and memory, *Scientific American*, 1956, 195, 42–46; and Human memory and the storage of information, *IRE Transactions on Information Theory*, 1956, Vol. IT-2, No. 3, 128–137. A more general discussion, however, can be found in A. A. Cleveland, The psychology of chess and of learning to play it, *American Journal of Psychology*, 1907, 18, 269–308.

Plan and the way all his other intentional behavior is guided by hierarchical Plans.

Some questions of efficiency should be raised at this point. Why do we bother to build up such elaborate hierarchies? Does this not add to what we already have to remember? A list of N words requires $N-1$ associations if we learn them as a chain. If we organize them into groups and form associations between those groups, we simply add to the number of associations we need. Isn't this just a make-work proposition? The efficient solution should be to use as few new associations as possible. A suspicious attitude toward these organizing tricks is reinforced by the observation that experienced memorizers of nonsense syllables say they can drop out all the translating and grouping and imagining, and concentrate directly upon connecting one syllable with the next.

The question raises a variety of problems. In the first place, experienced memorizers do change their strategy for memorizing. The change is prompted, at least in part, by increasing familiarity with nonsense syllables, less insecurity and anxiety about the task, more appreciation for the usefulness of rhythmic, as opposed to semantic, grouping, and by general exhaustion with the effort involved in doing it the way we described above. The matter needs careful examination, but it is the authors's impression that even the most hardened subjects never give up the practice of grouping the syllables into substrings, thus producing a kind of simple hierarchy, or Plan. What he gives up first is the translation of the nonsense syllables into words, which is what the novice spends most of his time doing. It is also interesting to note, however, that twenty-four hours later the novice will remember the list a good deal better than will the more professional memorizer.[5]

But we are still left with the fact of grouping and with questions about the necessity for this extra labor. The reason for it seems to be related to the rather severe limitation of our span of apprehension. The largest number of digits the average person can remember after one presentation is about seven, and if we want to be sure that he will never fail, we must reduce the number to four or five. Thus it is about

[5] Benton J. Underwood, Interference and forgetting, *Psychological Review*, 1957, 64, 49–60.

four or five symbols (words, elements, items, lists, things, chunks, ideas, thoughts, etc.) that will easily group in consciousness at one time as a new list to which we can attach a new label. Even lists as short as the names of the months are organized into the four seasons. The longest unorganized list that most of us ever learn is the alphabet, and even there one suspects that hierarchical traces could be detected in a child's learning process, traces that vanish when the recitation is, by endless repetition, transferred from a conscious, planned performance into "pure habit" so that the mouth can speak without guidance from above. As the learner groups and renames the elements in the list to be memorized, *he effectively shortens the length of the list.* It is as though he is trying to reduce the list to the number of units that can be held in mind simultaneously, since at that point there can be no serious problems in executing the Plan when the time comes to translate it into action. Miller once tried to explain the informational economies of grouping and renaming in the following terms:

> Since it is as easy to remember a lot of information (when the items are informationally rich) as it is to remember a little information (when the items are informationally impoverished), it is economical to organize the material into rich chunks. To draw a rather farfetched analogy, it is as if we had to carry all our money in a purse that could contain only seven coins. It doesn't matter to the purse, however, whether these coins are pennies or silver dollars. The process of organizing and reorganizing is a pervasive human trait, and it is motivated, at least in part, by an attempt to make the best possible use of our mnemonic capacity.[6]

Because the particular tricks that each person will use to group and rename the materials he is attempting to remember are quite variable and idiosyncratic, they pose formidable problems for the experimentalist. In his attempts to solve them, the experimentalist might very well turn into a clinician, for every subject must be individually studied and his performance interpreted in terms of the particular Plan that he constructed. In addition, there are all of the

[6] George A. Miller, Human memory and the storage of information, *IRE Transactions on Information Theory*, 1956, Vol. IT-2, No. 3, 129–137.

clinician's problems of discovering what the subject's Plan really was when the subject himself is not very clear about it. But the alternative, lumping everybody together and pretending they are doing the same thing, then discovering that only a statistical theory will fit the data, is a pure example of looking for the wallet only where the light is good. The kind of memorization that we are considering here is a process that goes on in one nervous system at a time, and the only way to study it is to see what each individual is doing. Only after that detailed look at each individual's strategy should we begin to recite the general features that characterize everyone.

The organizing, or planning, operations in memorization are perhaps easier to see and recognize when the material to be memorized consists of meaningful discourse, rather than nonsense syllables, mazes, etc. Imagine that you are cast in a play and that you have the job of memorizing your part. This is a great deal easier than memorizing nonsense syllables because you do not need to search for the translations into words and because the strings of words follow, by and large, grammatical rules that you have already learned. You first note that the play has four acts, that you are on in all four, and that your big scene is in Act III. In Act III you are on at the curtain, and first you talk to the maid about having cocktails ready for the guests, then there is the fight with Caspar, and finally the big love scene. In the love scene there are four attitudes to go through successively: indifference, interest, exploration, and expression of affection, ending with an embrace and a kiss. During the indifference part, there are about eight lines. In each line are one or more sentences. In each sentence are words, in each word are phonemes, in each phoneme are articulatory movements, in each movement are muscle twitches. And that is about as far as we can go. When you have memorized your part and are ready for the opening night, you will have imposed just such a hierarchical structure on your script and you will be able to move around in it without a slip. Your task during the performance will be greatly simplified by the fact that you are holding a conversation and that the other actors will be remembering the script too. But, as every actor knows, there are always those deadly moments when someone skips ahead two pages, thus leaving out essential facts that the audience must know in order to understand the play. Then the scramble begins to get those missing lines spoken, somehow, and the most exciting part of amateur acting, except for the curtain calls, is often connected with this adventure of trying to cover everything without letting the audience know that the author did not write it that way. Thus it is possible to revise and elaborate the Plan even after the material has been memorized. (One wonders whether the effects of skipping about during recitation might not provide some objective evidence for what the hierarchical structure really was. It is essentially the technique used by Müller and Schumann to reveal the rhythmic structure of a memorized list, and by Thorndike to show the importance of "belonging." [7])

When the items to be recalled are themselves familiar words, the learner is much freer to devise ingenious ways to solve his problem. He may, in fact, resort to mnemonic devices, if he knows any. The antagonistic attitude of experimental psychologists toward mnemonic devices is even more violent than their attitude toward their subject's word associations; mnemonic devices are immoral tricks suitable only for evil gypsies and stage magicians. As a result of this attitude almost nothing is known by psychologists about the remarkable feats of memory that are so easily performed when you have a Plan ready in advance. Anecdotes do not contribute to science, of course, but they sometimes facilitate communication—so we shall lapse momentarily into a thoroughly unscientific vein.

One evening we were entertaining a visiting colleague, a social psychologist of broad interests, and our discussion turned to Plans. "But exactly what is a Plan?" he asked. "How can you say that *memorizing* depends on Plans?"

"We'll show you," we replied. "Here is a Plan that you can use for memorizing. Remember first that:

[7] For a description of the work of Müller and Schumann, see Robert S. Woodworth, *Experimental Psychology* (New York: Holt, 1938), pp. 28–30. Woodworth's discussion of memory describes numerous studies showing the importance of organizational factors in memorization and is probably the root source of the present authors' dissatisfaction with much of the contemporary work in this field. "Belonging" as an aid to remembering was first discussed by E. L. Thorndike in *The Fundamentals of Learning* (New York: Teachers College, Columbia University, 1932).

> one is a bun,
> two is a shoe,
> three is a tree,
> four is a door,
> five is a hive,
> six are sticks,
> seven is heaven,
> eight is a gate,
> nine is a line, and
> ten is a hen."

"You know, even though it is only ten-thirty here, my watch says one-thirty. I'm really tired, and I'm sure I'll ruin your experiment."

"Don't worry, we have no real stake in it." We tightened our grip on his lapel. "Just relax and remember the rhyme. Now you have part of the Plan. The second part works like this: when we tell you a word, you must form a ludicrous or bizarre association with the first word in your list, and so on with the ten words we recite to you."

"Really, you know, it'll never work. I'm awfully tired," he replied.

"Have no fear," we answered, "just remember the rhyme and then form the association. Here are the words:

1. ashtray,
2. firewood,
3. picture,
4. cigarette,
5. table,
6. matchbook,
7. glass,
8. lamp,
9. shoe,
10. phonograph."

The words were read one at a time, and after reading the word, we waited until he announced that he had the association. It took about five seconds on the average to form the connection. After the seventh word he said that he was sure the first six were already forgotten. But we persevered.

After one trial through the list, we waited a minute or two so that he could collect himself and ask any questions that came to mind. Then we said, "What is number eight?"

He stared blankly, and then a smile crossed his face, "I'll be damned," he said. "It's 'lamp.'"

"And what number is cigarette?"

He laughed outright now, and then gave the correct answer.

"And there is no strain," he said, "absolutely no sweat."

We proceeded to demonstrate that he could in fact name every word correctly, and then asked, "Do you think that memorizing consists of piling up increments of response strength that accumulate as the words are repeated?" The question was lost in his amazement.

If so simple a Plan can reduce the difficulty of memorizing by a discriminable amount, is it not reasonable to suppose that subjects in a memorization experiment would also try to develop a Plan? Of course, they do not have a ready-made Plan of the kind just described. It takes subjects some time and some effort to construct Plans that will work for the sort of materials that we like to use in psychological experiments. In tests of immediate memory, for example, subjects seldom try any mnemonic tricks—with only one presentation of the material, there is little time to develop a Plan and little need for it, since the material will never be seen again. But without a Plan of some sort, the subject will never be able to recite a long list.

W. H. Wallace, S. H. Turner, and C. C. Perkins of the University of Pennsylvania have found that a person's capacity for forming associations is practically unlimited.[8] They presented pairs of English words to their subjects, who, proceeding at their own pace, formed a visual image connecting the two words. The list of paired associates was given only once. Then the subjects were given one member of each pair and asked to write the other. Starting with lists of twenty-five pairs they worked up to lists of 700 pairs of words. Up to 500 pairs, the subjects were remembering about ninety-nine percent; at

[8] Wallace H. Wallace, Stanley H. Turner, and Cornelius C. Perkins, *Preliminary Studies of Human Information Storage*, Signal Corps Project No. 132C, Institute for Cooperative Research, University of Pennsylvania, December 1957.

700 pairs it dropped to ninety-five percent. Ordinarily the subjects used about twenty-five seconds to form the association, but when they had become more experienced they could work accurately with less than five seconds per pair. The subjects were not selected for their special abilities; they were ordinary people, conveniently available for the experiment. Freed of the necessity to translate the items into familiar form, freed of the necessity to organize them by a Plan into a fixed sequence, freed of the necessity to work at a mechanically fixed pace, the subjects had nothing to do but sit there and form connections—and they did it almost without error until both they and the experimenters ran out of patience. What is more, little had been forgotten two or three days later.

But what of the traditional picture of an association as something to be constructed slowly through frequent contiguity and strengthened repeatedly by reinforcement? Slowly waxing and waning associations may be useful to characterize a conditioned salivary reflex, but they are not characteristic of human verbal learning. Irvin Rock has succeeded in demonstrating that in learning paired associates there is no increment in associative strength until the first correct response occurs, and that thereafter the association remains fully available to the learner.[9] Thus, the memorization of a list of paired associates is not delayed if, every time a pair is not recalled, a new pair is substituted in its place. In fact, subjects do not even notice that a substitution has been made. The association is not formed until the trial on which the learner has time to consider the pair of items; then it is formed and remembered throughout the remainder of the learning.

Observations such as these suggest that it is not storage, but retrieval, that is the real bottleneck in verbal learning. Building the connections seems to be far simpler than finding them later. A new association leading from A to B becomes merely one of many associations leading from A to something else. The time and effort that goes into a job of memorization is devoted to ensuring that there will be some way to get access to the particular association we want when

[9] Irvin Rock, The role of repetition in associative learning, *American Journal of Psychology*, 1957, 70, 186–193; Irvin Rock and Walter Heimer, Further evidence of one-trial associative learning, *American Journal of Psychology*, 1959, 72, 1–16.

the time comes to revive it. In this view of the problem, the memorizer's task is quite similar to a librarian's. In a large library it is essential to have books labeled by a code and filed on a shelf according to that code. If a book is moved accidentally to another shelf, it may remain lost for years. The librarian must mark the volumes, place them on the shelves in the correct places, enter cards into the central directory under two or three different schemes of reference—all that labor adds nothing to the information or entertainment contained in the book, but merely ensures that it may be possible to locate the book when its contents are relevant.

Memorizing is much too complex to lie open to such a simple analogy. The memorizer is more like a librarian who writes all his own books and is his own reading public. The point of the metaphor is simply that there is a great deal more to a memory—either in a library or a cranium—than the simple hooking of things together two at a time. Let us imagine that this hooking operation is available and that it is as cheap and easy as it would have to be to support the discursive human intellect. What do we do with it? Given that we can nail two boards together, how do we build a house?

CHAPTER 11

PLANS FOR SPEAKING

How much emphasis to place on language has always been something of a problem for psychologists. On the one hand, it is obvious that men are quite different from other animals and that most of the differences have their origin in man's verbal behavior. It is difficult to realize the full extent to which our mental accomplishments as human beings are evoked in us by learning to speak. But, on the other hand, the suggestion that men are very different seems like an anthropocentric retreat to pre-Darwinian dogmatism and medieval mysticism. How is it possible to recognize man's unique accomplishments without violating the concept of evolutionary continuity from animals to man?

One solution to this dilemma—and perhaps it is the simplest—is to argue that words are just like other responses, only more so. For instance:

> The essence of words is that they summarize many past experiences into a manageable unit; that is, they produce or represent a temporal integration of many diverse experiences. The use of words as a tool of thinking or reasoning or problem-solving, therefore, means that a huge number of past experi-

ences are being effective in determining present behavior. Language, or verbal mediating responses, represents an instance of extremely efficient central integration with which we, as educated human adults, are especially familiar. But language does not seem to introduce any really new psychological process; it may be thought of, rather, as an instrumental means or technique which enormously increases the speed and efficiency of processes already present to some extent in nonverbalizing animals.[1]

In short, language is nothing but an extremely complicated instance of behavioral processes that might better be studied in their simpler manifestations in animals. Some psychologists, however, carry this line of reasoning a step further and insist that it *must* be studied with animals. They argue that unless you can phrase your questions about man in such a way that the same questions could be asked of animals, you have not gotten to the heart of your problem. Thus, for example, they are willing to study brightness discrimination in man because the same experiment can be conducted with animals, but they will not ask a man to estimate numerical magnitudes of brightness because no one knows how that instruction could be given to a dumb beast. If words are needed to impart the instructions, so the argument runs, we cannot know whether the results are generated by the subject's history of verbal conditioning or by the stimulus magnitudes he is asked to estimate. Unless an inarticulate animal can be used as the subject, the experiment is certain to run aground on the treacherous shoals of introspection from which psychology has only too recently escaped.

[1] Henry W. Nissen, Axes of behavioral comparison, in A. Roe and G. G. Simpson, eds., *Behavior and Evolution* (New Haven: Yale University Press, 1958). Similar sentiments have been expressed by many other American students of animal behavior. However, Russian psychologists have, by and large, been keenly aware of the extent to which speech supports novel psychological processes in human beings. See, for example, A. R. Luria and F. Ia. Yudovich, *Speech and the Development of Mental Processes in the Child*. (Trans., Joan Simon) (London: Staples, 1959). Those authors write (p. 11–12) that, "Study of the child's mental processes as the product of his intercommunication with the environment, as the acquisition of common experiences transmitted by speech, has, therefore, become the most important principle of Soviet psychology which informs all research. . . . Intercommunication with adults is of decisive importance because the acquisition of a language system involves a reorganisation of all the child's basic mental processes; the word thus becomes a tremendous factor which forms mental activity, perfecting the reflection of reality and creating new forms of attention, of memory and imagination, of thought and action."

The psychologists who make this argument are, of course, a small minority. But they are a tough-minded group who are hard at work proving that psychology can be an experimental science. They know what data look like, they have high standards for what they will accept as evidence, and one violates their prejudices at one's own risk. In this matter, however, they have drawn the boundaries of scientific acceptability too narrowly. Consider their proposition: "A psychological process has not been fully, scientifically understood until it has been analyzed into component parts that can be studied experimentally in animals." One feels intuitively that there is something profoundly backward in such an approach to the study of man—nothing we ask about animals would have the slightest interest to anyone *except* in terms of standards imposed by the articulate, discursive intellect of man. The proposition is a challenge to search for exceptions—to search for some problem of human significance that psychologists must understand, but one that cannot be studied experimentally in animals. Or, to phrase the challenge in terms of the preceding quotation, is there any new and important psychological process that is introduced by language and that cannot be thought of as a technique to increase the efficiency of inarticulate processes?

No doubt there are many uniquely human problems we might choose, but the issues are illustrated sufficiently well by the problem of death. Man is the only animal that knows he is going to die. Should this be considered as a new and important psychological process introduced by language? Or is it just an improvement on nonverbal processes? A man can make his death a part of his Plans, as when he buys life insurance policies or draws a will, or he can even devise and execute a Plan that intends his own death. Indeed, we occasionally hear it said that a truly rational man would commit suicide immediately. But whatever one's evaluation of life, it must be admitted that the expectation of death provides a persistent theme in our art and literature, that it creates our estate-planning and life-insurance industry, that it motivates us to support our medical and public health authorities, that it is the foundation for much of our religion, that the fear of death is to the old what lust is to the young—in short, the anticipation of death influences our behavior in many pervasive ways. In order to understand human behavior and human institutions, therefore, it is necessary to know something about the way men look forward to their own deaths and prepare for the life they anticipate after death. But in order to study this important psychological phenomenon we must, according to the proposition we are considering, reduce it to "component parts that can be studied experimentally in animals." Could we impart to a rat the knowledge that his death is inevitable? We can teach an animal to recognize certain signs and to perform certain tricks, but the knowledge that all living creatures are mortal seems to be reserved for man alone. The anticipation of death cannot be studied with animals; therefore, according to the proposition, the effects on behavior of the anticipation of death cannot be studied scientifically.[2] The boundaries of science must be broader than that!

In the past, whenever psychologists have encountered methodological strictures against studying something that interested them, it was the stricture they gave up, not their interest. Presumably, that attitude will continue and psychologists will persist in asking questions about human beings that would not be appropriate or even intelligible if directed toward animals. Let us hope so, for human speech has provided man with a new mechanism of evolution that in a few brief centuries has set him apart from all other animals. The jealous guardian of Darwinian continuity merely blinds himself to the obvious facts. Almost nothing we could say about the psychologi-

[2] Which may help to explain why the matter has been so neglected by psychologists. (See I. E. Alexander, R. S. Colley, and A. M. Alderstein, Is death a matter of indifference? *Journal of Psychology*, 1957, 43, 277–283). The anticipation of death is something of a special problem for healthy-minded reflex theorists in any case. With a purely inductive conception of knowledge, it must be difficult to understand how the conditioning provided by 25,000 dawns could lead to anything but the conviction of immortality. It *might* be explained away in terms of the conditioning provided by the deaths of acquaintances, were it not for the fact that our society shields us so carefully from the emotionally disturbing sight of a dead body. (See D. O Hebb and W. R. Thompson, The social significance of animal studies, in G. Lindzey, ed., *Handbook of Social Psychology*, Vol. 1 [Cambridge: Addison-Wesley, 1954], p. 557.) Most of our acquaintances disappear sooner or later, but in modern societies we do not see them die except in unusual circumstances—war, catastrophe, or the like. Where could anything so morbid as the anticipation of one's own death take root and grow until it became one of the fundamental truths of our mental life? (See Sylvia Anthony, *The Child's Discovery of Death* [New York: Harcourt, Brace, 1940].) In neglecting this problem, psychologists conform to a general taboo on death that must be almost as strong in our society today as was the taboo on sex during the Victorian era. (See S. Freud, *Beyond the Pleasure Principle* [London: Hogarth Press, 1950].)

cal importance of language could be too extravagant—the speculations in Chapter 8 about the mechanism of hypnosis should suggest how crucial the present authors consider speech to be in controlling all the psychological processes in a human being.

The most important benefit we obtain from our capacity to represent things and events in verbal form, of course, is the capacity to share in and profit from the experience of others, living and dead. As a consequence, the Image we construct extends much farther than the bounds of our own experience and incorporates the conclusions of the great thinkers and explorers who have preceded us and have helped to shape our conception of the universe and of ourselves. But we also benefit from communicable Plans as well as from communicable Images. Skills are normally tacit, but by careful analysis and investigation we are often able to discover the principles underlying them and to formulate verbal instructions for communicating the skills to someone else. Our cultural heritage includes knowing *how* as well as knowing *what*. To explore these matters with the attention they deserve, however, would require a general psychology of knowledge—a far more ambitious project than the present authors are prepared to undertake.

A project of more reasonable proportions for a scientist to consider concerns the description of the speech skill itself, divorced from the cultural role that the skill fulfills or the content that the skill may enable us to convey. That is to say, instead of considering how speech is used to accomplish other things, let us consider in this chapter how linguistically acceptable sequences of sounds are themselves planned and executed.

At the motor extremities of the speech act, of course, are the marvelously delicate, swift, and synchronized movements of the tongue, teeth, lips, and velum. These coordinations comprise the subject matter of physiological phonetics and of phonology—although their study is fascinating, they do not raise psychological issues of the type we are considering in these pages. Let us move upward in the hierarchical organization of the speech skill, therefore, until we come to more molar units organized by a relatively more strategic part of the Plan. That is to say, let us move up into the level that might loosely be termed "grammatical."

We propose, now, to wander briefly into the domain of modern linguistics. The authors do not desire, nor are they competent, to summarize linguistic science.[3] Instead, we shall select the work of a single linguist and follow it slavishly. Our selection is based upon the fact that this linguist seems to agree so well with our own ideas about how human behavior in general, not merely in speech, is organized. (The agreement is not accidental, since many of our own ideas were stimulated by his example.) The linguist whose ideas we shall exploit is Noam Chomsky, and the ideas are presented summarily in his monograph, *Syntactic Structures*.[4] From considerations of grammar and syntax we hope to be able to gather some impression of how complicated the planning device must be in order to generate grammatical sentences. This result should provide a sort of lower bound for the complexity of the human planning equipment in general, for nonverbal as well as for verbal planning.

Sentences must be uttered one word at a time. Does that fact imply that they form a simple chain? That is to say, is the next word in the sentence chosen exclusively on the basis of preceding words? Or, is it chosen on the basis of words that will follow as well as words that have preceded it? Certainly introspection tells us we have very definite expectations about what we are going to say—our choice of words depends upon much more than the history of our utterance. We have a Plan for the sentence, and as we execute it we have relatively clear impressions of what we are going to say. William James described it far better than we can:

> And has the reader never asked himself what kind of a mental fact is his *intention of saying a thing* before he has said it? It is an entirely definite intention, distinct from all other intentions, an absolutely distinct state of consciousness, therefore; and yet how much of it consists of definite sensorial images, either of words or of things? Hardly anything! Linger, and the words and things come into the mind; the anticipatory intention, the divination is there no more. But as the words that replace it arrive, it welcomes them successively and calls them right if they agree with it, it rejects them and calls them wrong if they

---

[3] An excellent introduction to the problems and methods of linguistics can be found in H. A. Gleason, *An Introduction to Descriptive Linguistics* (New York: Holt, 1955).

[4] Noam Chomsky, *Syntactic Structures* (The Hague: Mouton, 1957).

do not. It has therefore a nature of its own of the most positive sort, and yet what can we say about it without using words that belong to the later mental facts that replace it? The intention *to say so and so* is the only name it can receive. One may admit that a good third of our psychic life consists in these rapid premonitory perspective views of schemes of thought not yet articulate.[5]

James is describing a state of consciousness associated with an intention to execute a Plan. The Plan of the sentence, it seems, must be determined in a general way even before it is differentiated into the particular words that we are going to utter.

Introspection is a fickle mistress, as every psychologist knows all too well. Before trying to invent some elaborate, anticipatory device for thinking about everything simultaneously, one should first explore the simpler possibilities. Let us try, therefore, to ignore our introspections, to forget the discussion of Plans, and to pretend that the next word in our utterance will depend only upon the words that have led up to it, but not upon any Plan for the words that may follow it. A nonanticipatory grammar would be exceedingly simple and, since the mathematics of those systems has been carefully studied under the general topic of "Markov processes," we would immediately know a great deal about the level of complexity of the sentence generator itself.[6] Moreover, such a grammar would permit a very simple correspondence between language-as-the-talker-generates-it and language-as-the-listener-receives-it. The listener can know only the past words of the sentence; he must make probabilistic inferences about its future developments. One might argue that, since the listener seems to need this probabilistic, "Markovian" equipment anyhow, it would be economical to let him use it when he stops listening and starts talking. But life, unfortunately, is not always as simple as we

[5] William James, *The Principles of Psychology*, Vol. I (New York: Holt, 1890), p. 253.
[6] The use of Markov processes to describe the message source is taken from C. E. Shannon, A mathematical theory of communication, *Bell System Technical Journal*, 1948, 27, 379–423. These ideas were made the basis of a grammatical theory by Charles F. Hockett, *A Manual of Phonology*, Indiana University Publications in Anthropology and Linguistics, Memoir 11, 1955. Some of the structural, or nonstochastic, aspects of these message sources are described by Noam Chomsky and George A. Miller, Finite state languages, *Information and Control*, 1958, 1, 91–112.

think it should be. It turns out that introspection is right, that purely historical models of the sentence source are too simple to account for the facts. The difficulties are instructive to anyone who would try to use simple stochastic chains of behavioral events as a general description of human behavior.[7]

There are two lines of argument calculated to dissuade one from using a left-to-right model of the sentence planner. One line is to show that it would be impossible to learn a language in that way. The other illustrates grammatical constructions that such a message source could not produce.

Suppose that we would like to learn how to generate and recognize all grammatical sentences up to some fixed length, say, twenty words. Information theorists tell us that English sentences carry about five bits per word on the average,[8] so we can guess that there must be about 2^{100} different strings twenty words long that we should learn how to cope with. It seems reasonable to assume that each of these 2^{100} different sequences would leave the system in a different internal state. In order to incorporate the ability to generate a particular one of these strings of words into our planner—to create one of the 2^{100} different internal states that would be required—the planner would have to hear the string at least once. That is to say, our left-to-right generator has no grammatical rules other than the ones that say, "Having produced the words X up to this point, you must choose your continuation from the set $\{Y\}$." In order for a child to learn all of the rules of this left-to-right variety that would be required for the generation of perfectly acceptable sentences of twenty words or less, he would have to hear the rule, or hear instances of it from which the rule would be derived. Thus there seems no alternative but to insist that a child must hear 2^{100} sentences before he can speak and understand English. That is about 10^{30} sentences. In order to appreciate how ridiculous this condition is, recall the fact that

[7] Eugene Galanter and George A. Miller, Some comments on stochastic models and psychological theories, in K. J. Arrow, S. Karlin, and P. Suppes, eds., *Proceedings of the First Stanford Symposium on Mathematical Methods in the Social Sciences* (Stanford: Stanford University Press, 1960 [in press]).

[8] This is a conservative estimate based on Shannon's data for letters. See C. E. Shannon, Prediction and entropy of printed English, *Bell System Technical Journal*, 1951, 30, 50–64. Repeated by N. G. Burton and J. C. R. Licklider, Long-range constraints in the statistical structure of printed English, *American Journal of Psychology*, 1955, 68, 650–653.

there are only about 3.15×10^9 seconds per century. In short, the child would have to hear about 3×10^{20} sentences per second in order to be exposed to all the information necessary for the planner to produce sentences according to these left-to-right rules of grammar, and that is on the assumption of a childhood 100 years long with no interruptions for sleeping, eating, etc., and perfect retention of every string of twenty words after one presentation! Just a little calculation will convince anyone that the number of internal states needed in a left-to-right system explodes before the system is capable of dealing with anything as complicated as a natural language, and that some other kind of sentence generator must be used.

Even if there were time to learn it all, the system we have imagined would not generate the set of sentences that native speakers of English recognize as grammatical. We set the upper limit at length 20—we had to set it somewhere—but there are many grammatical sentences longer than 20 words that the Markovian process could not generate and, conversely, the Markovian process would generate many strings longer than 20 words that would not be grammatical sentences. The model says something like this: Memorize verbatim all grammatical sentences and segments of sentences of 20 words or less in length, and then make longer utterances by fitting together these 20-word segments in all possible ways. If the rules for generating sentences were represented in this form in somebody's brain, there would be grammatical sentences longer than 20 words that he would not be able to recognize. If we raise the length to, say, 30 or 40 words, the task of learning the language becomes progressively more inconceivable and in the limit, when we demand that a child must memorize *all* sentences of *every* length, the notion reaches the extremes of absurdity. It is like learning the number system by memorizing all possible sequences of digits. To memorize the infinite number of grammatical sentences is to by-pass the problem of grammar completely.

The model is so unnatural that one is encouraged to search for a counterexample, a proof that a Markovian word generator with a finite number of internal states could not produce the set of all grammatical sentences. The counterexample for left-to-right grammars consists of showing that sentences can be grammatically embedded inside other sentences.[9] Consider the sentence, "The man who said X is here." Now we can substitute for X the sentence, "Either Y, or I quit." Let Y be the sentence, "If Z, then it will rain." And so we can continue indefinitely. Note that in each case there is a grammatical dependency extending across the sentence to be inserted. In the first, *man* and *is* are related and are separated by X. In the second, *either* and *or* are related and are separated by Y. In the third *if* and *then* are related and are separated by Z. And so on. In more abbreviated notation, we have $S = aXa'$, then $X = bYb'$, then $Y = cZc'$, etc., so that when the sentence Plan is executed we obtain $S = abcZc'b'a'$. In short, English grammar permits us to construct an indefinitely long sequence of these nested dependencies. (Such sentences are hard to understand, of course, but it is only human weakness, not grammar, that militates against them.) The problem is, however, that we cannot generate such sentences with a purely historical, left-to-right, type of message source. Since there can be an indefinitely large number of nested dependencies (no rule of grammar prohibits them), all of which must be remembered in the right order and simultaneously, the left-to-right sentence generator must have an indefinitely large memory, that is, an indefinitely large number of internal states. But indefinitely large memories are not currently available, in biological systems or elsewhere, so the left-to-right system must be unable to form certain grammatical sentences.[10] Q.E.D. Chains of words will not suffice.

[9] N. Chomsky, Three models for the description of language, *IRE Transactions on Information Theory*, 1956, Vol. IT-2, No. 3, pp. 113–124; On certain formal properties of grammars, *Information and Control*, 1959, 137–167.

[10] Victor Yngve has noted, in A model and an hypothesis about language structure, *Proceedings of the American Philosophical Society* (in press), that grammatical sentences must be generated by human beings who have a limited span of immediate memory; although there is no grammatical rule that limits the number of nested dependencies in an English sentence, there are psychological limits. Sentences with several nested dependencies are not ungrammatical, yet they are generally avoided in ordinary usage. Yngve illustrates the problem with *The House that Jack Built:* "This is the dog that the cow tossed" and "This is the cat that the dog worried" can be combined into a single sentence, "This is the cat that the dog that the cow tossed worried," a sentence with one dependency (cow tossed) nested inside another (dog worried). Now, however, if we add a third sentence, "This is the rat that the cat killed," the triple compound becomes, "This is the rat that the cat that the dog that the cow tossed worried killed." One more step in the nursery rhyme produces "This is the malt that the rat that the cat that the dog that the cow tossed worried killed ate," and grammar has clearly run riot; four dependencies nested in this fashion are totally unintelligible. In order to avoid such difficulties, we do not construct

Without laboring the point further, let us assume that a message source can know something about what it is going to say as well as about what it has already said. Let us imagine a scheme in which the whole sentence is manipulated as a unit and it is gradually developed according to a Plan—from the inside out, so to speak. Let us symbolize the whole sentence by the letter S. One of the first rules of the grammar will be that S can be rewritten as NP + VP, where we can think of NP as a noun phrase and VP as a verb phrase. This rule we would write as

(F1) $S \longrightarrow NP + VP,$

where the arrow indicates that the symbol S can be rewritten as NP + VP in the derivation of the eventual utterance. To expand the noun phrase into an article and a noun, we might write

(F2) $NP \longrightarrow T + Noun,$

and to expand the verb phrase into a verb and a noun phrase we might write

(F3) $VP \longrightarrow Verb + NP.$

(In a complete grammar, of course, there would have to be several alternative ways to expand NP and VP, but we wish to keep this example as simple as possible.) We have enough English grammar to complete the illustration, so let us add a few rules about vocabulary:

(F4) $T \longrightarrow$ a, the.
(F5) $Noun \longrightarrow$ boy, ball, stick.
(F6) $Verb \longrightarrow$ hit.

Now turn the grammatical machine loose and see what it produces. In order to get it started, feed it an S—tell it to speak. The only thing it can do with S is to apply rule F1 to it. The result is diagrammed in Figure 6. Next, we might expand either NP or VP, so suppose we use F2 first and obtain Figure 7. We continue in this way

---

sentences in the nested form; we leave them open, so to speak, for future elaborations presently unspecified: "This is the cow that tossed the dog that worried the cat that killed the rat that ate the malt that lay in the house that Jack built." Consideration of why the nested construction is so cumbersome, whereas the open-ended construction can be understood by small children, leads one to a conviction that whenever possible the sentence is planned so that it can be tactically elaborated in the order in which it will be uttered; the future of the sentence is stored in immediate memory in as brief and strategic a form as possible. Elaborating the tactical details of the Plan in the order they are needed serves to minimize the demands on the speaker's temporary memory.

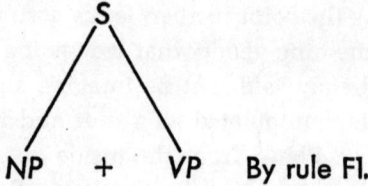

FIGURE 6. *First step in the formation of a sentence*

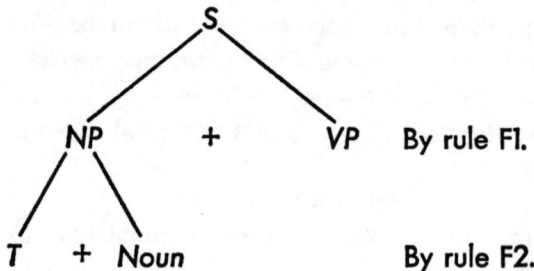

FIGURE 7. *The result of two steps in the formation of a sentence*

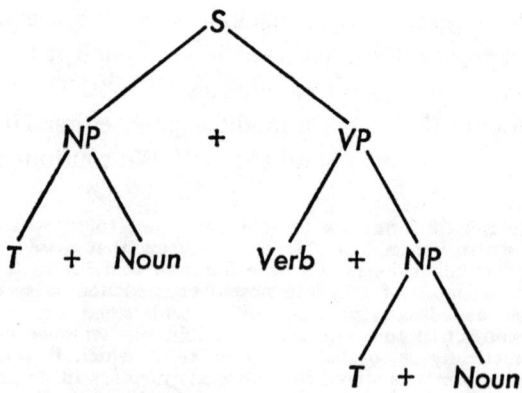

FIGURE 8. *Analysis of a sentence into its immediate constituents*

until finally we have produced the structure shown in Figure 8. At this point we are ready to use the vocabulary rules and so turn
$$T + Noun + Verb + T + Noun$$
into any one of a small variety of different sentences:

A boy hit the ball,
The stick hit a boy,
The ball hit a ball,

and so on. The machine is not very eloquent, but then, it is not a very elaborate machine.

It can be shown that sentence generators of this type have no trouble at all with the nested dependencies that are so embarrassing for the left-to-right planner. All that is needed are rules of the form $S \longrightarrow aXa$ and $X \longrightarrow bXb$ and $X \longrightarrow cXc$, etc. Such rules can settle the future and the past simultaneously and leave the growing tip of the sentence in the middle, rather than at the extreme right. Thus it is possible to answer one line of argument used against simple Markovian sources.

The other complaint, however, that the number of rules required must not be too great to be learned in a finite childhood, is still not met. Of course, only a few rules are needed to generate some sentences in the example above, but that proves nothing. Not until one begins to work seriously at the task of constructing an English grammar using only rules of this type does it become apparent what the problems are. Chomsky has discussed these in some detail and we shall not pursue them here. It is sufficient for us that some very great economies can be effected in the statement of the grammar if we permit ourselves to use a slightly more complicated kind of rule that enables us to rearrange as well as to rewrite. These more complicated rules are rules of transformation, rather than rules of formation.

One of the simplest examples is the transformation that carries active constructions into passive constructions: "John ate the apple" is transformed into "The apple was eaten by John." If the formal properties of this transformation are examined, it will be clear that the permutation involved cannot be accomplished by the simpler type of rules. Another common transformation is negation: "I will go" becomes "I won't go," "I can go" becomes "I can't go," "I have gone" becomes "I haven't gone." The negation is carried by

-n't, which acts as an affix on the auxiliary verb. But notice what happens when there is no auxiliary verb: "I go" becomes "I don't go." Since there is no auxiliary to which *-n't* can be affixed, the word *do* is introduced in order to carry it—a practice that has earned *do* a very bad reputation for irregularity, but which follows rather simply from a transformational form of grammar.[11] Notice that the transformation required to produce questions has the same problem. The general formula for the transformation is that *abc* becomes *bac.* Thus, "I will go" becomes "Will I go?" and "I can go" becomes "Can I go?" and "I have gone" becomes "Have I gone?" etc. But the rule cannot apply directly to the sentence "I go," and therefore it is necessary to introduce the *do* transformation here as in the case of negation. Then "I go" can become "I do go," in which form it can yield either the negation or the question, either "I don't go" or "Do I go?" We see, therefore, that the *do* transformation has a rather general role to play in the grammar of English.

These examples should suffice to suggest the nature of the grammatical transformations that we use to rearrange our simpler statements. Other transformations include those that combine two sentences into one by joining them with *and* or *or* and that enable us in various ways to build up long, complex, compound sentences.

The general picture of sentence generators that emerges from this analysis, therefore, is that we have a rather simple system for generating sentences like, "A boy hit a stick" (Chomsky calls these "kernel strings"). On top of that we have a system of transformations that operate upon the kernel strings to combine them or permute them, etc., into the endless variety of grammatical sentences. With such a theory it should be possible to do a fairly good job of speaking English grammatically with less than 100 rules of formation, less than 100 transformations, and perhaps 100,000 rules for

---

[11] An interesting case of "opposite speech"—all positive statements made in negative form, all negative statements made as positive assertions—has been described by J. Laffal, L. D. Lenkoski, and L. Ameen, "Opposite speech" in a schizophrenic patient, *Journal of Abnormal and Social Psychology,* 1956, 52, 409–413. The patient could interchange "yes" and "no," of course, without altering the structure of the rest of the sentence. But he would say, "I do go" rather than "I go," thus revealing the double transformation of negation—"I go" becomes "I don't go," which then becomes "I do go." In grammar, apparently, two negative transformations are not quite the same as none at all, for the *do* is left as a trace of the affix it had been introduced to carry.

vocabulary and pronunciation. Even a child should be able to master that much after ten or fifteen years of constant practice.

One of the most interesting features of Chomsky's analysis is that it provides for ambiguities. For example, "Flying planes can be dangerous" is recognized as ambiguous by speakers of English. Therefore, the grammar must provide two different Plans for generating it. According to one Plan it is a variant form of "Flying planes *are* dangerous," and according to the other Plan it is related to "Flying planes *is* dangerous." Most people are blissfully unaware of how many sentences are ambiguous in this way. When the ambiguity is noticed it becomes a rich source of humor, a kind of grammatical pun.

Note that the person must be aware of the underlying structure of the sentence in order to understand it or to know how to apply various transformations to it. "They are cooking apples" has one structure if it means "My friends are cooking apples," but a different structure if it means "Those apples are good only for cooking, not for eating." If the person has in mind the structure: (*They*) [(*are cooking*) (*apples*)], then he can apply a passive transformation to it and so obtain "Apples are being cooked by them." But if the person has in mind the structure (*They*) [(*are*) (*cooking apples*)], then the passive transformation is not relevant. If the complete hiearchy, and not just the terminal string of words organized by the hierarchy, were not represented cognitively, we would not know which transformations could be applied to it, and we would not be able to recognize the intrinsic ambiguity of the utterance.

The ability of the grammar to reproduce this kind of ambiguity is strong evidence for the adequacy of the grammatical formulation. One wonders how far this kind of test of a theory's adequacy can be extended beyond the purely linguistic domain. For example, two people who have memorized a string of symbols may recite them in exactly the same way, yet they may have quite different mnemonic Plans. An adequate theory should, hopefully, provide for both Plans. At the present time, however, no theory of verbal learning is anywhere near this level of sophistication.

There is a great deal about sentence generation left unexplained by this theory of grammar. If speaking were a game, then grammar would tell us what moves were legal, but not what moves were wise.

We cannot yet say how a talker selects the content of his utterances. But even within the relatively narrow scope of syntactics it is clear that people are able to construct and carry out very complicated Plans at a relatively rapid pace. This human ability may be unique to human speech, but that seems unlikely.

A study of grammatical systems is a particularly interesting way to approach the study of human Plans. The material is plentiful and relatively limited in type, it is easily described in writing, several alternative theories (that is, grammars) can be compared, reasonable intuitive agreement can be reached about acceptable and unacceptable sequences of responses, etc. With all these advantages, the scientific description of verbal behavior (by linguists, of course, not by psychologists) is far advanced over any other area of behavioral description and so provides a glimpse of what other behavioral theories may look like eventually. Karl Lashley once remarked:

> I have devoted so much time to discussion of the problem of syntax not only because language is one of the most important products of human cerebral action, but also because the problems raised by the organization of language seem to me to be characteristic of almost all other cerebral activity. There is a series of hierarchies of organization; the order of vocal movements in pronouncing the words, the order of words in the sentence, the order of sentences in the paragraph, the rational order of paragraphs in a discourse. Not only speech, but all skilled acts seem to involve the same problems of serial ordering, even down to the temporal coordination of muscular contractions in such a movement as reaching and grasping. Analysis of the nervous mechanisms underlying order in the more primitive acts may contribute ultimately to the solution of even the physiology of logic.[12]

This raises the question of whether Lashley, or the present authors, would endorse the ancient argument that the laws of grammar are the laws of thought, and whether they would support the more modern version advanced by Benjamin Lee Whorf, who wrote that "the forms of a person's thoughts are controlled by inexorable laws of pattern of which he is unconscious. These patterns are the un-

[12] Karl S. Lashley, The problem of serial order in behavior, in Lloyd A. Jeffress, ed., *Cerebral Mechanisms in Behavior, The Hixon Symposium* (New York: Wiley, 1951), pp. 121–122.

perceived intricate systematizations of his own language—shown readily enough by a candid comparison and contrast with other languages, especially those of a different linguistic family," [13] The question raises issues that extend far beyond the proper bounds of this discussion, but perhaps it is possible to clarify the situation somewhat by saying that the position advocated here does not commit the authors one way or the other with respect to the "Whorfian hypothesis." It is not only English grammar that is built around hierarchical Plans and their various transformations—the grammar of every language is constructed in that way, so a speaker's thought processes cannot be in any way unique on that account. Moreover, if the speculations of the present authors are correct, nearly all of man's behavior is similarly organized. We might speak metaphorically of a general grammar of behavior, meaning that the grammar of a language was only one example of a general pattern of control that could be exemplified in many other realms of behavior. But to say that the formal structure of the laws of grammar is *similar* to the structure of the laws of thought is very different from saying that the laws of grammar *are* the laws of thought, or that your thought must remain forever shackled to the conjugations and declensions of your native tongue.

How language is used for giving instructions, for descriptions, for asking questions, for making love, for solving problems, for making Plans, or organizing Images raises so many different psychological problems, each unique and special for each unique and special use of language, that no simple generalizations can cover them all. The way language enters into each of these situations can be determined only by studying the situations. The grammatical Plan, as we have said before, specifies only the legal moves in the social game of communication. The reasons for playing that game, however, cannot be deduced from its rules.

Let us close this chapter with a summary attempt to bring these linguistic observations closer to the general thesis of the present volume:

[13] B. L. Whorf, *Language, Thought, and Reality*, J. B. Carroll, ed. (New York: Wiley and the Technology Press, 1956), p. 252.

First, the pronunciation of a sentence in a normal manner is a skilled act, acquired after many years of practice. Like any skill, it must be guided by a Plan. That is to say, there must be a separate, distinct Plan for every separate distinct sentence we utter. The hierarchy of the Plan for some particular sentence corresponds with the way that sentence would be "parsed." The test phases of the TOTE units in this Plan involve comparisons of the uttered sounds and felt movements with the auditory and proprioceptive Images of what they should be. And the ultimate operational phase of the sentence Plan involves the movements of the speech musculature. We can refer to this as the "motor Plan" for the sentence.

Behind the motor Plan, however, is a process more difficult to understand, a process which generates the motor Plan itself. That is to say, there must be another level of Plan that operates on the motor Plan. We have encountered this notion already in Chapter 10, where we considered a Plan for generating a Plan to recall a memorized passage. The situation here is analogous. In order to keep the two straight, let us call this the "grammar Plan." The grammar Plan has been the central concern of this chapter. Its structure is the hierarchy of grammatical rules of formation and transformation. The object that it operates upon is tested for its "sentencehood." This reduces to a question of whether it has a noun phrase and a verb phrase. The test of whether it has a noun phrase fails and so sends the system off to generate one, etc., until eventually all the subtests and subsubtests are satisfied and the system returns to the main test, which now passes, and the motor Plan is complete. Given a complete motor Plan for a kernel string, it may be necessary to perform transformations upon it, so further elaboration of the grammar Plan would be required to do that.

There are, of course, many substantive, semantic decisions to be made in the operation of the grammar Plan. That is to say, when the test for a noun phrase fails and the operation of finding a noun phrase is begun, the system must have some way of determining which kind of noun phrase to select. Questions of selection, of course, require evaluation functions.[14] One way to conceive of it is to think

[14] The test phase of the TOTE would presumably consist of a list of acceptable alternatives from which the choice would be made according to the evalua-

that an Image of the result which the sentence should produce, or of the information it should convey, supplies criteria that must be met before the tests are passed. But how this aspect of the process might function would be completely different for, say, casual greetings and for the composition of a sonnet—criteria imposed by the Image undoubtedly exercise control over the rate at which the motor Plan can be fashioned. But here our speculations encounter larger issues that cannot be discussed intelligibly without a considerable development of the properties of the Image and the question of meaning, a development that the authors are not inclined to enter into here. For the moment it is sufficient to see verbal skills in the same frame of reference as other hierarchically organized skills, and to communicate the opinion that a system organized along these lines could speak gramatically—and might even be able to find something to say.

Where does this leave us with respect to the problem that opened this chapter? Does language introduce new psychological processes, or are all our verbally acquired skills foreshadowed by processes observable in lower animals? To the extent that language relies upon TOTE hierarchies and we have seen TOTE hierarchies in animals, there is nothing new here except a greater degree of complexity. But that comment is about as helpful as the remark that both animals and men are constructed of atoms. A more interesting question concerns the possibility that some new configuration of these basic components may have emerged. In particular, we might ask: Is the capacity to use Plans to construct Plans to guide behavior a new psychological process? A motor Plan may be instinctive, or it may be a skill acquired after long hours of practice—here men and animals are on an equal footing. But in the discussion of memorizing and even more clearly in the discussion of speaking we have found it necessary to believe that a motor Plan could be constructed very quickly and efficiently, not by rote, but by the operation of a higher-level Plan that had the motor Plan as its object. Something more is involved here than the usual discussions of insight versus trial-and-error—a

---

tion function supplied by the Image and the time available for making the choice. Some hint as to how this might work is given by the observation that in word association studies there is a strong tendency for the subject's reply to fall in the same syntactic category as the stimulus word. See R. S. Woodworth, *Experimental Psychology* (New York: Holt, 1938), pp. 347–348.

motor Plan could be insightfully selected by an organism that could not execute a Plan to construct a motor Plan. Perhaps some of the apes, even some of the higher mammals, might have the rudiments of this higher-level planning ability. If so, then man may indeed have to retreat into his greater complexity to explain his unique accomplishments. If not, we may have here the key to an evolutionary breakthrough as important as the development of lungs and legs.

CHAPTER 12

PLANS FOR SEARCHING AND SOLVING

Any Plan complicated enough to be interesting will include steps that are executed for no other reason than to pave the way for what we really want to do. In Chapter 2 these were referred to as the preparatory phases of the Plan—raising the hammer was a preparatory phase leading up to striking; it was the striking phase that accomplished the work, that is, changed the conditions involved in the tests for continuing or terminating the execution of the TOTE unit. There are, of course, many kinds of preparatory subplans. A necessary preparatory phase to hammering, as every carpenter knows, is the (frequently aggravating) subplan for locating a hammer. In its simplest form, this preparatory subplan consists of examining one object after another until something satisfactorily matches our concept of a hammer; only then are the conditions appropriate for initiating the next part of the Plan.

How do we conduct a search of this kind? Is there some kind of Plan that we follow? Certainly, there are some places of relatively high probability and we look there first. If these do not produce it, we may wander aimlessly about, poking into corners, often returning to look in the same place two or three times. Eventually it occurs to us that we should be systematic. So we start off in one room and search it from one end to the other, then move on to the next room, etc. Or we ask somebody if he knows where it is. Or we go next door and borrow one. If all else fails, we can go to the hardware store and buy a new hammer; then the old one is certain to reappear.

There is an item on an intelligence test that asks how you would find a ball that was lost somewhere in an open field. The correct answer is any systematic procedure for covering every inch of the field without looking in the same place twice. If the ball is in the field, the intelligent, systematic Plan for searching will lead you over it eventually. Systematic Plans are sometimes called "algorithms." People do not always use systematic Plans for searching because, in spite of the intelligence test, systematic Plans can be dull and inefficient. The alternative is to be unsystematic—in a clever way. If we try to short-cut the systematic Plan by guessing, asking for help, trying to remember where we saw it last, etc., the Plan we follow is said to be "heuristic."[1] A systematic Plan, when it is possible, is sure to work, but it may take too long, or cost too much. A heuristic Plan may be cheap and quick, but it will sometimes fail to produce the intended result.

One danger in executing search routines is that the object searched for may not exist. If the hammer is no longer in the house, even the most thoroughly systematic search, inch by inch, will not

[1] The recent revival of interest in *heuristic*—the art of discovery—seems to stem largely from the work of the mathematician G. Polya. His *How to Solve It* (Princeton: Princeton University Press, 1945) attempts to state the heuristic maxims of mathematical discovery, and this work was continued in *Mathematics and Plausible Reasoning*, 2 vols. (Princeton: Princeton University Press, 1954). Among psychologists it was principally K. Duncker who emphasized the discovery of the heuristic methods that people use. See K. Duncker, On problem-solving, L. S. Lees, trans., *Psychological Monographs*, 1945, No. 270. The study of *algorithms*—effective computational procedures—is an active branch of modern mathematics, a field usually referred to as the theory of recursive functions. A good introduction to the theory can be found in Martin Davis, *Computability and Unsolvability* (New York: McGraw-Hill, 1958). An algorithm is defined intuitively as any completely mechanical procedure for computing an answer in a finite number of steps. For some problems algorithms are known that are very efficient (e.g., finding the maximum of a function). For some problems algorithms are known that are not practical (e.g., exploring all possible continuations of a chess position). For some problems it is known that no algorithm exists and only heuristic methods are possible (e.g., showing that a particular logical proposition is not a theorem of quantification theory).

produce it—we have embarked on an impossible task. Since we are never absolutely certain in advance that the object can be found, the intelligent thing to do is to incorporate a stop-rule in the search Plan. That is to say, if the object is not found after some fixed time, or some given number of operations, or before some particular event occurs, the search will be halted and it will be assumed that the object in question does not exist. (The suspension of stop-orders during hypnosis has already been discussed in Chapter 8.) In all cases of human Plans for searching, a variety of such stop-rules will be built into the test phases. Many searches are instituted solely for the purpose of checking on the Image, either to confirm or infirm it. Such searches cannot occur unless we have a clear rule for determining when the Image is presumed to be infirmed because the object does not exist. We know surprisingly little about these stop-rules or the conditions that cause us to set them as we do. What makes us decide that the thing we are looking for does not exist? It is reasonable to suppose that both the probability of discovery and the utility of the object are involved in setting the stop-order, as well as the kind of Plan, systematic or heuristic, that is being executed.

Plans for searching for an object in the physical environment are usually rather simple. There is a perceptual test that defines the searcher's "set," plus an operational phase for orienting the receptors toward another object where the perceptual test can be repeated, etc., until an object is discovered that satisfies the test or until the stop-rule is effective. The search Plan holds a special interest for us, however, because it serves as a model for many other cognitive processes that, at first glance, we would not consider examples of searching at all. For example, we say that we "search" through our memory for a name, or an image, or an association. Or we "search" for the solution to a problem, an answer, or a method, or an insight. We speak of Edison testing thousands of substances in his effort to make an electric light as "searching" for a good filament, or Ehrlich as "searching" for a cure for syphilis, etc. These tasks have all the formal characteristics of search except that the object sought is not located in spatial coordinates.

In order to be explicit about the kind of search that is involved in solving problems, let us consider a problem that psychologists have studied rather extensively in the laboratory. Subjects are shown a collection of objects that differ from one another in several respects. For example, some may be large and others small, some may be red and others green, some may be circular and others triangular, some may have borders and others not, etc. All of the possible combinations are laid out neatly for the subject to see. He is told that some of the objects are examples of a "concept" and that the others are not. The concept could, of course, be a random sample from the set of objects, but no one has considered that condition worth studying. A concept is something like, "All the large, green ones," or, "All the ones with borders," etc. The subject can point to one of the objects and the experimenter will tell him whether or not that object is an example of the concept. The subject continues to ask about the various objects until he has attained the correct concept (that is, until he has read the experimenter's mind).

For example, imagine that there are three dimensions of variation, and that two values of each dimension are possible. In that case, there are $2 \times 2 \times 2 = 8$ different objects that have to be classified as instances of the concept or as not instances of it. If the dimensions were size, shape, and color, the eight objects might be as follows:

(1) Large, white circle (5) Small, white circle
(2) Large, white square (6) Small, white square
(3) Large, black circle (7) Small, black circle
(4) Large, black square (8) Small, black square

The various hypotheses that the subject could hold about the concept, however, might be the following:

(1) Large circles   (10) White squares
(2) Large squares   (11) Black circles
(3) Small circles   (12) Black squares
(4) Small squares   (13) Large things
(5) Large, white things   (14) Small things
(6) Large, black things   (15) White things
(7) Small, white things   (16) Black things
(8) Small, black things   (17) Circles
(9) White circles   (18) Squares

Obviously, we might have still other hypotheses, such as "all the objects," or "none of the objects," or disjunctions of the form "either large circles or small squares," or "everything except large circles," etc. The instructions that are given to the subject—and perhaps some instructions he assumes without being told—will determine the exact set of hypotheses that he is searching through.

This concept-learning task is commonly employed in experimental studies of thinking. It can be described as a search problem in almost the same terms as were used above for perceptual search problems. The subject is searching through a set of possible solutions for the correct one. The alternative solutions he is searching through are not the objects he sees, of course, but the set of possible hypotheses he could hold about the particular concept the experimenter has selected.[2] Each time he learns about the status of a new object, he reduces the size of the set of possible hypotheses that are compatible with the information he has received. The experimenter is interested to see in what order he will ask about the objects and how well he will be able to use all the information he has. The experiment enables us to study some of the heuristic Plans people will use for gathering information about the world they live in.

The concept of a set of alternative hypotheses that might be the solution of the problem is a very useful one, since it enables us to reduce many problems to a similar form—how to search most efficiently through a large set of possibilities. Sometimes the analogy can get a bit strained—it is difficult to think of writing a book as a process of selecting one out of all the possible ways 100,000 words could be strung together. The legendary monkeys who typed at random until they accidentally produced all the books in the British Museum could be hired to help the author, whose task would then be

[2] This insight seems to have occurred independently to Hovland and Whitfield at about the same time. See J. W. Whitfield, An experiment in problem solving, *Quarterly Journal of Experimental Psychology*, 1951, 3, 184–197; Carl I. Hovland, A "communication analysis" of concept learning, *Psychological Review*, 1952, 59, 461–472; Carl I. Hovland and Walter Weiss, Transmission of information concerning concepts through positive and negative instances, *Journal of Experimental Psychology*, 1953, 45, 175–182. The more general conception—that thinking, problem solving, concept attainment can be modeled after the search process—is a familiar one to psychologists; see, for example, the review by Donald M. Johnson, A modern account of problem solving, *Psychological Bulletin*, 1944, 41, 201–229, for a discussion of search and of plans of action in problem solving.

simply to read all they wrote and select the book he wanted. The reason this description seems unnatural is that we don't attack the problem of making a book in that way; and the reason we don't is that we use heuristic, rather than either systematic or random, Plans. But in spite of the psychological artificiality of such a notion, it provides a valuable formal tool for the analysis and understanding of problems and puzzles.

A systematic approach to learning a concept would be to write down all the possible hypotheses about the concept, as we did in the example above. Then the subjects could take the first hypothesis on the list and begin systematically to ask about the objects until he finds one that contradicts the hypothesis, at which point he could go on to the next hypothesis and start all over asking about the objects again. When he can proceed all the way through the entire set of objects without finding one that contradicts the hypothesis he is testing, then he knows that the hypothesis must be correct. In executing the Plan he makes no effort to remember anything or to understand anything—he plods systematically ahead, day after day, until a hypothesis checks out. This is an algorithm, a systematic Plan for solving the problem, and it is guaranteed to work—but it is not a very popular approach. Nobody has ever been known to use it in any of the hundreds of experiments that have been done with thousands of subjects. No subject would want to try it, and no experimenter would have the patience to let him.

Another systematic Plan, somewhat more intelligent, would be to write down all the possible hypotheses and then to test them all simultaneously. After asking whether an object is an example of the concept, the subject would then relate the answer to each hypothesis in turn—hypotheses that failed would be crossed off the list. This version of the Plan looks much more efficient to the experimenter because the subject asks him relatively few questions, but it is only trivially different from the preceding Plan. This version has occasionally been attempted, but without pencil and paper it is almost certain to fail—the cognitive strain is too great.

The actual behavior of subjects in this situation is quite different. Some people tackle the problem verbally, symbolically; others want to manipulate the objects, to group them perceptually this way and that; a few can alternate between the abstract and the perceptual strategies.³ Most people devise rather elaborate mnemonic Plans for remembering which objects are in which class, positive or negative.⁴ Each person has his own style, his own tricks, his own heuristic Plan for discovering the concept.

An interesting and important study of concept attainment by Jerome S. Bruner, Jacqueline Goodnow, and George Austin demonstrates that a subject's Plan for concept-learning can be discovered and analyzed.⁵ They were able to distinguish among several different heuristic strategies that their subjects used. For example, some subjects sampled at random, repeated their questions about the same object several times, and generally indicated that they had no good use for the information they were collecting. The people who do this tend to abandon it on repeated tests with more concepts.

An interesting Plan that many subjects developed was the following. First, locate a positive instance of the concept. Then find another object that is just like the positive one in all respects but one. If the first positive object is a *large,* red circle without border, then find the *small,* red circle without border and ask about it. If the answer is negative, then you know that size is important. If the answer is positive, then size has nothing to do with it. Next, repeat the test for color, then for shape, then for borders, etc., until the aspects are exhausted. This procedure is not the most efficient one imaginable, but it enables a person to explore the various hypotheses with a heuristic Plan that almost automatically keeps track of the information he has received. (As a matter of fact, this strategy would be an algorithm if no limit were placed on the number of instances about which the subject could inquire.) The cognitive strain is greatly reduced at only a slight penalty in extra objects examined.

When subjects are put under pressure to find a concept in the smallest possible number of questions, they may try to keep track of the entire set of hypotheses through which they are really searching.

[3] Eugenia Hanfmann, A study of personal patterns in an intellectual performance, *Character and Personality,* 1941, 9, 315–325.
[4] See, for example, Edna Heidbreder, The attainment of concepts, III: The process, *Journal of Psychology,* 1947, 24, 93–138.
[5] J. S. Bruner, J. Goodnow, and G. Austin, *A Study of Thinking* (New York: Wiley, 1956).

Subjects with mathematical or logical training are especially likely to try this heroic Plan. For problems of any degree of complexity it is almost certain to fail, because the person cannot keep all the implications of his information straight. When the pressure is applied, however, other subjects can frequently succeed by gambling. They use the Plan of changing aspects of a positive instance, as before, but now they change two or three at a time. If they change two aspects and are told that the result is still an example of the concept, then both of those aspects are known to be irrelevant, and they have settled two aspects with only one question. If the result is negative, however, they do not know which aspect of the two is important. With a little bit of luck, the Plan will sometimes work. The important point to note, however, is that there are many different heuristic Plans a subject may use. All involve the risk of failure, but some are more risky than others.

As another example of the important difference between systematic and heuristic Plans, consider an anagram. Imagine that we are given the letters EIMT and that the problem is to spell an English word with these letters. We can systematically work through all the $4! = 24$ orderings of these four letters, relying on our knowledge of the English vocabulary to provide the test. A more expensive, but more authoritative test would be to look for each string of letters in the Oxford English Dictionary. In this way we would be certain to discover TIME and MITE and ITEM and EMIT and any other solutions the anagram may have. It would be dull work and it would be slow, but we could certainly do it that way. As a matter of fact, if we could mechanize the dictionary test, the whole procedure might better occupy the time of a computing machine than of an adult man.

It is obvious that few normal people tackle problems, even problems as simple as an anagram, with a systematic Plan. In the case of an anagram, people might work backwards—guess some English word and then see if the letters can spell it. Or they might rely upon their feelings about the probabilities of letter pairs to guide them. For example, they would not bother to consider such possible solutions as TMIE, since they know that there are no English words beginning TM—. They would probably try to exploit the tendency for vowels and consonants to alternate in English; if they began with T, they would next form TI or TE. They would probably not bother to test any words ending in I. Now, note that most of these heuristic rules are fallible. Consonants and vowels do not always alternate. Some English words end in I. TM can occur in such words as posTMan, etc. It can easily happen, especially in longer anagrams with unique solutions, that one's intuitive feelings, or hunches, do not generate the solution at all, and one is then forced to adopt some exhaustive Plan for permuting the letters systematically until a word turns up. But usually these various bits of information about where it is worth while to look for the solution will be valuable and will produce correct solutions more quickly. For most problems the only Plans we have are heuristic, and much of the study of thinking can be reduced rather generally to the study of the heuristic Plans people use for generating proposed solutions that are worth testing.

The idea that problem-solving can be represented as searching through a large set of possibilities until we find one that solves the problem may seem odd at first, and somewhat novel to a person who has taken his heuristic Plans for granted and who has never bothered to consider the multitude of alternatives he doesn't need to reject because he doesn't even think of them. But the notion is familiar to mathematicians, who have reflected on the heuristic art a great deal more than most of us. For example, Poincaré wrote:

> What, in fact, is mathematical discovery? It does not consist in making new combinations with mathematical entities that are already known. That can be done by anyone, and the combinations that could be so formed would be infinite in number, and the greater part of them would be absolutely devoid of interest. Discovery consists precisely in not constructing useless combinations, but in constructing those that are useful, which are an infinitely small minority. Discovery is discernment, selection.[6]

Exhaustive Plans can be used to solve some mathematical problems, but unless the problem is simple, the number of hypotheses that would need to be systematically explored usually makes them impractical. The mathematician A. M. Turing illustrated the inefficiency of systematic Plans several years ago—he considered the number of

[6] Henri Poincaré, *Science and Method*, F. Maitland, trans. (New York: Dover, 1952), pp. 50–51.

arrangements that would have to be looked at in the process of systematically solving a common puzzle consisting of sliding squares to be arranged in a particular way. The number was 20,922,789,888,000. Working continuously day and night and inspecting one position per minute the process would take four million years.[7] In a similar spirit, Newell, Shaw, and Simon have considered the set of all possible sequences of expressions in propositional logic and tried to estimate what fraction of them were proofs of theorems in the second chapter of Whitehead and Russell's *Principia Mathematica*. Working at the speed of modern electronic computers, it would take, they surmised, hundreds of thousands of years of computation if the machine used a systematic "British Museum algorithm." [8] Obviously, Whitehead and Russell did not proceed in that fashion; they must have worked heuristically.

It is fairly obvious that without a little discernment and selection among the alternatives we are willing to consider, we will not live long enough to solve anything. A heuristic is a way of exercising discernment—but it always runs the risk that the solution will be discarded inadvertently along with the millions of apparently useless combinations. Thus we arrive at a typically human dilemma—slow and sure, or fast and risky? All of us are cognitive gamblers—some more than others, but most of us more than we realize.[9]

The reduction of thinking and problem-solving to a matter of efficient techniques for searching is, of course, quite attractive to anyone who takes the general thesis of this book seriously. We think of a test phase and an operational phase alternating until the operations turn up something that passes the test. Solving a problem is a matter of turning up a lot of likely hypotheses until either one satisfies the test or the stop-rule is applied.

[7] Quoted in M. Polyani, *Personal Knowledge* (Chicago: University of Chicago Press, 1958), p. 126.
[8] Allen Newell, J. C. Shaw, and Herbert A. Simon, Empirical explorations of the logic theory machine: A case study in heuristic, *Proceedings of the Western Joint Computer Conference* (Los Angeles: February 1957), 218–230.
[9] *A Study of Thinking* by Bruner, Goodnow, and Austin suggests several ways to do psychological research on the economic analysis of the costs and values of different strategies for processing information in thinking and problem-solving. See also E. Galanter and M. Gerstenhaber, On thought: the extrinsic theory, *Psychological Review*, 1956, 63, 218–227, for a discussion of the relations among payoffs, achievements, problem complexity, and the subject's strategies in solving problems.

But is the search process an adequate model for everything that we would normally call thinking and problem-solving? Some people would argue that it is not. For example, there is a distinction between "problems to find" and "problems to prove" that goes back at least to 300 A.D. and the Greek mathematician Pappus, whose discussion of heuristic is one of the oldest to be preserved.[10] The aim of a "problem to find" is to locate an object—a hammer, a concept, an invention, or the value of x. The aim of a "problem to prove" is to show conclusively that some clearly stated assertion is either true or false. It is obvious that a "problem to find" involves a search, but can a "problem to prove" also be formulated that way?

If we think of a "problem to prove" as involving a clear statement of what is given and a clear statement of what is to be proved, then we can consider the solution of the problem to depend upon discovering a path—a sequence of steps—that leads from one to the other. When the problem is to establish that A (the given) implies C (to be proved), we must search for some X such that A implies X and X implies C. We search through a large set of X until we find one, B, that provides a path: A to B to C. (Of course, B may also involve a sequence of two or more steps.) Pappus discussed the solution of "problems to prove" in just these terms, so it is scarcely an innovation to point out that the search for a path to connect two things is just a more complicated version of the search for any other kind of unknown. But whereas the search for an unknown is satisfied when a particular hypothesis or number is selected, the search for a path is really a search for a Plan. In short, we are once more confronted by the necessity to think of one Plan as testing and operating upon another Plan, a level of complexity we have met before in discussing remembering and speaking.

In the more complex kinds of problem-solving, therefore, we must have some way to generate alternative Plans and then to operate on them, test them, evaluate them. These metaplans—Plans for forming other Plans—will be discussed in the next chapter, along with some of the techniques available for studying the properties of these complicated systems.

For the moment, however, we want to pursue the question of the

[10] Cited in Polya, *How to Solve It*, pp. 141–147.

search process as a paradigm for thinking and problem-solving. There is one feature of any search process that is absolutely indispensable —the searcher *must* be able to recognize the thing he is looking for. No doubt everyone has had the experience of going to meet a perfect stranger because the problem of identification was forgotten when the appointment was made. Exactly the same helpless impotence afflicts the thinker who cannot recognize the solution to his problem. If a satisfactory test exists, the problem is said to be "well defined."

The test of a search TOTE need not be simple. The way a chemist tests to see if he has sulphur may involve several steps and much time. The way a mathematician tests to see if he has determined the correct value of x may be similarly tedious. And the question of whether a particular Plan leads to a valid proof can require a considerable amount of skill and judgment. The test phase may be extremely complex and the ability to perform it adequately is not always a trivial matter. If there is any single caution that should be emphasized more than the others when considering search as the paradigm of problem-solving, it is this: There are important problems whose solutions cannot be identified in a finite number of steps, so that no satisfactory test is possible. We can get caught looking for a solution that we would not be able to recognize if we had it. When we use the search paradigm for problem-solving, we must remember that it includes cases where the person cannot recognize what he is looking for.

An interesting and important example of a problem for which no test exists is the following: We have spoken (see Chapter 2) of the possibility of a TOTE hierarchy falling into a "loop" of tests. The prototest may fail, sending the system into a series of TOTEs, all of which pass, thus returning the system to the prototest, which fails again, sending the system into the same series of TOTEs again, etc. In this situation it is necessary to have a stop-order to break up the loop—only so much time, or so many operations, or so much fatigue, etc., will be tolerated before the execution of the Plan is halted. But we also know that sometimes our stop-orders are issued too soon— that what appeared to be a loop really was not—and that if we had persisted a bit longer the Plan would have worked. What we would like, therefore, is some way to apply the stop-order only when we are really in a loop, but not to apply it when we merely appear to be but really are not. That is to say, we would like to have some test that we could perform on our Plans that would tell us in advance whether they would work in a finite number of steps or whether they would fall into a loop and go on forever without success. But no such test exists. The "halting problem" is unsolvable. The only thing we can do is to adopt an arbitrary criterion that reflects the value to us of the outcome.[11] We can say, "I will try to do it in this way and if, after N years, I have not succeeded, then I will stop." The problem is then to determine N as a function of the importance of the problem.

An alternative to the stop-rule is a modification of the conditions that are imposed in the test phase. After searching unsuccessfully for a pen, we settle for a pencil. After searching unsuccessfully for a concept that will identify every good risk, a banker finally settles for a concept that will work 19 times out of 20. After searching unsuccessfully for a Plan that will integrate two incompatible Plans into one, a person settles for one or the other. Half a loaf is better than no loaf. There are, fortunately, many ways to compromise with reality, and people probably revise the Image as often as they give up the Plan.

In ordinary affairs we usually muddle ahead, doing what is habitual and customary, being slightly puzzled when it sometimes fails to give the intended outcome, but not stopping to worry much about the failures because there are too many other things still to do. Then circumstances conspire against us and we find ourselves caught failing where we must succeed—where we cannot withdraw from the field, or lower our self-imposed standards, or ask for help, or throw a tantrum. Then we may begin to suspect that we face a problem. But at first it is not clear what the problem is, or what test would have to be satisfied by any solution. There is an important kind of thinking that goes on at this stage—the stage in which the problem becomes defined—and it is not obvious that the search paradigm is the best way to discuss it. Indeed, the very act of discussing it seems to

---

[11] The psychological aspects of the halting problem involve persistence, satiation, level of aspiration—aspects that have been studied primarily by Lewin and his students. For a review of this work, see Leonard Carmichael, ed., *Manual of Child Psychology* (New York: Wiley, 1946), Chapter 16, especially pp. 823–832.

lend to it a degree of clarity and objectivity that makes it difficult to remember how ineffably confused we are before a problem is well defined. We search about, exploring a hunch, gambling that we might get a good idea if we spent some time on this or that, fiddling with a few examples, trying to imagine what is missing or what we could get rid of, but never being certain precisely what we are searching for. We are trying to construct a better Image of the situation. Whereas the subject in a psychological experiment has the problem explained to him and can be reasonably confident that a solution exists, the average person is not sure there really is a problem, or, if there is, that any simple test for its solution can be found, or, if the test exists, that any solution can be found that will meet the test. There is a great deal more uncertainty in an actual problem-solving situation than there is in its laboratory counterpart. The statement of the problem is revised repeatedly as we struggle with it, learn more about it, and build a richer, clearer Image of it. Given an adequate Image, of course, the test required to define the problem should, if it exists, form a part of it. Frequently the problem may become well defined and the test for a solution become obvious at just about the same instant that the solution for it is found.

During the period when we are fumbling about, trying to clarify the Image in order to discover a test that will define the problem, we still use heuristic tricks, but we frequently use them without any feedback, without any assurance that they are taking us nearer to the definition or the solution of a problem. It is a little like trying to develop a good filing system without knowing exactly what the file will be used for.[12] We may revise it several times, as we learn more about what must go into it, thus deliberately reverting to a confused state in the hope of putting it back together again in a more useful or novel form. It would be quite wrong to believe that all problems are given in a well-defined form and that thinking consists merely of

---

[12] In his *Heuristic Aspects of the Artificial Intelligence Problem*, Group Report 34–55, Lincoln Laboratory, Massachusetts Institute of Technology, 17 December 1956, M. L. Minsky discusses in rather general terms a "character generator" that classifies situations and keeps a record of which heuristic methods have been successful with which classes of problems. What we have called "building an Image of the problem situation" may correspond to the development of a useful classification scheme in Minsky's discussion—in which case the analogy to a filing system would be quite appropriate.

searching through a set of alternatives for one that will work. In fact, some people argue that once the problem has been well-defined the "real" thinking is all over—that carrying out the search for a solution is just a mechanical exercise in which it is possible to be efficient or ingenious, but not creative. The opinion is extreme, of course, but it makes us remember that many people represent their problems in terms of clarifying their Image, rather than in terms of forming a Plan to discover the solution. Once the Image is correct, they argue, the Plan will follow directly. The answer to this argument is that, unfortunately, it happens to be false. But there is enough truth in it to make us pause.

Is there an alternative to the search paradigm of thinking? Of course, there are several. For example, instead of discussing every problem as a search for an object, or a concept, or a Plan, we might just as well have discussed them as attempts to *predict* what is going to happen. We predict the hammer will be found in the workshop, then test the prediction by looking there. We predict that object X will be called a positive instance of the concept, and so we inquire about it in order to test the prediction. We predict that such and such a sequence of steps will generate a proof, so we execute them in order to test the prediction. It should be apparent that this substitution of prediction for search is merely a new way of discussing the TOTE units involved; the test phase remains the same, but the operate phase is now called "predicting" instead of "searching." Nevertheless, the substitution has heuristic value, for it encourages us to look at the same processes in a different way and so enriches our understanding of them.

The prediction paradigm for thinking and problem-solving tends to direct our attention more to the Image than to the Plan, because the test of the prediction provides us with a confirmation or infirmation of the Image that supported the prediction. Galanter and Gerstenhaber comment that "imaginal thinking is neither more nor less than constructing an image or model of the environment, running the model faster than the environment, and predicting that the environment will behave as the model does."[13] According to this view, the elements with which the problem-solver seems to work are

[13] Galanter and Gerstenhaber, *op. cit.*, p. 219.

his perceptual image of the situation before he does anything, his imagination image of what the situation will be like if he takes a particular course of action, his perception of the situation after he does something, his image of some ideal situation that he might hope to attain, etc. And each of these images must have some evaluation on a utility scale, and the decision to execute a particular Plan will depend upon the payoff function defined by these utilities. Descriptions of problem-solving and thinking that place the emphasis on the Image frequently correspond better to our personal intuitions about what is going on—the imaginal part of the process is much more accessible to awareness than is the part that deals with the formation of a Plan. An ordinary person almost never approaches a problem systematically and exhaustively unless he has been specifically educated to do so. It is much more natural for him to visualize what is and what ought to be and to focus on the gap between them than to visualize some huge set of alternative possibilities through which he must search. In other words, the phenomenological aspects of problem-solving are more frequently connected with alternative Images than with alternative Plans.

Thus we see there are at least two ways to represent the information-processing that goes on during thinking and problem-solving. According to the prediction paradigm, the main source of trouble in solving problems arises from the inadequacy of the Image of the problem situation. It is necessary to collect more information, to attempt various organizations, to destroy old Images in order to replace them by new, to transfer Images from more familiar situations. In order to verify an Image as it develops, it is necessary to make predictions and to test them, to probe for the places where our knowledge is thin and our understanding weak. We may not have the leisure to collect all the information we could use and we may need to settle for an Image that is only approximate. Moreover, the information we need is not "given" with some guarantee that it is relevant or important—we have to dig for it, and even then the data we gather may be useless once we achieve a stable cognitive structure. The process of making predictions may itself involve considerable time and expense, so that we must be quite circumspect about the predictions we decide to test.

All of these comments can be paralleled in the search paradigm: The main source of trouble in solving problems arises from the fact that the set of alternatives may be extremely large, perhaps infinite, and the acceptable solutions may be scattered haphazardly so that they are hard to find. In few situations are we completely free to start examining exhaustively and systematically all the various possible permutations of atomic elements. If a test is expensive to apply, we will want to find a solution with as few applications as possible. Moreover, alternative hypotheses are seldom "given" in the sense that we need merely point to the one we want—usually they must be generated according to rules. The process of generating potential solutions may itself involve considerable time and expense. We cannot dismiss the task of searching efficiently as a mere mechanical exercise suitable only for second-rate thinkers.

Sometimes one of these representations will be more helpful, sometimes the other, depending upon whether the heart of the difficulty lies in the construction of a better Image or the elaboration of a better Plan. Both can, the authors believe, be discussed in terms of the TOTE schema. In the context of this book, however, we must concentrate our attention principally upon the latter kind of problem. In the next chapter, therefore, we shall consider how people formulate heuristic Plans to search for the answer to well-defined problems. This emphasis, however, should not be understood to mean that the authors wish to reject the vast domain of ill-defined problems or to deny the critical importance of refining our Images. For as our Images become more accurate and more elaborate and more useful, we will become able to define more and more problems—to translate them from the domain of mere difficulties into the domain of practical problems, to make them into something we can solve instead of something we must ignore or overpower or circumvent.

CHAPTER 13

THE FORMATION OF PLANS

Where do Plans come from? Probably the major source of new Plans is old Plans. We change them around a little bit each time we use them, but they are basically the same old Plans with minor variations. Sometimes we may borrow a new Plan from someone else. But we do not often create a completely new Plan.

Consider the origins of the Plans we have discussed: Instincts are inherited Plans and so are not created by the individual who executes them. Habits and skills are most frequently acquired by imitation or verbal instruction from another person, although they may develop inadvertently as we attempt to cope with the pattern of events around us. Shared Plans are normally communicated to us as participants, but even when we help to originate a new shared Plan we usually try to form it along lines already familiar. Plans for remembering attempt to exploit familiar situations and previously established associations. When we speak we usually try to say something that is not completely predictable, but the novelty of what we say is always subject to well-established grammatical Plans that we are not at liberty to revise. Even in thinking and problem-solving we are continually executing Plans tediously mastered at school.

This attitude toward the question of where we get our Plans resembles the attitude of Boston matrons toward their hats: "My dear, we don't *get* our hats, we *have* them." The analogy could be improved, however, if they had a few hats and only the pattern for many others. When we say that most Plans are remembered, not created, we do not mean that the Plan is stored in memory ready for execution down to the very last muscle twitch. Often it is a metaplan that is stored—a metaplan from which a large number of different Plans can be generated as they are needed.

When do we store Plans directly and when do we store Plans for generating Plans? For example, the Plan for reciting the alphabet is probably stored—memorized—directly, like any other motor skill. And so is the Plan for counting, at least through the first few hundred integers. But as the numbers begin to get large it is likely that we work in terms of a metaplan, a set of rules for generating $N+1$ from N, rather than with a direct Plan for uttering the successive integers. There are interesting questions here concerning the mental economies involved—how frequently must a Plan be used before it is worth our while to memorize it directly rather than to remember a Plan for reconstructing it?

A kind of low-level creativity is displayed by any system complex enough to have mataplans. For example, in using an electronic computer to make calculations involving logarithms, a decision must be made whether to store a table of logarithms in the computer's memory or to give the computer a formula for calculating logarithms as they are needed. If the table is used, the logarithm will be rapidly found if it is in the table, but the computer will be unable to handle any numbers whose logarithms it has not been given explicitly. If the formula is used the process will be slower, but the computer will be able to "create" the logarithms of numbers it has not seen before. Therein lies a great advantage of formulas, sets of rules, metaplans: They are easily stored, and when there is time to use them they can be projected into an infinite variety of unforeseen situations. The advantages of having Plans to generate Plans is so great that no intelligent automaton, living or dead, could get along without them. They not only permit the electronic computer to seem creative in a trivial way with logarithms, they permit men to be creative in significant ways in a wide variety of situations.

Consider some well-defined problem, such as finding a proof of a mathematical expression, and note the levels of metaplanning that are involved. The expression is itself a Plan that can be used to carry out some particular arithmetic operations—it has its own hierarchical organization and can be analyzed in much the same way a sentence can be parsed. The proof is a sequence of those mathematical expressions and will characteristically have its own hierarchical structure. Thus, the proof is also a Plan. And it is a metaplan because the objects it operates on are themselves Plans. But the system cannot stop there. There is a third level of planning that we discover as soon as we think of the procedures that the mathematician used in order to generate the proof. If the proof is a path leading from the expressions that were given to the expression that was to be proved, then the mathematician had to explore a great variety of possible paths in order to find this one. As we noted in Chapter 12, searches are generally conducted according to some kind of Plan, usually a heuristic Plan. So we must have a heuristic Plan for generating a proof Plan for transforming a mathematical Plan for performing certain computations. Does it stop there? Is it necessary to add the students of heuristic—mathematicians, computer engineers, psychologists, teachers, etc.—who may someday be able to specify hierarchical organizations for generating heuristics? Is it possible for all Plans to have metaplans that write 'em, and so on *ad infinitum*? Or is heuristic the end of the line? It seems that heuristic Plans are as far as one can go in this regression, for the methods used to discover new heuristic Plans would themselves be heuristic Plans. A plausible account of heuristic Plans, therefore, will provide the general outlines within which a theory of thinking about well-defined problems can eventually be constructed.

In his popular text, *How to Solve It,* Polya distinguishes four phases in the heuristic process:

—First, we must understand the problem. We have to see clearly what the data are, what conditions are imposed, and what the unknown thing is that we are searching for.

—Second, we must devise a plan that will guide the solution and connect the data to the unknown.

—Third, we must carry out our plan of the solution, checking each step as we go.

—Fourth, we should look back at the completed solution, reviewing, checking, discussing, perhaps even improving it.

Obviously, the second of these is most critical. The first is essentially what we have described in Chapter 12 as the construction of a clear Image of the situation in order to establish a test for the solution of the problem; it is indispensable, of course, but in the discussion of well-defined problems we assume that it has already been accomplished. The third is what we have described as the execution of a Plan, and although it may be costly or require much skill, we assume that it can be performed in a straightforward manner. The fourth phase is important for the student who wants to develop his ability to solve problems, for it facilitates storing the method for future use. However, it is in the second phase, the actual formation of a Plan, that something creative must happen. As Polya describes it:

> We have a plan when we know, or at least know in outline, which calculations, computations, or constructions we have to perform in order to obtain the unknown. The way from understanding the problem to conceiving a plan may be long and tortuous. In fact, the main achievement in the solution of a problem is to conceive the idea of a plan. This idea may emerge gradually. Or, after apparently unsuccessful trials and a period of hesitation, it may occur suddenly, in a flash, as a "bright idea." [1]

Polya presents the heuristic devices that mathematicians use in the form of questions, a kind of dialogue between a teacher and a student. The first question to ask is whether you know of a related problem. Usually there are many related problems and the problem is to choose the right one. A suggestion that points toward an essential common point is: Look at the unknown and try to think of a familiar problem that has the same or a similar unknown. If this does not suggest a plan, can you restate the problem? If you cannot solve

[1] G. Polya, *How to Solve It* (Princeton: Princeton University Press, 1945), p. 8.

the proposed problem, perhaps you can solve some related problem. Can you decompose it into several simpler problems? Perhaps you can work backwards—from what antecedent could the desired result be derived? Each of these heuristic devices is discussed by Polya in terms of specific examples.

Consider this puzzle: How can you bring up from the river exactly six quarts of water when you have only two containers, a four-quart pail and a nine-quart pail? The answer is not immediately apparent. What related problem can we solve? We could get eight quarts by twice filling the small pail and emptying it into the large pail. Or we could get five quarts by filling the larger nine-quart pail and then pouring off as much as we can into the smaller, four-quart pail. But the desired amount is six quarts. We are not making much progress working forwards from the given conditions to the desired result. Perhaps we could work backwards. What is the situation we are trying to reach? Imagine six quarts of water in the large pail. From what antecedent condition could this be derived? If the large container were filled and we could pour out three quarts, we would have the desired result. From what antecedent condition could this be derived? If the small pail already held one quart, we would have the condition we need. From what antecedent could this be derived? We could measure one quart by filling the nine-quart pail, discarding four quarts twice with the small pail, and then pouring the remaining one quart into the small pail. And so, by working backwards, we reach something that we know how to do. If we now reverse the whole process, we have our plan for measuring out the six quarts. This heuristic principle—said to have been described first by Plato—is to concentrate on the unknown and to try to see what could have led to it; it works not only in solving water-measuring problems but in a great variety of other problems as well. (The principle is perhaps most apparent when we note how easy it is to run a multiple-T maze from the goal box to the start, and how difficult it is to find the right path in the opposite direction.) Working backwards is one of many heuristic methods known to all good problem-solvers.

A critic of the present argument would have the right at this point to register a number of protests. His complaints might run something like this: (1) Metaplans that generate metaplans that generate still more Plans are far too complicated. A good scientist can draw an elephant with three parameters, and with four he can tie a knot in its tail. There must be hundreds of parameters floating around in this kind of theory and nobody will ever be able to untangle them. (2) These rough, heuristic rules of thumb, these probes and questions, these maxims and proverbs can be used only by people with enough intelligence to understand them and see how to apply them. They cannot be seriously proposed as unambiguous components of a scientific theory. (3) Even if we took this approach seriously, there is no way to put it to the test of experimentation. The evidence for it is not even simple introspection—the argument is based on what must lie behind introspection. It violates all the rules of the behavioristic tradition and threatens to set psychology back at least N years (where N measures the intensity of the critic's emotional response).

These are good criticisms and they must be met. The answer to the first one is clear enough: If the description is valid, then the fact that it is very complicated cannot be helped. No benign and parsimonious deity has issued us an insurance policy against complexity. However, there is no need to become discouraged on that account, for within the past decade or so electronic engineers have begun to develop computing machines that are big enough and fast enough to serve as models for testing complicated theories. Describe the theory carefully, translate the description into a computer program, run the program on a computer, and see if it reacts the same way organisms do. Now that we know how to write such programs—especially since the work of Newell, Shaw, and Simon [2]—we can begin to test ideas that would probably have seemed impossibly complicated to an earlier generation of psychologists. Computer engineers have only just begun to explore the possibilities of self-programming automata —we can look forward to many new discoveries as they learn more and more about what Norbert Wiener calls "the problems of organized complexity."

[2] The earliest description of the use of list structures to develop flexible information-processing languages in order to simulate cognitive processes with heuristic programs seems to be in the paper by Allen Newell and Herbert A. Simon, The logic theory machine: A complex information processing system, *IRE Transactions on Information Theory*, 1956, Vol. IT-2, No. 3, 61–79.

The possibility of using electronic computers gives us an answer to the second criticism, as well. If the heuristic devices that thinkers say they are using can be translated into programs that reproduce the results obtained by the person, then we have every reason to believe that the heuristic device was a true description of his procedure in solving the problem. If the heuristic method is ambiguous, the program simply will not work. With this test available, therefore, heuristic rules of thumb can indeed be proposed as elements of a serious theory of thinking.

The proposal that a theory of thinking and problem-solving should include all the heuristic rules men have discovered does not originate with the present authors, of course. It has a long and distinguished history, for it appears implicitly in almost every subjective description of the problem-solving process. Without a good supply of heuristic methods no artist could create, no scientist could discover, no technician could invent. In most cases, however, the discussions of heuristic schemes have been little more than catalogues of useful tricks.[3] Only recently have workers begun to explore the possibility that the catalogue might be converted into a coherent theory.

Marvin Minsky, noting the extent to which language guides our problem-solving efforts, has suggested that one way to develop a theory of heuristic would be to design or evolve a language through which the machine can be given heuristic suggestions which it can try to realize in a variety of reasonable ways.[4] We would then be able to communicate with the machine in much the same way Polya communicates with his students. Of course, the machine would have to provide an intelligent description of what it was trying to do, for otherwise it would be difficult to know what suggestions to make. But the machine would slowly accumulate its own private catalogue of heuristic tricks, just as the student does. Then we could take the machine apart and see how it worked—an analysis to which few

[3] For example, in Abraham A. Moles, *La Création Scientifique* (René Kister: Geneva, 1957), there is a list of twenty-one different heuristic methods that Moles has been able to distinguish and exemplify in the historical development of science and technology.

[4] M. L. Minsky, *Heuristic Aspects of the Artificial Intelligence Problem*, Group Report 34-55, Lincoln Laboratory, Massachusetts Institute of Technology, 17 December 1956, p. III-23.

students are willing to submit. In Minsky's view, which is broadly the same as the present authors', verbal information provides an organism with "a set of instructions for constructing, in its head, out of parts available there, a machine to perform a response of the desired kind." [5] As he points out, a machine that uses language as we do would have to contain a fairly powerful, general-purpose machine that, under the direction of linguistic signals, could construct a variety of special-purpose machines. If such a machine was told to try to construct a Plan by working backwards, for example, it would presumably know how to do so. Children acquire their store of heuristic methods by listening to verbal suggestions and then trying to execute them, and perhaps that is also the best way to let the machines evolve. If we want to develop a self-programming automaton, maybe we should let it learn the way we do.

Yet the fact that students of heuristic talk about such schemes does not mean that they are able to carry them out. Our critic should not be put off by appeals to authority or by evidence that computers are both impressive and fashionable. Talk about self-programming machines could create an impression that all of psychology's problems have been locked tightly in a box labeled "Plan Generator," never to be opened again. In order to meet the criticism head-on, therefore, we should, even before considering the third complaint, give some more concrete description of how heuristic Plans can be realized in actual machines.

Let us consider chess and the way a computer might use heuristic Plans in order to play that game. One's first thought, perhaps, is to compute all possible continuations from a given position, then choose one that led to a checkmate of the opposing king. Unfortunately, even the fastest electronic computers we have would be unable to execute that exhaustive Plan in a reasonable period of time. It is necessary, therefore, to use heuristic Plans. But what heuristic Plans do we have for playing chess? These can be found in any chess manual for beginners; they include such maxims as, "Try to control the four center squares," or "Always make sure your King is safe before you attack," or "Do not attack the opposing position until your own position is developed," etc. How can these heuristic principles be used to control what the machine will do?

[5] *Ibid.*, p. III-18.

Newell, Shaw, and Simon have analyzed the traditional chess heuristics into six independent "goals": (1) King safety, (2) material balance, (3) center control, (4) development, (5) King-side attack, and (6) promotion of Pawns.[6] This ordering of the goals is significant, because the machine always tries to achieve them in that same order. That is to say, first the machine will look to see if its King is safe. If not, it will try to defend it; if so, it will go on to the next goal. The next thing the machine will do is to check up on the possible exchanges, to make sure that its pieces are adequately protected. If not, the machine will protect them; if so, the machine will turn next to center control. Can it move its Pawns into the center? If so, it is done; if not, the machine turns to development, then to attacking the King; and finally, if none of those goals leads to a good move, the machine will consider the Pawn structure.

Associated with each of the goals is a set of rules for generating moves that are relevant to that goal. For example, when the machine applies the center-control heuristic, it will first propose moving Pawn to Queen 4, then Pawn to King 4, then will propose moves that may prevent the opponent from making these two key moves, then propose moves that prepare for making these moves (e.g., adding defenders to the Queen 4 or the King 4 squares, or removing some block to moving the Queen's Pawn or the King's Pawn).

When the move generator has proposed something to do, the machine does not automatically accept it, of course. The proposal must be evaluated to see if it really achieves the desired results. The evaluation cannot be limited to a single goal, however, for a move that would look very good to the center-control Plan might utterly destroy the King's position, or lose a piece, etc. The proposed move must be analyzed in terms of all six goals. The value of a move is a vector. The value of a move for center control is obtained by counting the number of blocks there are to making the two key Pawn moves. The component representing material balance will assign the conventional numerical values to the pieces, examine certain continuations until no further exchanges are possible, and note the

---

[6] Allen Newell, J. C. Shaw, and H. A. Simon, Chess-playing problems and the problem of complexity, *IBM Journal of Research and Development*, 1958, 2, 320–335. This article contains, in addition to the description of their own work, an account of the history of the problem beginning with Shannon's paper in 1949 (see footnote 25 in Chapter 3).

change in material. (The evaluation of moves with respect to material balance is exceedingly complex and involves numerous other heuristic principles.) And so the evaluation proceeds through the different goals.

Now, when the machine has found a move that all the different heuristic goals approve, the move may still not be made. There may be an even better move possible. Thus, the machine has the problem of making a choice among the moves after they have been evaluated. There are several different ways it could proceed, but there is one thing it cannot do: It cannot wait until all the possible proposals have been made and evaluated in order to select the one with highest value. There are far too many proposals possible. Newell, Shaw, and Simon suggest that the simplest choice procedure is to set an acceptance level arbitrarily (a mechanical "level of aspiration") and simply to take the first acceptable move. In order to avoid the possibility that no conceivable move would meet the criterion, a stop-order can also be imposed; save the best move discovered up to this point and, if the time-limit expires before an acceptable move has been found, make the best one that was found.

In order to be completely concrete, we should examine the routines used to generate and evaluate the moves in more detail, but that would take us too far from the main argument of this book. A critic who still doubts that heuristic rules can be incorporated into completely deterministic programs suitable for guiding the behavior of an automaton will have to pursue his doubts into the original articles themselves. We should, however, pause long enough to try to express the Newell, Shaw, and Simon program in the language used in the present book—not because it adds anything to their description, but simply to make clear that their work does indeed illustrate, and lend credibility to, the less explicit notions about information-processing that we have applied to psychological questions in these pages.

There are several ways that TOTE hierarchies could be organized to play chess, all of them using the heuristics that Newell, Shaw, and Simon have programmed, but the one that seems simplest and nearest to the spirit of their work has two major subplans, one for generating the moves, the other for evaluating them. The prototest could be the question, "Who plays next?" If the machine is to play, the operational phase, "Make a move," is executed. This operation has two tests, "What move?" and, when that has been answered, "Is that the best move?" The operational phase of the move generator has six tests, all of the intuitive form, "If you do not have a move, why not try to X?" where X is one of the six goals. If no move has been selected, then the operational phase of X will be executed. In the case of center control, for example, it will consist of a string of tests of the form, "Have you tried P-Q4?" "Have you tried P-K4?" "Have you tried to prevent him from moving P-Q4?" and so on. Each of these can be further elaborated. Eventually a legal move is selected and then control is transferred to the evaluation routine. This also has six parts, one for each of the goals; and each question, "How does it affect the safety of the King?" or "How does it affect the balance of material?" etc., has associated with it operational phases which are more or less elaborate according to how difficult the question is to answer. We could, if it seemed desirable, permit any of the six individual evaluation routines to reject a proposed move if it tested out too badly with respect to that particular goal—that decision would make it difficult for the machine to offer sacrifices, however, so it is probably wiser to postpone any rejections until the result of all six evaluation routines are collected and compared with similar evaluations of other moves. Amateur chess-players are not always that wise, however, and will frequently reject a move because of some glaring disadvantage—only to discover its compensating advantages later when they study the games of a master. It is not our present purpose to offer alternatives to the Newell, Shaw, and Simon program, however, but merely to illustrate that their heuristic programs do not confute or conflict with the idea of Plans presented here.

There are many other heuristic devices that we might discuss. One of the most interesting is the use of a "diagramming heuristic" in a geometry program written by H. L. Gelernter and N. Rochester.[7] They used the heuristic programming techniques developed by

[7] H. L. Gelernter and N. Rochester, Intelligent behavior in problem-solving machines, *IBM Journal of Research and Development*, 1958, 2, 336–345. The idea seems to have originated at the Dartmouth Summer Research Project on Artificial Intelligence in 1956, particularly in discussion among John McCarthy, Marvin L. Minsky, and Nathaniel Rochester.

Newell, Shaw, and Simon in order to make a computer tackle geometry problems in the same fashion as a high-school student. Geometric proofs are typically rather long and it is almost impossible to discover them by any exhaustive procedure of trying all possible sequences of transformations. In this situation the human geometer will draw a figure that contains the essential conditions of the problem and then study the figure until he develops some Plan for the proof. He may check with other figures in order to make sure he is not trapped by some accidental property of the one figure he has used. Or he may, following standard heuristic methods, try to restate the problem or analyze it into steps that create new problems, then construct figures to help him prove those ancillary problems. The ways in which he exploits this Image of the problem are quite interesting and complex, and it is a challenging task to try to convert them into explicit rules that can be programmed for a machine. The rules would be such things as, "If the figure has an axis of symmetry and it is not drawn, then draw it." Or, most important, "If two line segments or angles are to be proved equal, determine by measuring on the diagram whether they are corresponding parts of apparently congruent triangles." When the machine discovers by measurement that certain things are equal or proportional, it can set these up as hypotheses and inquire whether, if they are true, they will contribute to the construction of a proof.

It is certainly true, as our critic pointed out, that these systems become extremely complicated. There is, however, a kind of backhanded comfort to be found in that fact. Most scientific advances have reduced man's dignity, moved him out of the center of the universe, given him apes for cousins, subjected his brain to the fickle endocrines and his mind to the unconscious forces of lust—the reduction of his cognitive processes to machine operations would seem to be the final, crushing blow. At least we can take comfort in the fact that we are too complicated to reduce to simple machines. Thus far the human brain seems to be the most amazing computing machine ever devised—nothing else we know even approaches it. The more carefully we analyze the information-processing that must go on in order to solve even the simplest problems, the more respect we gain for this beautiful piece of biological equipment.

Before we try to meet our critic's final objection, however, let us consider two more heuristic methods. These two are quite general methods described by Newell, Shaw, and Simon and tested for their effectiveness in enabling a computer to solve problems in logic, chess, and trigonometry.[8] They refer to them as "means-ends analysis" and the "planning method." The former attempts to analyze a problem into a sequence of subproblems, and the latter attempts to find a plan by ignoring some of the complicating factors in the situation. Undoubtedly there are many other heuristics that we use to solve problems, but these two are certainly ubiquitous, important, and powerful.

The means-ends analysis runs something like this: First, see if you know any way to transform the given into the desired solution. If no way is known, then try to reduce the difference between them; find some transformation that reduces the difference, and then apply it. Then try the first step again—see if you know any way to transform the new version of the given into the desired solution. If not, search again for a way to reduce the difference, etc. Each time the difference is reduced, the problem gets a little easier to solve. Intuitively, the heuristic works something like this: "I want to get from A to B, but I do not know how. What is the difference between what I have and what I want to get? The difference is D. How can I reduce D? Operator T will reduce D, but I do not see how to apply it. Transform A so that operator T will apply to it. Now apply operator T and get a new object A'. The new problem is to get from A' to B, but I do not know how. What is the difference?" And so the means-ends analysis continues.[9] The argument attempts to make progress by substituting for the achievement of any goal the achievement of a set of easier goals. Its success will depend upon how shrewdly the measure of difference is defined and the transformations are selected.

No doubt it is obvious that any method we can discover for

[8] Allen Newell, J. C. Shaw, and Herbert A. Simon. Report on a general problem-solving program. *Proceedings of the International Conference on Information Processing*, Paris, 1959 (in press).

[9] What Newell, Shaw, and Simon call "means-ends analysis" is similar to the theory of productive thinking described by K. Duncker. From his analysis of the situation and of the goal, the person locates a source of difficulty that he then attempts to remove. See K. Duncker, On problem-solving, L. S. Lees, trans., *Psychological Monographs*, 1945, No. 270. The important advance over Duncker's work, of course, is to be completely explicit in terms of a computer program.

breaking up a big problem into smaller problems will tremendously simplify the solution. This approach is valuable when the solution can be characterized by several simultaneous attributes. That is to say, if a situation differs from the goal with respect to *both* attribute A and attribute B, we can try to factor the problem into two parts. Instead of looking for a Plan to remove both differences simultaneously, we can search first for a set of Plans that will take care of attribute A, then search through that smaller set of Plans for one that will also handle attribute B. When we proceed in this way we are free to decide in which order to search for each aspect, in which order to eliminate the differences. In the language of children's games, we get progressively "warmer" as we solve each successive component of the problem.

A second very general system of heuristic used by Newell, Shaw, and Simon consists in omitting certain details of the problem. This usually simplifies the task and the simplified problem may be solved by some familiar plan. The plan used to solve the simple problem is then used as the strategy for solving the original, complicated problem. In solving a problem in the propositional calculus, for example, the machine can decide to ignore differences among the logical connectives and the order of symbols and to look only at what the symbols are and how they are grouped. The logical operators that add, delete, or regroup symbols are then applied to the abstracted propositions, regardless of their connectives. The steps required to get the right symbols correctly grouped then serve as a possible strategy for a complete proof. The critical feature, of course, is whether or not the neglect of the details changed the problem so much that the solution of the simple problem was irrelevant.

Most heuristic methods involve some way to use the information already acquired. If correct solutions are literally scattered at random through the set of possible solutions, then previous search through one part of the solutions can be of no aid to the subsequent search through the remainder. However, in most situations where men have been successful in solving problems, the successful solutions lie in a neighborhood of successful solutions. *Hamlet,* for example, is still an excellent play even when an actor accidentally changes a few of Shakespeare's lines, thus changing it into another, but very similar, play. The general concept of biological evolution is a good one, even though the sequence of development of different species may in some instances require revision in the light of future evidence. When we get into situations where the modification of any slight detail of a correct solution changes it into an incorrect solution—as in opening a combination lock, for example—we are usually unsuccessful. When the best solution is in a neighborhood of good solutions, however, it is possible to explore the neighborhood of any relatively successful solution to see if a better one turns up near by.

If a set of possible solutions are, in this loose sense, clustered together in a space defined by the attributes, or dimensions, of the problem, it may be possible to simplify the problem by ignoring one or two of the attributes entirely. If the simplified problem can be solved, the steps in its solution can suggest a Plan for solving the original problem. With luck, the steps that led to a successful region in the smaller space may still lead to a successful region in the larger space. This is the sort of heuristic we use, for example, when we try to find ways to settle disputes between nations by thinking how we might settle similar disputes between individuals. Another example is the use of the diagram heuristic by Gelernter and Rochester—the steps involved in solving the problem posed by a particular diagram may provide a Plan suitable for proving the general theorem.

Means-ends analysis and the planning method are two of the most powerful heuristic methods used by Newell, Shaw, and Simon in their development of a general problem-solving program, one general enough to deal with a wide range of well-defined problems in essentially the same way. Once they have succeeded, their computer programs will indeed have risen above the level of heuristic "catalogues," such as those offered by Polya and others, to the status of a heuristic "theory" of thinking.

After studying this pioneering work by Newell, Shaw, and Simon it is quite difficult to recapture one's innocent respect for parsimony in psychological theories. Certainly, we can no longer think that anyone who postulates complicated information-processing by an organism is appealing to mysterious, vitalistic, ambiguous, or unscientific principles. Complicated information-processing according to heuristic principles is not only conceivable—it has actually been accomplished, demonstrated on existing computers. Henceforth, it is not necessary to suspect metaphysical booby traps in every psychological process more complicated than a conditioned reflex. The work of Newell, Shaw, and Simon shows in detail how the processes of solving problems can be compounded out of more elementary processes that can be executed by machines. And it shows that those elementary processes, properly organized, can in fact solve complex problems; no ghostly assistance from an undefined source, human or divine, is needed.

But, while all of this work is clear progress in dealing with the problems of organized complexity, we still have hanging over our heads the third complaint by our patient critic. He may by now have finally granted that heuristic methods can be incorporated into machines, but he must still feel that the behavioral evidence can never be collected for really testing these ideas. It is a serious complaint. If people must be this complicated, and if things this complicated cannot be studied experimentally, then scientific psychology must be impossible. It is a complaint that, if true, would certainly be important to prove.

But is it true? Certainly, if one interprets "scientific" to mean that all of a subject's verbal reports must be ignored, then it will be impossible to study thinking at the level of complexity required for programming computers or for understanding the neurology and physiology of the brain. But are such Spartan strictures necessary? They would protect us from long, violent disputes about "imageless thoughts," perhaps, because they would make it impossible to say anything at all about thoughts, but that is a high price to pay for consonance.

The most valuable approach seems to be the "thinking aloud" method used by Binet, Duncker, Claparède, and many others.[10] Unlike the usual introspective or retrospective methods that require a subject to analyze his experience into meaningless mental contents—sensations, images, feelings—thinking aloud requires merely that the person talk while he is working, that he should comment on what he is doing, what he is looking for, what his intentions are, what objects or relations catch his attention, etc. As Claparède pointed out, the

[10] E. Claparède, La genèse de l'hypothèse, *Archives de Psychologie*, 1934, 24, 1–154.

method has many shortcomings—the task of talking may inhibit the thought processes, or slow them down, it may make the process sound more coherent and orderly than it would otherwise be, the referents for some of the utterances are not clear, the subject may fall silent at just the critical moment when the experimenter would most like to know what he is doing. But when the method is used intelligently and conscientiously, it can provide a tremendous amount of information about the detailed process of thought. The problem is not so much to collect the data as it is to know what to do with them.

The subject will say, in effect, "I want to do A, but before I can do A I have to prepare for it by doing B." He then proceeds to do B, which may lead on to unforeseen consequences that prevent his ever returning to do A. Nevertheless, the consideration of A was an essential step in the thought processes leading to B. If we are to develop an adequate heuristic description, one that will solve the problem in the same manner as the subject, it must consider A, then do B. But if we had not recorded the things the subject said he was considering, along with the things he actually did, the task would be hopeless. It is actually easier to simulate the person's spoken thoughts than to simulate only the decisions that appear in his behavior. Since thinking aloud permits more of the person's thought processes to project through the plane of perception, it helps to limit the variety of conceivable descriptions to a handful that are reasonably accurate.

Newell, Shaw, and Simon have found that the subject's description of what he is doing is exactly the kind of data they need to formulate a theory that will predict his behavior.[11] They ask a subject to derive one logical expression from another by the application of a given set of transformation rules. The subject talks about the task as he does it. He may look at the two expressions he is given and say that the one he has to start with has too many propositions to the left of the main connective, so he will have to get rid of some (an application of the "planning method"). He looks at the list of transformations until he finds one that gets rid of things to the left of the main connective, so he would like to apply that. But then he realizes that he cannot, because the proposition he wants to transform has

[11] H. A. Simon in an invited address before the Eastern Psychological Association in Atlantic City, April, 1959.

"and" in it, whereas the rule he wants to apply works only for "or." So, he says, the job is to get that connective changed in order to apply the transformation that will shorten the left side. He looks for a transformation that turns "and" expressions into "or" expressions and elects to try it as his first step. Now, it is possible to find a fairly simple set of heuristic methods to describe what this subject is doing (e.g., his method is to make the propositions more important than the connectives in guiding the choice of transformations), and to predict that he would mention the left-shortening transformation before he adopted the connective-changing transformation. But if the only datum that the experimenter records is the bald fact that the subject's first choice of a transformation was the connective-changing transformation, it is impossible to see how the subject's strategy can be inferred.

It is tempting to say that a successful theory "predicts the subject's verbal behavior." In fact, no one is yet much interested in the verbal behavior as behavior, but only in the meaning of what is said. The subject may say, "Use number 8 next," or, "Let's try that one again," or any of a variety of equivalent verbal behaviors, yet these differences are ignored when testing the adequacy of the theory. Obviously, therefore, the interest lies in the subject's Plan, not in his specific actions.

When the psychologist says that his subject in these experiments was following such-and-such a Plan, or was using a particular metaplan for generating Plans to solve the problem, it is clear that this is a hypothetical statement. The Plan, or the metaplan, represents the psychologist's theory about that chunk of observed behavior. Obviously, we can never know whether or not we have *the* theory for any domain of inquiry. There is always a variety of alternative Plans that could have led the subject to exhibit the same behavior; the best we can hope to do is to select the simplest one compatible with all the facts. But, because this kind of ambiguity is such a pervasive feature of behavioral analysis, it is important to reduce it as far as possible. In this endeavor, the subject's verbal report has one great recommendation in its favor, because language, for all its notorious shortcomings, is still the least ambiguous of all the channels open from one human being to another.

CHAPTER 14

SOME NEUROPSYCHOLOGICAL SPECULATIONS

"A hole is to dig." The child amuses us with his operational definitions. "A knife is to cut." "A book is to read." "Milk is to drink." Each concept is defined by the concrete operations that it customarily evokes. The child is learning what to do with things. Or, to put it in our present language, the child is building up TOTE units by associating a perceptual Image used in the test phase with an action pattern used in the operational phase of the unit. The number of these TOTE units that a child must learn is enormous and he probably learns them, initially at least, by following this simple verbal formula that associates a subject with a predicate. It is not enough for the child simply to be able to name the object or to distinguish it from other objects. He must know what actions can be released when the test phase indicates the object is now at hand.

Children, however, are not the only ones who produce definitions of this type. Kurt Goldstein has widely publicized the fact that they can appear after certain types of brain damage.[1] The unfortunate patient is confronted with a knife, or with a picture of a knife. He is unable to supply the name. But if he is given the object, he knows how to use it. He may indicate that he recognizes it by making the gestures that imitate its use. He may even say, "It is to cut with," thus echoing the child. According to Goldstein's interpretation, this behavior on the part of the patient indicates an impairment of the "abstract attitude." The injury to the brain leaves the patient with a simpler, more concrete way of dealing with his world. Goldstein's famous theoretical analysis of the abstract-concrete dimension of mental life is one way of looking at the symptoms he describes in the patients. Another, more in keeping with the proposals made in this book, suggests that the brain can be damaged in such a way that some of the simplest processes of retrieving stored information cannot be performed, but other Plans normally initiated by the *object* are left intact. The patient may have lost the ability to execute the Plans involved in naming objects, but retained the ability to execute all other Plans. Or the patient may have lost the ability to recall a Plan by internal, verbal processes and be completely dependent upon external memory devices.

In any case, there seems to be good evidence for the age-old belief that the brain has something to do with the mind. Or, to use less dualistic terms, when behavioral phenomena are carved at their joints, there will be some sense in which the analysis will correspond to the way the brain is put together. Psychological problems may not be solved by making measurements on the brain; but some more modest aim may be accomplished. A psychological analysis that can stand up to the neurological evidence is certainly better than one that can not. The catch, obviously, is in the phrase "stand up to," since considerable prejudice can be involved in its definition. In any case, each time there is a new idea in psychology, it suggests a corresponding insight in neurophysiology, and vice versa. The procedure of looking back and forth between the two fields is not only ancient and honorable—it is always fun and occasionally useful.

The present authors determined to follow tradition and to look

[1] Kurt Goldstein and Martin Scheerer, Abstract and concrete behavior: an **experimental** study with special tests, *Psychological Monographs*, 1941, No. 329.

at the nervous system through the same theoretical spectacles. In fact, the brain was never far from the focus of discussion. Innumerable alternative interpretations of the available neuropsychological data were invented and discarded. In the hope of communicating the flavor of the arguments, this chapter reports a few of the ideas that were considered. However, the authors feel somewhat less than confident that they have discovered the one best line to pursue.[2]

The arguments revolved around a three-way analogy: The relation of a Plan to the mind is analogous to the relation of a program to a computer, and both are analogous to the relation of X to the brain. Question: What is X?

Of these three systems, the one we know most about is the computer. When a large, modern, general-purpose computer is turned on in the morning and sits there warming up, purring through its magnetic drums and scratching its multivibrators, it is not yet a true computing machine. It will not begin to act like a computing machine until it is given some instructions. Depending upon what kind of instructions it is given it may act like any one of an infinite variety of different computing machines that might have been built with the particular instructions locked in and unchangeable. But without the instructions, or program, the computer will do no processing of information. It may have all kinds of fascinating data stored in its memory or being fed into it from the outside, but without a program nothing can happen. A computer must have a program.

Now, as soon as someone suggests that people are like computing machines—and we hear that said every day—it should become clear that if the suggestion is true, people must have programs, also. If a man is like a computer, then the man must have somewhere available an organized set of instructions that he attempts to execute. That is to say, the man must have a Plan. By taking the analogy between man and computer with complete sincerity is one driven to

[2] One reason for much of the trouble in reaching an agreement about the way the brain works was that two of the authors stubbornly persisted in trying to talk about it in terms appropriate to the dry hardware of modern digital computers, whereas the third was equally persistent in using language appropriate to the wet software that lives inside the skull. After a decade of cybernetics you might think the translation from one of these languages into the other would be fairly simple, but that was not the case. The relation between computers and brains was a battle the authors fought with one another until the exasperation became unbearable.

search literally for the source of instructions that guide human behavior. The preceding pages try to describe the results of that search in psychological terms. Now we are interested to see what results the same attitude might produce in neurology.

In the broadest, crudest terms, what is the pattern to be transferred from computers to brains? There are many ways to build electronic computers, but most machines seem to involve a *memory*—where both the program and the data and any intermediate results and the final answer can all be stored—with facilities for transferring information into it and out of it, and a *processing unit*—where the actual operations of comparison, addition, multiplication, shifting, etc., are performed. The computer begins by taking the first instruction on the program and moving it from the memory to the processing unit. Whatever instruction is in the processing unit has control over what the machine will do, so it executes the instruction and goes on to the next instruction, etc., etc., with tremendous speed and blind persistence until an instruction tells it to stop. The instruction that is temporarily in the processing unit can be said to be the one that the computer is "attending to" at the moment. Note that the center of attention is a fixed place and that symbols are shifted *into and out of it* from the memory; the center of attention does not go wandering around through the memory itself, as a beam of light might scan a darkened room. No doubt there is nothing *necessary* about this pattern for computers, but at least it is familiar and we know that it will work.[3]

Is it possible to locate parts of the brain that correspond, however crudely, to these parts of a computer? To look for some particular place in the brain to represent a locus of consciousness, or a focus of attention, or whatever it is that corresponds to a computer's proc-

[3] We have considered only the possibility that the nervous system performs one operation at a time; an equally plausible alternative would be to allow different parts of the brain to perform computations at the same time. At the London Symposium on Mechanization of Thought Processes in 1958 Oliver Selfridge of the Lincoln Laboratory gave a talk entitled, "Pandemonium: a Paradigm for Learning," in which he described a hierarchical organization of parallel computers that could learn to recognize patterns and illustrated its operation in terms of a machine that would learn to recognize manually keyed Morse code. Ulric Neisser, in *Hierarchies in Pattern Recognition* (Group Report 54-9, Lincoln Laboratory, Massachusetts Institute of Technology, 9 October, 1959), explores some of the virtues of Pandemonium as a model of human cognition in general.

essing unit, is a naïve and impossible oversimplification. But the alternative metaphor—that a focus of activity moves about in the brain carrying consciousness with it from place to place—seems just as *ad hoc* in the light of available evidence. Regardless of what consciousness may be, however, the computer analogy would say to look for some particular place that could be used to store programs and data, that is, to serve as the memory. And it would tell us to look for another part of the brain into which an instruction could be transferred when the time arrived for the execution of that instruction.

After several months of discussion, the present authors were almost (but not quite) convinced that you could put the names of parts of the brain on slips of paper, scramble them up, draw two at random, assign them in either order to serve either as the memory or as the processing unit, and you would be able to interpret *some* evidence *somehow* as proof that you were right. One notion, for example, is that the cerebral cortex provides the memory unit, that the limbic areas somewhere house the processing unit, and that the cerebellum is a digital-to-analogue converter in the output system. The primary projection areas could provide short-term storage for images that would be operated upon by programs stored in the adjacent association areas. And so on. It is wonderful to see how these analogies can blossom when they are given a little affection.

Eventually, however, even the most optimistic theorist feels the need for evidence. What does the neurologist have to contribute to this discussion? In the broadest, crudest terms, once again, what pattern can be discerned in the organization of the brain?

Like Caesar's Gaul, the brain is divided into parts, a conceptual operation that always reflects a conviction that when two things live close together they probably cooperate with each other. A fourfold division of the forebrain can be made: first into an internal core vs. an external portion; then, each of these can be divided into two parts. The internal core is made up of limbic systems and a frontal "association area." The external portion is divided into projection systems for the different sense modalities and a posterior "association area."[4]

[4] The evidence on which these divisions are based has been summarized by Karl Pribram, Comparative neurology and the evolution of behavior, in A. Roe and G. G. Simpson, eds., *Behavior and Evolution* (New Haven: Yale University Press, 1958), Chapter 7, pp. 140–164.

These divisions are based on neuroanatomical evidence, but they also indicate relatively consistent differences in the kinds of psychological functions that they serve. Concerning the major division into an internal core and an external portion, Pribram comments as follows:

> [It is assumed] that the internal core is primarily related to changes in central nervous system excitability; that the external portion serves propagation of patterns of signals; that the internal core is primarily concerned in mechanisms necessary to the performance of behavior sequences while the external portion is related to informational processes necessary in discriminative behavior.[5]

The reader who has come this far through the present text should react with interest to this division of the brain into an internal part that handles sequences of acts and an external part that handles discrimination. Once the present distinction has been drawn between the Plan and the Image, it is almost inevitable that one should identify the internal core as the part of the brain involved in planning (i.e., "sequences") and the external portion as the part of the brain involved in our organized system of facts and values (i.e., "discrimination"). Thus, one begins to think of the internal core as a place that governs the execution of Plans; of the limbic portions of the internal core, along with their closely related subcortical centers, as if they performed the functions of a processing unit in a computer; and of the frontal lobe, which is the "association area" in the inner core system, as a "working memory" where various Plans could be temporarily stored (or, perhaps, regenerated) while awaiting execution.

There are problems with this schema, of course. One difficulty is the disposition of different motivational processes. Since it has been argued in these pages that values are part of the Image, consistency would demand that evaluation must be mediated by the external portion of the forebrain. However, current research on the limbic areas —the part of the inner core that might govern the execution of the Plan—suggests that they are involved in motivational processes in a most intimate fashion. Thus we seemed to face a dilemma, which took some careful analysis of the behavioral evidence to resolve. The matter is quite important, so let us pursue it here and now.

[5] *Ibid.*, p. 143.

Analysis of the functions of the limbic systems of the forebrain has been one of the outstanding achievements of neurophysiology during the 1950's. These systems are located deep in the center of the brain, and because they are difficult to get at surgically, they were neglected until recently. In spite of a great deal of research, however, the functions that these structures serve in normal behavior have eluded precise specification. The trouble stems from the fact that a wide variety of seemingly unrelated effects on behavior result when these regions are stimulated electrically or are surgically destroyed. Two different points of view have been adopted in the various attempts to explain the observed behavior: (1) The limbic systems comprise the substrate concerned with motivational and emotional behavior, motivation and emotion being conceived as primitive, instinctual, "visceral" reactions.[6] (2) The limbic systems are primarily concerned with "memory."[7] Clinical and experimental observations can be advanced, of course, to support both of these interpretations.

What sort of evidence is there for the first view, that the limbic systems are concerned with primitive motivational-emotional processes? For one thing, homeostatic mechanisms are abundant in the central core of the nervous system and are located especially around the third and fourth ventricles of the rostral end of the neuraxis. Take, for example, the thirst mechanism. Goats have been made to drink large quantities of water by injecting a few drops of concentrated table salt solution into the third ventricle. The osmoreceptors in this region of the brain are activated and the goats continue to drink water until an equilibrium is reached. That is to say, they drink until a sufficient amount of water is absorbed from the gut through the vascular system and into the cerebrospinal fluid to return its salinity to normal. This is the kind of "motivational" process one finds situated in the internal core. Should the present authors be embarrassed and revise their opinion about the relegation of dynamic factors to the Image on the basis of such evidence? Not at all. The thirst homeostat is a Plan, a relatively simple, innate TOTE unit.

[6] P. D. MacLean, The limbic system with respect to self-preservation and the preservation of the species, *Journal of Nervous and Mental Diseases*, 1958, 1, 1–11.

[7] B. Milner, Psychological defects produced by temporal lobe excision, in *The Brain and Human Behavior*, Research Publication, Association for Research in Nervous and Mental Disease, XXXVI (Baltimore: Williams and Wilkins, 1958), Chapter VIII, pp. 244–257.

As elsewhere, the TOTE phases, once they have been initiated, run themselves off until the incongruities that activated them are resolved. The organism will continue activities that tend to complete the TOTE sequence: i.e., the organism will show "intentional behavior." A statement that the animal "intends to quench its thirst" seems more appropriate than a statement that the animal values water. The distinction made in Chapter 4 between values and intentions is crucial here. What would really be surprising would be to discover that a lesion in the central core could cause a man to reverse, say, his preference for Rembrandt over Picasso, or for capitalism over communism. The evaluative factors involved in such choices as these must be mediated somehow in the external portion of the forebrain.

In the normal animal—one which does not have concentrated salt solution in its third ventricle—the number of swallows of water taken is determined by the amount of water the body needs, and the drinking will terminate long before there has been time for any dilution of the cerebrospinal fluid. What terminates the TOTE unit activity for drinking in this case? Presumably the number of swallows is recorded—we hesitate to say "counted," since that might be misunderstood as meaning that the animal pronounced the names of integers subvocally as it drank—and is compared with some predetermined number that depends upon the body's water balance. After each swallow the amount of drinking that has been done is compared with the predetermined amount that is to be done and when the two are equal the TOTE unit is terminated. How the number can be predetermined is not clear, but presumably it depends upon previous experience in some way. We might think of the information about how-many-swallows-are-needed-as-a-function-of-how-much-water-deprivation-has-been-endured as forming a part of the Image, a stored relationship, which must be drawn upon, activated, before the TOTE unit for drinking is set up for execution. Therefore, the present authors are not disconcerted to discover that lesions in the limbic systems of the central core disrupt the execution of such behavior.

This distinction between the automatic execution of TOTE units concerned with vital functions and the evaluation of these same functions in the Image can be illustrated by an actual case. Bilateral surgical ablation of certain parts of the limbic systems characteristically result in excessive eating and obesity. One patient, who had gained more than one hundred pounds, was examined at lunch time. Was she hungry? She answered, "No." Would she like a piece of rare, juicy steak? "No." Would she like a piece of chocolate candy? She answered, "Um-humm," but when no candy was offered she did not pursue the matter. A few minutes later when the examination was completed, the doors to the common room were opened and she saw the other patients already seated at a long table, eating lunch. She rushed to the table, pushed others aside, and began to stuff food into her mouth with both hands. She was immediately recalled to the examining room and the questions about food were repeated. The same negative answers were obtained again, even after they were pointedly contrasted with her recent behavior at the table. Somehow the lesion had disrupted the normal relation between the evaluation of an object and the execution of Plans for obtaining it—between Image and Plan—a fact that we interpret as further evidence for a clear separation between value and intention, the two aspects of motivated behavior. Just how the lesion could have such an effect is a topic to which we shall return shortly.

What sort of evidence is there for the second view, that the limbic systems are concerned with memory? A large lesion in the limbic systems in man (more extensive than that described in the patient above) can produce a very odd type of memory loss. Patients with lesions in this part of the internal core of the forebrain are able to repeat correctly a series of digits that they have just heard for the first time. On this test of immediate memory they are practically as efficient as they were before the lesion occurred. Moreover, their memory for events prior to their surgical operation is apparently normal. But if distracted, they are unable to carry out a sequence of orders. If you are called away for ten or fifteen minutes in the middle of administering some test to such a patient, when you return he will not be able to continue where he left off. He will not recall where he was in the task. In fact, he will not even recall that there was any task or that he had ever seen you before. Such a patient can be directed to a grocery store where he can purchase the items on a written list without having to refer to that list any oftener than would a person with an intact brain. But once he has completed the shopping he does not recall what he is supposed to do with his purchases and he is completely incapable of finding his way home. Unless given new instructions at this point he will wander about aimlessly until something in the environment sets off a habitual reaction, such as waiting for a red light to change before he crosses a street. His behavior is not organized into a Plan, but rather is a mere concatenation of discrete acts.

On the surface, this peculiar defect of memory would not seem to have anything in common with the disturbed thirst and hunger mechanism mentioned above. Yet this patient's behavior illustrates perfectly what would happen if a person were unable to formulate Plans for remembering (cf. Chapter 10). Given an external Plan written out on a sheet of paper, the patient can carry on quite well.

Neurobehavioral studies conducted on animals support this notion that the limbic systems of the internal core of the forebrain play an essential role in the execution of Plans. Ablation and stimulation of various structures within these systems interfere with feeding, fleeing, fighting, mating, and maternal behavior. Two kinds of effects are obtained, depending on which of the major divisions of the limbic systems is experimentally involved.

The first kind of effect we have already met in the patient at lunch time. It seems to involve a failure of some sort in the test phase of the TOTE unit. Either the test will not indicate that the operational phase should occur, or the test will not indicate that it should terminate. If a lesion is made in one spot, the animal will starve to death in the presence of food. If the location of the lesion is shifted slightly, the animal will eat continuously as though it is impossible for him to stop. (Interestingly enough, preferences among foods are not disturbed; monkeys will still prefer peanuts to lab chow and prefer lab chow to feces.)

When a normal baboon is handed a lighted match for the first time he will grab it and put it into his mouth and perhaps set his whiskers afire in the process. He douses his snout in a water trough. When he is offered another lighted match he may reach for it, but he will stop before he grabs it, or if he does take it, he will fling it into the trough or out of the cage. If he has had an ablation of the amygdaloid complex—one of the major subdivisions of the limbic systems

—he behaves quite differently. If he reaches for the first match he will continue to reach for subsequent matches, and each time he will complete the entire sequence of putting it into his mouth, firing his whiskers, and dousing his snout. The test phase of the TOTE unit which initiates the actions of oral exploration cannot be modified in the light of experience.

In a similar fashion, sexual activity, once it has been initiated, will be displayed by these operated animals under circumstances in which normal animals show no such behavior.[8] And the effects of such lesions on fleeing can also be understood. The animals develop a conditioned avoidance reaction only with great difficulty: they apparently cannot establish the conditioned stimulus as part of the test phase of the avoidance behavior. And once conditioned avoidance has been established it is very easily extinguished—perhaps the animal is unable to terminate other TOTE units in which he is engaged in time to make the conditioned response.[9]

An effect of lesions in this part of the limbic systems, therefore, can be interpreted as a disruption of the test phase of different TOTE units. TOTE units that are already established may get their testing routines "jammed," so that the test always passes or always fails. And experience in the situation does not enable the operated animal to learn new testing procedures to substitute for the ones he has. An interesting sidelight on this inability to impose new tests on a TOTE unit comes from electrophysiological studies of cortical conditioning. The electrical activity produced in the visual cortex under ordinary circumstances by visual stimulation can be conditioned, after several paired auditory-visual presentations, to occur when only the auditory stimulus is given. The only selective ablation that is known to interfere with this conditioning process is that of the limbic structures we have been considering.[10]

Interference with the test phase of various TOTE units is only

---

[8] J. D. Green, C. D. Clemente, and J. de Groot, Rinencephalic lesions and behavior in cats: an analysis of the Klüver-Bucy syndrome with particular reference to normal and abnormal sexual behavior, *Journal of Comparative Neurology*, 108, 1957, 505–545.

[9] L. Weiskrantz, Behavioral changes associated with ablation of the amygdaloid complex in monkeys, *Journal of Comparative and Physiological Psychology*, 1956, 49, 381–394.

[10] F. Morrell and H. H. Jasper, Electrographic studies of the formation of temporary connections in the brain, *EEG and Clinical Neurophysiology*, 1956, 8, 201.

one of two kinds of symptoms that are produced by lesions in the limbic systems. A second kind of symptom appears as damage to the hierarchical relation between TOTE units. In order to execute a plan of any complexity at all it is necessary to keep track of where in the plan one has gotten. What happens when the hierarchical structure of TOTEs is disrupted is nicely illustrated by the behavior of a mother rat with limbic lesions. When a normal mother rat is faced with a situation in which her brood has been strewn around the cage, she will pick up one baby rat and carry it to the nest, go back to pick up another and return it to the nest, etc., until all the youngsters are safely back in the nest. This behavior does not appear when the mother has had a surgical operation to remove the cingulate cortex —another of the major subdivisions of the limbic systems. The surgically operated mother will pick up an infant, carry it part way to the nest, drop it in favor of another which may be carried to the nest only to be removed on subsequent trips. After half an hour of this the baby rats are still strewn all over the nest and, eventually, are left to die.[11] Similar disorganization occurs when these operated animals try to hoard food, an activity that is quite common among normal rodents when they become hungry.

A little can be surmised about how the hierarchical relation between TOTE units is accomplished in the nervous system. The amygdala seems to be necessary to the test phase of many innate TOTE units. Under normal conditions the electrical activity recorded from the amygdaloid complex changes only when the animal is startled or when, as a result of conditioning, his "attention" is focused on some environmental event. However, when the hippocampus—still another subdivision of the limbic systems—is inactivated by ablation or by massive electrical stimulation, the electrical activity recorded from the amygdala changes whenever the animal touches, or hears, or catches sight of *any* environmental event. It is tempting to speculate that the hippocampus normally protects the amygdala from all incoming information except that appropriate for the TOTE unit currently in control. The hippocampus could perform this "gating" func-

[11] J. S. Stamm, The function of the median cerebral cortex in maternal behavior of rats, *Journal of Comparative and Physiological Psychology*, 1955, 87, 77–88.

tion via the reticular formation in the internal core of the brain stem, which, in turn, is known to influence the receptors, the afferent pathways into the central nervous system, and the activities of the entire external portion of the forebrain. Thus the hippocampus may be intimately involved in the business of keeping the brain at work on the successive steps in the Plan and preventing it from being shunted haphazardly about by every fluctuation in the environment.[12] If so, it would fit very nicely into our conception of how the hierarchy of TOTEs (within the operational phases of their proto-TOTEs) can be established.

The frontal "association areas," sometimes referred to as "the organ of civilization," are intimately connected with the limbic systems to form the internal core of the forebrain. This most forward portion of the primate frontal lobe appears to us to serve as a "working memory" where Plans can be retained temporarily when they are being formed, or transformed, or executed. This speculation appears to be consistent with the fact that animals with lesions in the frontal lobes have difficulty with the delayed-reaction and the delayed-alternation tests. Both of these tasks require the animal to follow an internally stored Plan of action. The behavioral evidence is complicated, however, and it may well be that it is the transformation of Plans, rather than merely the storage of them, for which the frontal lobes are required.

The effects of frontal ablation or lobotomy on man are surprisingly subtle. Very few of the usual psychometric tests turn up any deficits at all. One that frequently shows a deficit is the Porteus maze, a pencil-and-paper labyrinth that would seem to require some planning. It should not be difficult to devise many more tests of planning ability and to use them on these patients. Clinical observations of their behavior would encourage us, at least in some cases, to expect that such tests would succeed in diagnosing the patient's difficulties. Such a patient is apt to "fall apart" when some minor detail goes awry in the Plan he is executing. If he is preparing dinner when the trouble occurs, he may not be readily capable of reshuffling the parts of the

---

[12] M. A. B. Brazier, ed., *The Central Nervous System and Behavior*, Transactions of the Second Conference, February 22–25, 1959, Josiah Macy, Jr., Foundation.

Plan. Segments of the Plan may simply be omitted—the vegetables are served raw—or the whole dinner may be lost. Even if these speculations prove to be wrong in detail, the notion that the frontal "association areas" are intimately linked to the limbic systems in the transformation and execution of Plans is worth pursuing. Clinical and laboratory observations that investigate *how* rather than *what* behavior is changed by the frontal lesions have hardly begun.

One fairly obvious consequence of looking at the relation of brain and behavior in the way proposed here is that we need a much more elaborate and precise theory than we have about an organism's Plans before we can predict what any particular lesion may do to him. Overly simple indicators, such as the strength, rate, or latency of some isolated movement pattern, will only delude us into thinking the processes are simpler than they really are. The ethologists are among the few students of behavior who have been willing to look for the Plan behind the actions and to describe it literally in the kind of flow diagrams that an engineer would need in order to construct a machine to perform the same functions. Given such a detailed specification of what is guiding the muscle twitches it may then be possible to see certain critical points at which the behavior can be disrupted by lesions in certain parts of the brain. To hope for relations between brain structures and crude, *ad hoc,* statistical indicants of some loosely defined abstraction called "response" is apt to be very misleading. The problem of specifying what constitutes a "stimulus" for an organism has long been recognized to be more difficult than it appears on the surface; the chapters in this book must make it equally clear that the mechanism that generates any "sequence of responses" may not be as simple as it may at first seem.

One of the most interesting aspects of brain function, therefore, is how Plans are constructed in the first place, how they are formed. The present discussion has been confined to the more limited task of describing how Plans must be executed. These speculations may throw some light on the functions of the limbic systems. But the authors are not sure where or how the brain might generate Plans. When a familiar Plan is remembered and only slightly modified to fit a new situation, we might find that its selection depended somehow upon the posterior "association areas" in the external portion of the forebrain—selecting a Plan from memory is closely related to using the Image, and the Image, in turn, would seem to be mediated by the external portion. Perhaps the decision to execute a particular Plan is equivalent to transferring control from the posterior "association areas" to the frontal "association areas." Perhaps.

These speculations about the functions of the central nervous system take on a kind of finality and solidity when they are committed to paper that they did not have so long as they remained conversational. The authors know how fuzzy their own Image of this marvelous organ is and how oversimplified or arbitrary these statements must appear. Yet the notions of a reflex telephone system with an enigmatic switchboard, or inhibitions and excitations rippling majestically over the surface of the brain, or little homunculi inside the pineal glands of little homunculi inside the pineal glands of little homunculi *ad infinitum*, or empty black boxes that absorb S's and emit R's, are so thoroughly unsatisfactory that, although the present ideas may be wrong, they are likely to be a great deal less wrong than the metaphors many psychologists have used heretofore. Anybody who tries to do the research needed to put this approach to test will discover things that he would not otherwise have thought to look for.

EPILOGUE

As our debate progressed and our conception of Plans became clearer, a conviction grew on us that we were developing a point of view toward large parts of psychology. We then began to wonder how we might best characterize our position so as to contrast it with others more traditional and more familiar. The question puzzled us. We did not feel that we were behaviorists, at least not in the sense J. B. Watson defined the term, yet we were much more concerned—in that debate and in these pages, at least—with what people did than with what they knew. Our emphasis was upon processes lying immediately behind action, but not with action itself. On the other hand, we did not consider ourselves introspective psychologists, at least not in the sense Wilhelm Wundt defined the term, yet we were willing to pay attention to what people told us about their ideas and their Plans. How does one characterize a position that seems to be such a mixture of elements usually considered incompatible? Deep in the middle of this dilemma it suddenly occurred to us that we were subjective behaviorists. When we stopped laughing we began to wonder seriously if that was not exactly the position we had argued ourselves into. At least the name suggested the shocking inconsistency of our position.

As a matter of fact, we recognized that we had been drifting in that direction for several years. In 1957, for example, Pribram, in the course of reviewing the interrelations of psychology and the neurological disciplines for "Project A," made this comment:

> As a rule, the extreme behaviorist has become overly suspicious if the psychological concepts derived from behavioral observation too closely resemble those derived introspectively (the "mental"). The position accepted here is that behaviorally derived concepts *are* to be compared with those derived introspectively. Two extremes must be avoided, however. When the behaviorally derived concepts, because of a lack of empirical evidence, are indistinguishable from those derived from introspection, confusion results; when the two classes of concepts are so distinct that no relation between them is recognizable, the behaviorally derived concept is apt to be trivial.

We hope that in these pages we have hit some sort of happy compromise between these two extremes and that we can both distinguish and compare the *Plan* with the *Behavior*. But the point is that the need for reconciliation has bothered us for some time. Galanter had struggled with the same problem in a discussion of thinking:

> Classical theories of thinking fall into two general (and oversimplified) categories. These classes of theories have been termed variously (a) S-R, association, trial-and-error, or sign theories; and (b) image or model theories. . . . It is difficult to specify the behavioral manifestation or identification of an image, and in addition, image theories rarely give more than a slipshod account of how the image comes into its full-blown existence. Even so, the fuzzy description of the role of images in complex thinking does a fuzzy kind of justice to our introspections. . . . Most early theorists attempted a synthesis. Such synthesizing went out of vogue during the "behavioral revolution," and now most psychologists espouse either an S-R theory or a cognitive theory. Our ultimate aim is to try again the development of a synthetic theory.[1]

Again we note the theme—how to pull together two conceptions that were both necessary yet apparently incompatible. Our aim is still to develop a synthetic theory. But now we think that a clear description

---

[1] E. Galanter and M. Gerstenhaber, On thought: the extrinsic theory, *Psychological Review*, 1956, 63, pp. 218–219.

of the role of Plans is the link that will hold the two together—that will make subjective behaviorism possible.

Why not be subjective behaviorists? The objection, of course, is that "subjective" and "behaviorism" do not go together. We might as well talk about a black whiteness, or a square circle. But almost every behaviorist has smuggled into his system some kinds of invisible gimmicks—internal responses, drives, stimuli, or whatnot—that are as "objective" as John Locke's ideas used to seem to be. Everybody does it, for the simple reason that you cannot make any sense out of behavior unless you do. J. B. Watson himself talked about "covert speech," which is certainly a kind of subjective behavior. Of course, we could call our Plans by some such operationally acceptable name as "intervening variables" and so pretend that we are *really* talking about tacit behavior, but what would that accomplish? If a behaviorist is willing to introspect on what he would do if he found himself in the predicament that his rats are in, then he is, in our opinion, a subjective behaviorist whether he admits it or not.

What matters to us far more than a name, however, is whether or not we have glimpsed an important aspect of human intelligence. Psychologists who have been content to describe the mind as though it were, in turn, nothing but a description of its own experience have scarcely noticed how sedentary they seem to others, especially to those who are more concerned with actions and results. At first the behaviorists seemed to be the men of action. But the correction they should have supplied was somewhere lost in the rituals and taboos of objectivity. Eventually, they too slipped into a tradition of description until they differed from their colleagues only in the fact that the object they described was behavior, not mind. Indeed, it scarcely jars our modern ear to hear behavior called an *object* for description.

Description is of course important. Even more, it is *essential* to science that we have accurate descriptions available. But there is another ingredient required, one that we seem to forget and rediscover in every generation of psychologists, at least since Brentano's Act first competed with Wundt's Content. Life is more than a thing, an object, a substance that exists. It is also a process that is enacted. We have a choice in our approach to it. We can choose to describe it, or we can choose to re-enact it. Description in its various ramifications is the traditional approach of the scientist. Re-enactment has been the traditional approach of the artist. And just as description depends upon an Image, re-enactment depends upon a Plan.

Re-enactment has lived on the technological borders of pure science for a long time—the planetarium is an astronomer's re-enactment of the solar system, the model is an engineer's pre-enactment of his structure, the wind tunnel is an aeronautical re-enactment of the atmosphere—but it has usually played a supporting role. If a description is correct and accurate, re-enactments based upon it should closely resemble the natural phenomenon that was described. Now, however, re-enactment is emerging as a scientific alternative in its own right. The development of modern computing machines, more than anything else, has given scientists the tools required to re-enact, or simulate, on a large scale, the processes they want to study. The program for a computer that re-enacts a process is becoming just as acceptable a theory of that process as would be the equations describing it. There is still much that needs to be clarified in this new application of the artist's ancient attitude, but clarification will not lag far behind application. And as the understanding of these complex systems grows, the need to distinguish between introspectively derived and behaviorally derived concepts should decline—until eventually both our experience and our behavior will be understood in the same terms. Then, and only then, will psychologists have bridged the gap between the Image and Behavior.

INDEXES

INDEX OF AUTHORS

Alderstein, A. M., 142n
Alexander, I. E., 142n
Allport, G., 114, 122
Ameen, L., 152n
Anscombe, B. E. M., 61n
Anthony, S., 142n
Arrow, K. J., 146n
Ashby, W. R., 3, 42n
Attneave, F., 28n
Austin, G., 165n, 168n

Baerends, G. P., 79
Baernstein, H. D., 46n
Barker, R. G., 15n, 96n
Bartlett, F. C., 7
Beach, F., 74
Beebe-Center, J. G., 54n
Bennett, G. K., 46n
Bergson, H., 45n
Bernstein, A., 55n
Bigelow, J., 42
Binet, A., 192
Bishop, G., 24n
Book, W. F., 86
Boothe, A. D., 53n
Boring, E. G., 46n
Boulding, K. E., 1, 2
Bradner, H., 46n
Brazier, M. A. B., 207n
Brower, R. A., 53n
Bruner, J. S., 165n, 168n
Bryan, W. L., 86
Burton, N. G., 146n

Campbell, D. T., 88n
Cannon, W. B., 43
Carmichael, L., 121n, 171n
Carroll, J. B., 14n, 52n
Chauncey, H., 122n
Cherry, C., 28n
Chomsky, N., 3, 14n, 15–16, 23, 52, 144, 145n, 148n
Claparède, E., 192n
Clark, W. A., 50n
Clemente, C. D., 205n
Cleveland, A. A., 130n
Colley, R. S., 142n
Craik, K., 50
Crozier, W. J., 44n

Davis, M., 46n, 160n
de Groot, J., 205n
Dennis, W., 43n, 44n
Descartes, R., 42
Dewey, J., 30n, 43n
Dinneen, G. P., 50n
Driesch, H., 45n
Duda, W. L., 50n
Duncker, K., 160, 189n, 192

Ebbinghaus, H., 69, 70
Ellis, W. D., 60n
Ellson, D. G., 46n
Elsasser, W. M., 45n
Estes, W. K., 9n

Farley, B. G., 50n
Festinger, L., 32n

Index of Authors ▪ 217

Freud, S., 69, 142n
Frick, F. C., 52n

Galanter, E., 47, 51, 146n, 168n, 173, 212
Gardner, M., 55n
Gelernter, H. L., 51, 55n, 56n, 187, 191
Gerstenhaber, M., 51, 168n, 173, 212n
Gleason, H. A., 144n
Goldstein, K., 195, 196
Goodnow, J., 165n, 168n
Gorn, S., 46n
Green, J. D., 205
Green, W., 119n
Guthrie, E. R., 9, 10

Haibt, L. H., 50n
Hall, E. T., 101n
Hanfmann, E., 165n
Harter, N., 86
Hartley, D., 44n
Hebb, D. O., 9, 50n, 51, 142n
Heidbreder, E., 165n
Hilgard, E. R., 9n
Hockett, C. F., 145n
Holland, J. H., 50n
Holt, E. G., 44
Hovland, C. I., 163n
Hull, C., 15n, 41n, 44–45, 46n
Hunter, W. S., 88

Irion, A. L., 125n

James, W., 11, 12, 64, 144, 145n
Jasper, H. H., 205
Jeffress, L., 11n, 154n
Johnson, D. M., 163n
Jung, C. G., 122n

Karlin, S., 146n
Kister, J., 55n
Kluckhohn, C., 102n
Kluckhohn, F., 102n
Kochen, M., 47
Köhler, W., 10
Kreuger, R. G., 46

Laffal, J., 152n
Lashley, K., 10, 88n, 154
Lees, L. S., 160, 189
Leibnitz, G., 42
Lenkoski, L. D., 152n
Lewin, K., 11, 60, 61, 64–68, 102n, 121n, 171n

Lewis, C. I., 59, 71
Licklider, J. C. R., 146n
Lindzey, G., 142n
Locke, J., 213
Locke, W. N., 53n
Loeb, J., 44
Lorenz, K., 75
Lotka, A. J., 44n
Luchins, A. S., 120n
Luria, A. R., 140n

McCarthy, J., 32n, 49n, 56n
McCulloch, W. S., 3, 49
McGeoch, J. A., 125n
MacKay, D. M., 3, 32n, 50, 51n
MacLean, P. D., 201n
McNemar, O., 120n
Mandler, G., 88n
March, J. G., 101
Miller, G. A., 3, 28n, 52, 53n, 54n, 130n, 132n, 145n, 146n
Milner, B., 201n
Milner, P. M., 50n
Milton, G. A., 119n
Minsky, M. L., 3, 49n, 55n, 172n, 183, 184
Moles, A. A., 183n
Morrell, F., 205n
Müller, G. E., 134
Murchison, C., 44n
Murray, J. A., 102n

Neisser, U., 198n
Newell, A., 3, 15n, 16, 17n, 37n, 55n, 56, 96n, 168, 182, 185–193
Nissen, H. W., 140n

Pavlov, I. P., 6, 23, 91n
Pearson, K., 42n
Perkins, C. P., 136
Perky, C. W., 110
Pitts, W., 49
Plato, 181
Poincaré, H., 167
Polya, G., 160n, 169n, 179, 180, 183, 191
Polyani, M., 87n, 168n
Pribram, K., 199n, 212

Rapaport, D., 60n, 68n
Rashevsky, N., 49n
Riesman, D., 119
Roberts, M., 55n
Rochester, N., 50n, 51, 55n, 187, 191

218 ▪ *Index of Authors*

Rock, I., 137
Roe, A., 140n, 199n
Rosenblueth, A., 42
Ross, T., 46n
Ruch, T. C., 91, 92
Russell, B., 168

Saltzman, I. J., 130n
Samuel, A. L., 55n
Scheerer, M., 196n
Schlosberg, H., 86n, 127n
Schneider, D. M., 102n
Schumann, F., 134
Selfridge, O., 50n, 198n
Shannon, C. E., 3, 28, 32n, 49n, 52n, 55n, 145n, 146n
Shaw, J. C., 3, 15n, 16, 17n, 37n, 55n, 56, 96n, 168, 182, 185–193
Sherrington, C., 23, 24
Simon, B., 91n
Simon, H. A., 3, 15n, 16, 17n, 37n, 55n, 56, 96n, 101, 168, 182, 185–93
Simon, J., 140n
Simpson, G. G., 140n, 199n
Skinner, B. F., 21, 22
Sluckin, W., 27n
Smith, W. A. S., 51n
Stamm, J. S., 206n
Stephens, J. M., 46n
Stevens, S. S., 91n
Sullivan, H. S., 115n
Suppes, P., 146n

Taylor, D. W., 120n
Thompson, W. R., 142n
Thorndike, E. L., 134n

Thorpe, W. H., 75n
Tinbergen, N., 75, 76, 78, 79
Tolman, E., 8, 9, 13, 44n, 61n
Troland, L. T., 44
Turing, A. M., 46, 167
Turner, S. H., 136

Ulan, S., 55n
Underwood, B. J., 131

von Neumann, J., 3, 90n

Walden, W., 55n
Wallace, W. H., 136
Walton, A., 46n
Ward, L. B., 46n
Watson, J. B., 104, 211, 213
Weiskrantz, L., 205n
Weiss, W., 163n
Weitzenhoffer, A. M., 104, 106, 107
Wells, F. L., 120n
Wells, M., 55n
White, L. D., 17n
Whitehead, A. N., 168
Whitfield, J. W., 163n
Whorf, B. L., 154, 155
Wiener, N., 3, 27n, 28, 42, 43, 182
Wisdom, J. O., 27n
Woodworth, R. S., 32n, 37, 86, 127, 134n, 157n
Wright, H. F., 15n, 96n
Wundt, W., 211

Yngve, V., 148n
Yudovich, F. Ia., 140n

Zeigarnick, B., 68

INDEX OF SUBJECTS

ablation, 203, 204
accessibility, of Plans, 100
activity
   patterns of, 12, 13
   spontaneous, of nerve, 24
adaptive concatenations, 79
algorithms, 160, 164
ambiguities, 153
amnesias, 109, 110
amygdaloid complex, 204
anagram, 166
analogue computer, 90n
ancillary Plan, 110, 111
anesthesias, 109, 113
anxiety, 116
apprehension, span of, 131
aspiration, level of, 171n
association, 60, 129
attention, 65, 198, 206
automatization, of Plans, 82
automation, self-programming, 184

behavior
   configuration of, 12
   emotional, 201
   hierarchical organization of, 13, 15
   instinctive, 73
   intentional, 202
   levels of, 13, 14, 78
   motivated, 61
   multiple causation of, 95
   organization of, 13

behavior (*Continued*)
   stimulus control of, 75
   verbal, 14, 139 ff.
behaviorism, 125
   subjective, 211, 213
bicycle riding, 87
borrowed Plans, 113
brain, 196, 197
   amygdaloid complex, 204
   association area, 200
   cerebellum, 91, 92, 199
   cerebral cortex, 199
   cingulate cortex, 206
   external portion, 199
   frontal association area, 199, 207, 208
   hippocampus, 206, 207
   internal core, 199, 200, 201
   limbic systems, 199, 200 ff.
   osmoreceptors, 201
   posterior association areas, 208
   projection systems, 199
   reticular formation, 207
   subcortical centers, 200
   ventricles, 201
   visual cortex, 205
   waves, 111
brightness discrimination, 140
British Museum algorithm, 163, **168**

catatonia, 113, 116
cerebellum, 91, 92, 199

cerebral cortex, 199
chaining, 77, 78, 84, 144
character disorders, 123
chess, 55, 184, 185
cingulate cortex, 206
circular reflexes, 44
cognitive
   strain, 164, 165
   structure, 63
cognitive theory, 11
   criticism of, 9, 10, 41
commitment, 116
communicable Plans, 82, 89, 143
communication, 155
compatible Plan, 97
compulsive person, 119
computer, 178, 197
   analogue, $90n$
   digital, 48, $90n$
   electronic, 46
   memory of, 49, 54
concatenation, 77, 78, 204
   adaptive, 79
concept, 162
   attainment, 165
   learning, 163
   positive instance of, 165
conditioned avoidance, 205
conditioning, cortical, 205
confirmation of Image, 161
conflicting Plans, 97
consciousness, 111, 145, 198
   of Plans, 65
consummatory acts, 76, 77
   hierarchical organization in, 77
control, 27, 28, 198
coordination of Plans, 96, 98, 120
cortical conditioning, 205
creativity, 178, 179
   in thinking, 173
culture, 95, 119, 123
cybernetics, 2, 3, 26, 49

death, 141
defense mechanisms, 116
dependencies, nested, 148
depression, agitated, 115
desertion of Plans, 98
detail of Plans, 119
digital computer, 48, $90n$
digital-to-analogue converter, 91, 92, 199
discrimination, 200
   of brightness, 140

disorganization, 206
dual personality, 97
dynamic property, 118
   of instincts, 73
   of Plans, 62 ff.

efficiency, 96, 131
emotional behavior, 201
   excitation of, 116
emotions, 98, 114
entelechy, 42, $45n$
environment, internal representations of, 7 ff.
ethical guilt, 98
ethology, 74, 75
evaluation, 62, 156
evolution, 38, 142
execution of Plans, 17, 59, 61, 64, 69, 105, 116
external memory devices, 68, 70

feasibility of Plans, 70, 113
feedback, 26, 42, 51, 91
   loop, 30
   mechanism, 43
   sensory, 44, 91
flexible Plan, 67, 78, 82, 89, 96, 120
formation of Plans, 69, 177
frontal association area, 199, 207, 208

gambling, 166
generator of Plans, 184
grammar, 144, 145 ff.
   of behavior, 155
   dependency in, 148
   level of, 143
   machine, 149
   Plan, 155, 156, 177
   sentences and, 146
   theory of, 153
grouping, 131
guilt, ethical and moral, 98

habit, 81, 82, 177
hallucinations, 111
halting problem, 171
hebephrenia, 115
heuristic Plan, 160, 163, 167, 168, 179
hierarchy
   of consummatory acts, 77
   of behavioral units, 85
   instinctive, 76
   in organization of behavior, 15, 32
   in organization of word list, 155

hierarchy (*Continued*)
  in Plans, 155
  structure of, 33
hippocampus, 206, 207
homeostatic mechanisms, 27, 201
human Plans, 154
hypnosis, 103, 106 ff.
  anesthesias in, 109
  inducing, 106
  levels of, 108
  speech during, 107
hypotheses, 162
  alternative, 163, 175
hysteria, 116

ideo-motor action, 12
Image, 1, 2, 5 ff., 17, 157, 202
  alternative, 174
  in computer, 50 ff.
  confirmation of, 161
  definition of, 17
  imaginative, 110
  infirming of, 161
  perceptual, 110, 195
  Plan symbolized in, 116
  public, 98
  revising of, 171
  use of, 2
imagery, 129
imaginal thinking, 173
imagining, 131
imitation, 177
imprinting, 75
incongruity, 26, 31, 82, 202
inflexible Plan, 67, 74, 78, 89, 96
information, 27, 28
  processing, 91, 174, 188
  processing languages, 16
innate Plan, 74, 78
innate releasing mechanism, 75
inner speech, 71, 105, 111
insight, 10, 157
instinctive Plan, 74, 78
instincts, 73, 74, 93, 177
  dynamic aspects of, 73
  innate character of, 73
  motivational aspects of, 73
  as Plan, 74, 177
  reproductive, 76
instruction, 155
  verbal, 177
integration of Plans, 95
intelligence, artificial, 55

intention, 59, 60, 62, 202
  dynamic property of, 61
  forgotten, 69
  invariance of, 63
  to learn, 129
intercalated act, 84
internal core of brain, 199, 200, 201
interruption of Plans, 67
intervening variables, 213
introspection, 117, 127, 140, 182
involuntary Plans, 74, 81, 82, 116

kernel strings, 152

language, 14, 38, 104, 139
  in animals, 140
learning, 83
  rote, 130, 131
  verbal, 137, 153
lesion of brain, 203, 204, 207, 208
  symptoms of, 206, 207
life space, 60
limbic systems, 199, 200, 201–205, 208
linguistics, 144
lists, 15, 132, 134
lobotomy, effects of, 207
loop, 37, 170
  feedback, 30

machine imagery, 51
Markov processes, 52, 145, 147
maze, Porteus, 207
meaningful discourse, 133
meaningfulness, 125
means-end analysis, 189, 191
mediating organization, 8
memorization, 128
memory
  of computer, 49, 198
  external devices for, 68, 70, 196
  function, 66
  immediate, 148, 203
  and limbic system, 201, 203
  loss, 203
  trace, 127
  unit, 199
  working, 64, 200, 207
message source, 148
metaplan, 129, 169, 178, 179
mnemonic devices, 134, 136
mnemonic Plans, 165
model
  left-to-right, 146
  mechanical, 42
  stochastic, 47

motion study, 85
motions, sequence of, 13
motivation, 61, 95, 201
   and instincts, 73
   processes of, 200
motor Plan, 156
motor skills, 81, 82, 93
motor unit, 13, 32, 83
   polyphase, 37

needs, 64
negation, 151
negative evaluation, 62, 63
nerve, spontaneous activity of, 24
nested dependencies, 148
neural nets, 49
neuropsychology, 195
neurotic personality, 97
nonrecurrent Plans, 130
nonsense syllables, 70, 126, 127
operationism, 126
organizations, 99
osmoreceptors, 201
outline, 15

pain, 109
paired associates, 136
paranoid reaction, 115
parataxic modes, 115
payoff function, 174
persistence, 121
personality, 117, 122
   neurotic, 97
persuasion, 103
phase sequences, 51
physiological limit, 110
planlessness, 112
planning
   higher-order, 128
   method of, 189, 191, 193
   social, 99
   speed of, 120
Plans, 2, 5, 16, 29, 31, 33, 37, 38, 50, 62, 63, 102, 104
   accessability of, 100
   alternative, 174
   ancillary, 110, 111
   automatized, 82
   borrowed, 113
   communicable, 82, 89, 143
   compatible, 97
   complex, 72
   conflicting, 97
   coordination of, 96, 98, 120

Plans (*Continued*)
   detail of, 119
   definition of, 16
   desertion of, 98
   dynamic properties of, 64
   efficient, 96
   execution of, 17, 59, 60, 64, 65, 69, 105, 116
   exhaustive, 167
   feasible, 70, 113
   fixed, 78
   flexible, 67, 78, 82, 89, 96, 120
   formation of, 69, 177
   generator, 184
   grammatical, 155, 177
   for hammering nails, 34
   heuristic, 160, 163, 167, 168, 179
   hierarchical, 16, 155
   for housekeeping, 108
   human, 154
   inflexible, 67, 74, 78, 89, 96
   inherited, 74, 177
   innate, 74, 78
   instinctive, 74, 78
   integration of, 95
   interruption of, 67
   involuntary, 74, 81, 82, 116
   locked in, 81, 89
   mnemonic, 165
   nonrecurrent, 130
   openness of, 121
   pruning of, 115
   public, 98, 101
   ready-made, 134 ff.
   reconstructing, 178
   relevant, 113
   remembering, 204
   retrieval of, 121
   revision of, 70
   rigid, 78
   search, 161
   several at once, 78, 79
   shared, 177
   source of, 119
   span of, 119
   stopping, 105
   stored, 178
   symbolized in Image, 116
   systematic, 160, 166
   voluntary, 82, 89
   working memory, 65
polyphase motor units, 37
posterior association areas, 208
posthypnotic suggestion, 111

prediction paradigm, 173, 174
primary projection, 199
priorities, 101
problem
   non-numerical, 54
   search, 163
   simplified, 191
   solving, 167, 169, 178
   well-defined, 170
processing unit, 198
program, 15n, 16, 28, 37n, 48, 56, 184, 197
projection systems, 199
protaxic modes, 115
proximal stimulus, 25
psychometrics, 118

quasi-need, 60

ready-made Plans, 134 ff.
recall, of interrupted tasks, 65, 66
recitation, 130
reconstructing Plans, 176
re-enactment, 214
reflex, 21, 24, 77
   circular, 44
   conditioned, 46
reflex arc, 6
   criticism of, 18, 22–25
   definition of, 22
reflex theorist, 7, 41
reinforcement, 7, 30, 118, 128
remembering, 125, 177
   Plans for, 204
repression, 69
reproductive instinct, 76
resumption, of interrupted tasks, 65, 66
reticular formation, 207
retrieval of Plans, 121
retroflex, 44
revision
   of Image, 171
   of Plans, 70
rhythmic grouping, 128
risk in Plans, 166
roles, social, 99, 100
Rorschach ink-blot test, 119
rote learning, 130, 131
rules, 151

schema, 7
schizophrenic, 115

search, 159 ff.
   Plans, 161
   problem, 163
   routines, 160
sentence, 144, 145
   generators, 151, 152
   planner, 146
sequence
   of acts, 200
   of motions, 13
sensory feedback, 44, 91
servomechanism, 31, 44
sexual activity, 205
shared plans, 99, 100, 177
short-term storage, 199
simulation, 47, 50
skills, 81, 82, 93, 156, 177
   acquisition of, 86, 87
   development of, 85
   verbal, 157
sleep, 105
solution, neighborhood of, 191
span
   of apprehension, 131
   of Plans, 119
speaking, 139
   in hypnosis, 107
space, 101
statistical theory, 133
steady state, 24
stimulus, 208
   magnitude, 140
   reinforcement, 7, 118
   response relation, 6
stochastic chains, 146
stochastic models, 47
stop-orders, 121, 170
stop rule, 33, 109, 110, 161, 168
stopping of Plans, 105
stored Plans, 178
strategy, 32, 74, 83, 119
   definition of, 17
   habitual, 89
   integrated, 90
   for learning, 129
   perceptual, 165
   verbalized, 89
style, 118
subcortical centers, 200
subplans, 96, 159
suggestion, posthypnotic, 111
suicide, 141
symptoms, of lesions of limbic systems, 206

synapse, 24, 45n
syntax, 144, 154

taboo, 112
tactics, 32, 74, 119
   definition of, 17
   during hypnosis, 107
   idiosyncratic, 84
talking, 145, 193
tasks, interrupted, 65, 66
teleological argument, 42
tension system, 66, 67
test
   delayed alternation, 207
   delayed reaction, 207
   perceptual, 161
   proximal stimulus, 25
test phase, of TOTE, 25, 29, 109
thinking, 163, 169, 178
   aloud, 192
   creative, 173
   imaginal, 173
thirst, 201
thought
   control, 112
   imageless, 192
   laws of, 155
threshold, 25
time, 101, 123

TOTE, 27, 29, 32–38, 62, 63, 75, 170, 175, 195, 202
   hierarchy of, 63, 98, 156, 186, 206
   operational phase, 37
   pattern as hypothesis, 31
   test phase, 109
trait, 122
translating, 131
translation, mechanical, 52, 53, 54
trial-and-error, 52, 157
tropism, 44, 77
transfer, of previous learning, 125
Turing machine, 46, 49
two-phase motor units, 32

units of action, 13, 32
utility scale, 174

valence, 60
values, 59, 62, 122, 200
   differences in, 118
ventricles, 201
visual cortex, 205
volition, 111
voluntary Plans, 82, 89

Whorfian hypothesis, 155
will, 12, 71, 104, 112
working memory, 64, 200, 207